SVG Essentials

SVG Essentials

J. David Eisenberg

O'REILLY®

Beijing · Cambridge · Farnham · Köln · Paris · Sebastopol · Taipei · Tokyo

SVG Essentials

by J. David Eisenberg

Published by O'Reilly & Associates, Inc., 1005 Gravenstein Highway North,
Sebastopol, CA 95472.

O'Reilly & Associates books may be purchased for educational, business, or sales
promotional use. Online editions are also available for most titles (*safari.oreilly.com*).
For more information contact our corporate/institutional sales department:
(800) 998-9938 or *corporate@oreilly.com*.

Editor: Simon St.Laurent

Production Editor: Jeffrey Holcomb

Cover Designer: Ellie Volckhausen

Interior Designer: David Futato

Printing History:

February 2002:   First Edition.

ISBN: 0-596-00223-8
[M]

To my Mother and my late Father,
for their advice and love through the years.

Table of Contents

Preface

SVG Essentials introduces you to the Scalable Vector Graphics XML application. SVG, a recommendation from the World Wide Web Consortium, uses XML to describe graphics that are made up of lines, curves, and text. This rather dry definition does not do justice to the scope and power of SVG.

You can add SVG graphics to an Extensible Stylesheet Language Formatting Objects (XSL-FO) document, and convert the combined document to Adobe PDF format for high-quality printouts. Mapmakers and meteorologists are using SVG to create highly detailed graphic images in a truly portable format. All of the diagrams in this book were originally created in SVG before being sent to the art department at O'Reilly. As you learn and use SVG, you're sure to think of new and interesting uses for this emerging technology.

Who Should Read This Book?

You should read this book if you want to:

- Create SVG files in a text or XML editor

- Create SVG files from existing vector data

- Transform other XML data to SVG

- Use JavaScript to manipulate the SVG document object tree

- Serve SVG or SVG-source graphics over the Web

Who Should Not Read This Book?

If you simply want to view SVG files, you need only acquire a viewer program or plug-in for the Web, download the files, and enjoy them. There's no need for you to know what's going on behind the scenes unless you wish to satisfy your lively intellectual curiosity.

If you wish to create SVG files with a drawing program that has SVG export capability, just read that program's documentation to learn how to use that program feature.

If You're Still Reading This...

If you've decided that you should indeed read this book, you should also be aware that most of the people who use this book will be fairly advanced users, quite probably from a technical background rather than a graphics design background. We didn't want to burden them with a lot of basic material up front, but we did want the book to be accessible to people with no background in XML or programming, so we created a number of introductory chapters—and then put them in the back of the book as appendixes. If you haven't used XML or stylesheets (and this could include some of the technical folks!) or have never programmed, you might want to turn first to the appendixes. A complete list of all the chapters and appendixes with details on what they contain is given later in this preface.

If you're one of the technical types, you definitely need to be aware that this book will *not* make you a better artist, any more than a book on word processing algorithms will make you a better writer. This book gives the technical details of scalable vector graphics; to create better art, you need to learn to *see*, and the book you should read in addition to this one is *The New Drawing on the Right Side of the Brain*, by Dr. Betty Edwards.

This book gives you the essentials of SVG; if you want to find out all the information, straight from the source, you should go to *http://www.w3.org/ Graphics/SVG/Overview.htm8*.

About the Examples

All the examples in this book except for those in Chapter 11 have been tested with the Batik SVG viewer on a system running Linux (the Mandrake distribution). The Batik SVG viewer is an application of the software developed by the Apache Software Foundation's Batik project. This cross-platform software is written in Java and is available as open source under the Apache Software License. For full details, visit *http://xml.apache.org/batik/*.

Since Batik produces only static output, I could not use it for the examples in Chapter 11. Those examples were tested with the Adobe SVG Viewer. Adobe has been deeply involved in promoting SVG as a standard, and their viewer, which can be downloaded from *http://www.adobe.com/svg/viewer/install/*, is a nearly complete implementation of the SVG 1.0 specification. It offers JavaScript and ECMA Script support in Netscape, Internet Explorer, and RealPlayer 8. As of this writing, it is available for Windows and Macintosh OS X. An unsupported Linux version is also available at *http://www.adobe.com/svg/viewer/install/old.html*.

Another SVG viewer, also written in Java, is available from Australia's Commonwealth Scientific and Industrial Research Organization (CSIRO) Mathematical and Information Sciences department. This viewer, which has not been updated since December of 2000, is available at *http://sis.cmis.csiro.au/svg/*. The same group has implemented a subset of SVG for Pocket PCs; it is available for license at *http://www.cmis.csiro.au/sis/SVGpocket.htm*.

As you look through the illustrations in this book, you will find that they are utterly lacking in artistic merit. There are reasons for this. First, each example is intended to illustrate a particular aspect of SVG, and it should do so without additional visual distractions. Second, the author becomes terribly depressed when he looks at other books with impossibly beautiful examples; "I can never draw anything that looks like this," he thinks. In an effort to save you from similar distress, the examples are purposely as simple (or simplistic) as possible. As you look at them, your immediate reaction will be: "I can certainly use SVG to draw something that looks far better than this!" You can, and you will.

Organization of This Book

Chapter 1, *Getting Started*
> This chapter gives a brief history of SVG, compares raster and vector graphics systems, and ends with a brief tutorial introducing the main concepts of SVG.

Chapter 2, *Coordinates*
> How do you determine the position of a point in a drawing? Which way is "up?" This chapter answers those questions, showing how to change the system by which coordinates are measured in a graphic.

Chapter 3, *Basic Shapes*
This chapter shows you how to construct drawings using the basic shapes available in SVG: lines, rectangles, polygons, circles, and ellipses. It also discusses how to determine the colors for the outline and interior of a shape.

Chapter 4, *Document Structure*
In a complex drawing, there are elements that are reused or repeated. This chapter tells you how to group objects together so they may be treated as a single entity and re-used. It also discusses use of external images, both vector and raster.

Chapter 5, *Transforming the Coordinate System*
If you draw a square on a sheet of stretchable material, and stretch the material horizontally, you get a rectangle. Skew the sides of the sheet, and you see a parallelogram. Now tilt the sheet 45 degrees, and you have a diamond. In this chapter, you will learn how to move, rotate, scale, and skew the coordinate system to affect the shapes drawn on it.

Chapter 6, *Paths*
All the basic shapes are actually specific instances of the general concept of a *path*. This chapter shows you how to describe a general outline for a shape by using lines, arcs, and complex curves.

Chapter 7, *Patterns and Gradients*
This chapter adds more to the discussion of color from Chapter 3, discussing how to create a color gradient or a fill pattern.

Chapter 8, *Text*
Graphics aren't just lines and shapes; text is an integral part of a poster or a schematic diagram. This chapter shows how to add text to a drawing, both in a straight line and following a path.

Chapter 9, *Clipping and Masking*
This chapter shows you how to use a clipping path to display a graphic as though it were viewed through a circular lens, keyhole, or any other arbitrary shape. It also shows how to use a mask to alter an object's transparency so that it appears to "fade out" at the edges.

Chapter 10, *Filters*
Although an SVG file describes vector graphics, the document is eventually rendered on a raster device. In this chapter, you'll learn how to apply raster-oriented filters to a graphic to blur an image, transform its colors, or produce lighting effects.

Chapter 11, *Animating and Scripting SVG*

Since SVG is an XML application, you can use Java and JavaScript to dynamically control a graphic's attributes. This chapter also shows you how to use SVG's built-in animation capabilities.

Chapter 12, *Generating SVG*

Although you can create an SVG file from scratch, most people will have existing vector data or XML data that they wish to display in graphic form. This chapter discusses the use of programming languages such as Java, Perl, and XSLT to create SVG from these data sources.

Chapter 13, *Serving SVG Files*

This chapter shows a servlet that transforms XML to SVG, and then to PNG format, for delivery to browsers that do not have SVG viewer plug-ins.

Appendix A, *The XML You Need for SVG*

SVG is an application of XML, the Extensible Markup Language. If you haven't used XML before, you should read this appendix to familiarize yourself with this remarkably powerful and flexible format for structuring data and documents.

Appendix B, *Introduction to Stylesheets*

You can use stylesheets to apply visual properties to particular elements in your SVG document. These are exactly the same kind of stylesheets that can be used with HTML documents. If you've never used stylesheets before, you'll want to read this brief introduction to the anatomy of a stylesheet.

Appendix C, *Programming Concepts*

If you're a graphic designer who hasn't done much programming, you'll want to find out what programmers are talking about when they throw around words like "object model" and "function."

Appendix D, *Matrix Algebra*

To fully understand coordinate transformations and filter effects in SVG it's helpful, though not necessary, to understand matrix algebra, the mathematics used to compute the coordinates and pixels. This appendix highlights the basics of matrix algebra.

Appendix E, *Creating Fonts*

TrueType fonts represent glyphs (characters) in a vector form. This appendix shows you how to take your favorite fonts and convert them to paths for use in SVG documents.

Appendix F, *Using SVG with Other XML Applications*
> Since SVG is an application of XML, it can work with other XML appli-
> cations. This appendix shows you how to put SVG into XHTML and
> XSL Formatting Objects.

Conventions Used in This Book

Italic
> Is used to introduce new terms, as well as for email and URL
> addresses.

`Constant width`
> Is used for code examples and fragments.

`Constant width bold`
> Is used to highlight a section of code being discussed in the text.

`Constant width italic`
> Is used for replaceable elements in code examples.

 The owl icon represents a note.

 The turkey icon represents a warning.

This book uses *callouts* to denote "points of interest " in code listings. A
callout is shown as a white number in a black circle; the corresponding
number after the listing gives an explanation. Here's an example:

```
Roses are red,
    Violets are blue. ❶
Some poems rhyme;
    This one doesn't. ❷
```

❶ Violets actually have a color value of #9933cc.

❷ This poem uses the literary device known as a "surprise ending."

Request for Comments

Please address comments and questions concerning this book to the publisher:

O'Reilly & Associates, Inc.
1005 Gravenstein Highway North
Sebastopol, CA 95472
(800) 998-9938 (in the United States or Canada)
(707) 829-0515 (international/local)
(707) 829-0104 (fax)

We have a web page for this book where we list errata, examples, or any additional information. You can access this page at:

http://www.oreilly.com/catalog/svgess

To comment or ask technical questions about this book, send email to:

bookquestions@oreilly.com

For more information about our books, conferences, software, Resource Centers, and the O'Reilly Network, see our web site at:

http://www.oreilly.com

Acknowledgments

I'd like to thank Simon St.Laurent, the editor of this book, for his guidance and comments, which were always right on the mark. He also told me in an email, "we already know that you know how to write," which is one of the nicest things anyone has ever told me.

Thanks also to Edd Dumbill, who wrote the document which I modified only slightly to create Appendix A. Of course, any errors in that appendix have been added by my modifications.

Thanks also go to Antoine Quint and to David Klaphaak and the SVG Quality Engineering team at Adobe, who did the technical review of the manuscript. Your comments have helped improve many aspects of this book.

Jeffrey Zeldman is the person who first put the idea in my head that I, too, could write a book, and for that I thank him most sincerely.

I also want to thank all the people, foremost among them my brother Steven, who, when I told them I was writing a book, believed in me enough to say, "Wow, that's great."

1

Getting Started

SVG, which stands for *S*calable *V*ector *G*raphics, is an application of XML that makes it possible to represent graphic information in a compact, portable form. Interest in SVG is growing rapidly, and tools to create and view SVG files are already available from major companies. This chapter begins with a description of the two major systems of computer graphics, and describes where SVG fits into the graphics world. The chapter concludes with a brief example that uses many of the concepts that we will explore in detail in the following chapters.

Graphics Systems

The two major systems for representing graphic information on computers are raster and vector graphics.

Raster Graphics

In raster graphics, an image is represented as a rectangular array of picture elements or pixels (see Figure 1-1). Each pixel is represented either by its RGB color values or as an index into a list of colors. This series of pixels, also called a bitmap, is often stored in a compressed format. Since most modern display devices are also raster devices, displaying an image requires a viewer program to do little more than uncompress the bitmap and transfer it to the screen.

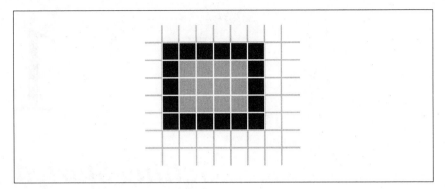

Figure 1-1. Raster graphic rectangle

Vector Graphics

In a vector graphic system, an image is described as a series of geometric shapes (see Figure 1-2). Rather than receiving a finished set of pixels, a vector viewing program receives commands to draw shapes at specified sets of coordinates.

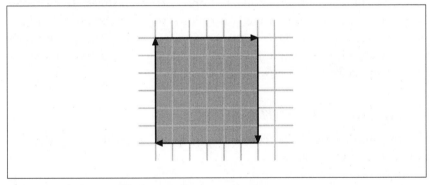

Figure 1-2. Vector graphic rectangle

If you think of producing an image on graph paper, raster graphics work by describing which squares should be filled in with which colors. Vector graphics work by describing the grid points at which lines or curves are to be drawn. Some people describe vector graphics as a set of instructions for a drawing, while bitmap graphics (rasters) are points of color in specific places. Vector graphics "understand" what they are—a square "knows" it's a square and text "knows" that it's text. Because they are objects rather than a series of pixels, vector objects can change their shape and color, whereas bitmap graphics cannot. Also, all text is searchable because it really is text, no matter how it looks or how it is rotated or transformed.

Another way to think of raster graphics is as paint on canvas, while vector graphics are lines and shapes made of a stretchable material which can be moved around on a background.

Uses of Raster Graphics

Raster graphics are most appropriate for use with photographs, which are rarely composed of distinct lines and curves. Scanned images are often stored as bitmaps; even though the original may be "line art," we want to store the image as a whole and don't care about its individual components. A fax machine, for example, doesn't care what you've drawn; it simply transmits pixels from one place to another in raster form.

Tools for creating images in raster format are widespread and generally easier to use than many vector-based tools. There are many different ways to compress and store a raster image, and the internal representation of these formats is public. Program libraries to read and write images in compressed formats such as JPEG, GIF, and PNG are widely available. These are some of the reasons that web browsers have, until the arrival of SVG, supported only raster images.

Uses of Vector Graphics

Vector graphics are used in:

- Computer Assisted Drafting (CAD) programs, where accurate measurement and the ability to zoom in on a drawing to see details are essential

- Programs such as Adobe Illustrator, which are used to design graphics that will be printed on high-resolution printers

- The Adobe PostScript printing and imaging language; every character that you print is described in terms of lines and curves

- The vector-based Macromedia Flash system for designing animations, presentations, and web sites

Because most of these files are encoded in binary format or as tightly packed bitstreams, it is difficult for a browser or other user agent to parse out embedded text, or for a server to dynamically create vector graphic files from external data. Most of the internal representations of vector graphics are proprietary, and code to view or create them is not generally available.

Scalability

Although they are not as popular as raster graphics, vector graphics have one feature that makes them invaluable in many applications—they can be scaled without loss of image quality. As an example, here are two drawings of a cat. Figure 1-3 was made with raster graphics; Figure 1-4 is a vector image. Both are shown as they appear on a screen that displays 72 pixels per inch.

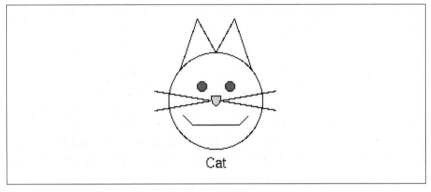

Figure 1-3. Raster image of cat

Figure 1-4. Vector image of cat

When a display program zooms in on the raster graphic, it must find some way to expand each pixel. The simplest approach to zooming in by a factor of four is to make each pixel four times as large. The results, shown in Figure 1-5, are not particularly pleasing.

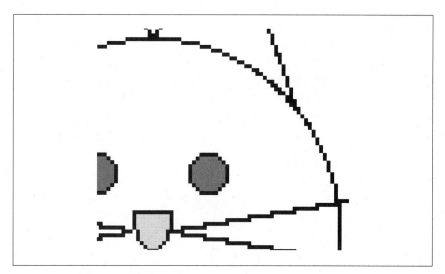

Figure 1-5. Expanded raster image

Although it is possible to use techniques such as edge-detection and anti-aliasing to make the expanded image more pleasing, these techniques are time-consuming. Furthermore, since all the pixels in a raster graphic are equally anonymous, there's no guarantee that an algorithm can correctly detect edges of shapes. Anti-aliasing results in something like Figure 1-6.

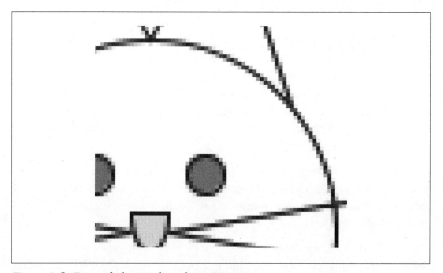

Figure 1-6. Expanded anti-aliased raster image

Expanding a vector image by a factor of four, on the other hand, merely requires the display program to multiply all the coordinates of the shapes by four and redraw them at the full resolution of the display device. Thus, Figure 1-7, which is also a screenshot from a 72 dot per inch screen, shows crisp, clear edges on the lines with significantly less of the stair-step effects of the expanded raster image.

Figure 1-7. Expanded vector image

SVG's Role

In 1998, the World Wide Web Consortium formed a working group to develop a representation of vector graphics as an XML application. Because SVG is an XML application, the information about an image is stored as plain text, and it brings the advantages of XML's openness, transportability, and interoperability.

CAD and graphic design programs often store drawings in a proprietary binary format. By adding the ability to import and export drawings in SVG format, applications gain a common, standard format for interchanging information.

Since it is an XML application, SVG cooperates with other XML applications. A mathematics textbook, for example, could use XSL Formatting Objects for explanatory text, MathML to describe equations, and SVG to generate the graphs for the equations.

The SVG working group's specification is an official World Wide Web Consortium Recommendation. Some applications such as Adobe Illustrator and Jasc WebDraw export drawings in SVG format. On the Web, SVG viewer plug-ins let users view presentations with many of the same scripting and animation capabilities that Flash has. Since the SVG files are XML, text in the SVG display is available to any user agent that can parse XML.

Creating an SVG Graphic

In this section, we will write an SVG file that produces the image of the cat that we showed earlier in the chapter. This example introduces many of the concepts that we will explain in further detail in subsequent chapters. This file will be a good example of how to write an example file, which is not necessarily the way you should write an SVG file that will be part of a finished project.

Document Structure

We start Example 1-1 with the standard XML processing instruction and DOCTYPE declaration. The root <svg> element defines the width and height of the finished graphic in pixels. The <title> element's content is available to a viewing program for use in a title bar or as a tooltip pointer, and the <desc> element lets you give a full description of the image.

Example 1-1. Basic structure of an SVG document

```
<?xml version="1.0"?>
<!DOCTYPE svg PUBLIC "-//W3C//DTD SVG 1.0//EN"
    "http://www.w3.org/TR/2001/REC-SVG-20010904/DTD/svg10.dtd">

<svg width="140" height="170">
<title>Cat</title>
<desc>Stick Figure of a Cat</desc>
<!-- the drawing will go here -->
</svg>
```

Basic Shapes

We draw the cat's face by adding a <circle> element. The element's attributes specify the center *x*-coordinate, center *y*-coordinate, and radius. The (0,0) point is the upper left corner of the picture. *x* coordinates increase as you move horizontally to the right; *y* coordinates increase as you move vertically downwards.

The circle's location and size are part of the drawing's *structure*. The color in which it is drawn is part of its *presentation*. As is customary with XML applications, we want to separate structure and presentation for maximum flexibility. Presentation information is contained in the style attribute. Its value will be a series of presentation properties and values, as described in Appendix B, in the section "Anatomy of a Style." We'll use a stroke color of black for the outline, and a fill color of none to make the face transparent. The SVG is shown in Example 1-2, and its result in Figure 1-8.

Example 1-2. Basic shapes—circle

```
<?xml version="1.0"?>
<!DOCTYPE svg PUBLIC "-//W3C//DTD SVG 1.0//EN"
    "http://www.w3.org/TR/2001/REC-SVG-20010904/DTD/svg10.dtd">

<svg width="140" height="170">
<title>Cat</title>
<desc>Stick Figure of a Cat</desc>

<circle cx="70" cy="95" r="50" style="stroke: black; fill: none"/>;

</svg>
```

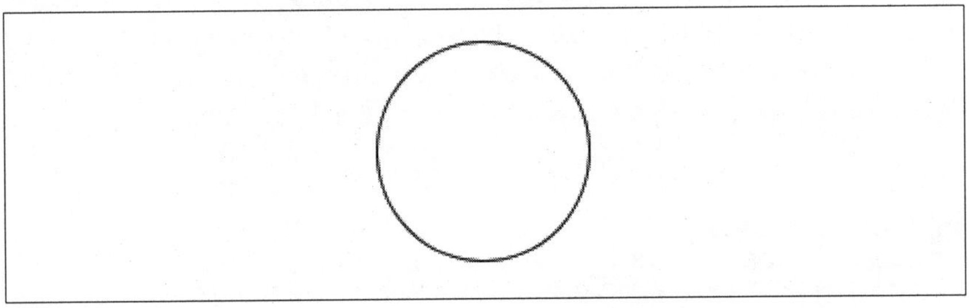

Figure 1-8. Stage one—circle

Specifying Styles as Attributes

Now we add two more circles for the eyes in Example 1-3. Although their fill and stroke colors are really part of the presentation, SVG does allow you to specify them as individual attributes. In this example we specify the fill and stroke colors as two separate attributes rather than inside a style attribute. You probably won't use this method often; we'll discuss it further in Chapter 4, in the section "Presentation Attributes." We've put it here just to prove that it can be done. The results are shown in Figure 1-9.

The <?xml ...?> and <?DOCTYPE?> have been omitted to save space in the listing.

Example 1-3. Basic shapes—filled circles

```
<svg width="140" height="170">
<title>Cat</title>
<desc>Stick Figure of a Cat</desc>

<circle cx="70" cy="95" r="50" style="stroke: black; fill: none"/>
<circle cx="55" cy="80" r="5" stroke="black" fill="#339933"/>
<circle cx="85" cy="80" r="5" stroke="black" fill="#339933"/>

</svg>
```

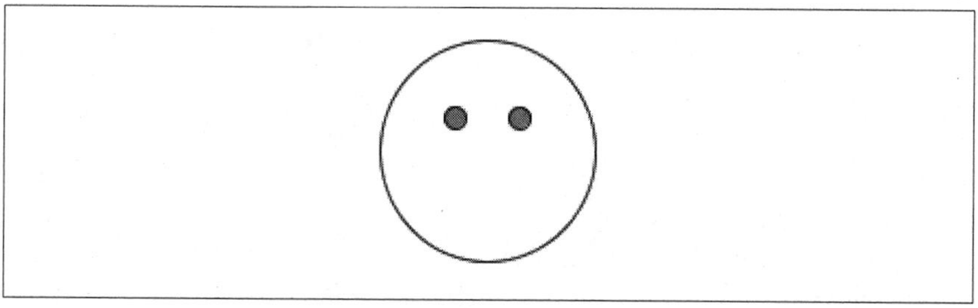

Figure 1-9. Stage two—face and eyes

Grouping Graphic Objects

Example 1-4 adds the whiskers on the right side of the cat's face with two <line> elements. We want to treat these whiskers as a unit (you'll see why in a moment), so we enclose them in the <g> grouping element, and give it an id. A line is specified by giving the *x*- and *y*-coordinates for its starting point (x1 and y1) and ending point (x2 and y2). The result is displayed in Figure 1-10.

Example 1-4. Basic shapes—lines

```
<svg width="140" height="170">
<title>Cat</title>
<desc>Stick Figure of a Cat</desc>

<circle cx="70" cy="95" r="50" style="stroke: black; fill: none;"/>
<circle cx="55" cy="80" r="5" stroke="black" fill="#339933"/>
<circle cx="85" cy="80" r="5" stroke="black" fill="#339933"/>
<g id="whiskers">
    <line x1="75" y1="95" x2="135" y2="85" style="stroke: black;"/>
    <line x1="75" y1="95" x2="135" y2="105" style="stroke: black;"/>
</g>
</svg>
```

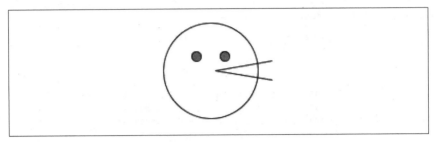

Figure 1-10. Stage three—right whiskers

Transforming the Coordinate System

Now we will <use> the whiskers group, and transform them into the left
whiskers. Example 1-5 first flips the coordinate system by multiplying the
x-coordinates by negative one in a scale transformation. This means that
the point (75, 95) is now located at at the place which would have been
(-75, 95) in the original coordinate system. In the new scaled system, coordinates increase as you move *left*. This means we have to translate
(move) the coordinate system 140 pixels right, the negative direction, to
get them where we want them as shown in Figure 1-11.

Example 1-5. Transforming the coordinate system

```
<svg width="140" height="170">
<title>Cat</title>
<desc>Stick Figure of a Cat</desc>

<circle cx="70" cy="95" r="50" style="stroke: black; fill: none;"/>
<circle cx="55" cy="80" r="5" stroke="black" fill="#339933"/>
<circle cx="85" cy="80" r="5" stroke="black" fill="#339933"/>
<g id="whiskers">
    <line x1="75" y1="95" x2="135" y2="85" style="stroke: black;"/>
    <line x1="75" y1="95" x2="135" y2="105" style="stroke: black;"/>
</g>
<use xlink:href="#whiskers" transform="scale(-1 1) translate(-140 0)"/>

</svg>
```

The transform attribute's value lists the transformations, one after another,
separated by whitespace.

Other Basic Shapes

Example 1-6 constructs the ears and mouth with the <polyline> element,
which takes pairs of *x*- and *y*-coordinates as the points attribute. You separate the numbers with either blanks or commas as you please. The result
is in Figure 1-12.

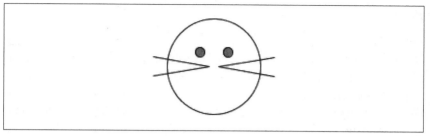

Figure 1-11. Stage four—left whiskers

Example 1-6. Basic shapes—polylines

```
<svg width="140" height="170">
<title>Cat</title>
<desc>Stick Figure of a Cat</desc>

<circle cx="70" cy="95" r="50" style="stroke: black; fill: none;"/>
<circle cx="55" cy="80" r="5" stroke="black" fill="#339933"/>
<circle cx="85" cy="80" r="5" stroke="black" fill="#339933"/>
<g id="whiskers">
    <line x1="75" y1="95" x2="135" y2="85" style="stroke: black;"/>
    <line x1="75" y1="95" x2="135" y2="105" style="stroke: black;"/>
</g>
<use xlink:href="#whiskers" transform="scale(-1 1) translate(-140 0)"/>
<!-- ears -->
<polyline points="108 62,  90 10,  70 45,  50, 10,  32, 62"
    style="stroke: black; fill: none;" />
<!-- mouth -->
<polyline points="35 110, 45 120, 95 120, 105, 110"
    style="stroke: black; fill: none;" />
</svg>
```

Figure 1-12. Stage five—ears and mouth

Paths

All of the basic shapes are actually shortcuts for the more general <path>
element, which Example 1-7 uses to add the cat's nose. The result is in
Figure 1-13. This element has been designed to make specifying a path, or
sequence of lines and curves, as compact as possible. The path in Example 1-7 translates, in words, to: "Move to coordinate (75,90). Draw a line
to coordinate (65,90). Draw an elliptical arc with an *x*-radius of 5
and a *y*-radius of 10, ending back at coordinate (75,90)."

Example 1-7. Paths

```
<svg width="140" height="170">
<title>Cat</title>
<desc>Stick Figure of a Cat</desc>

<circle cx="70" cy="95" r="50" style="stroke: black; fill: none;"/>
<circle cx="55" cy="80" r="5" stroke="black" fill="#339933"/>
<circle cx="85" cy="80" r="5" stroke="black" fill="#339933"/>
<g id="whiskers">
    <line x1="75" y1="95" x2="135" y2="85" style="stroke: black;"/>
    <line x1="75" y1="95" x2="135" y2="105" style="stroke: black;"/>
</g>
<use xlink:href="#whiskers" transform="scale(-1 1) translate(-140 0)"/>
<!-- ears -->
<polyline points="108 62,  90 10,  70 45,  50, 10,  32, 62"
    style="stroke: black; fill: none;" />
<!-- mouth -->
<polyline points="35 110, 45 120, 95 120, 105, 110"
    style="stroke: black; fill: none;" />
<!-- nose -->
<path d="M 75 90 L 65 90 A 5 10 0  0 0 75 90"
    style="stroke: black; fill: #ffcccc"/>
</svg>
```

Figure 1-13. Stage six—nose

Text

Finally, since this picture is so crudely drawn, there's a good chance that
people will not know it is a cat. Hence, Example 1-8 adds text to the picture as a label. In the `<text>` element, the x and y attributes which specify
the text's location are part of the structure. The font family and font size
are part of the presentation, and thus part of the `style` attribute. Unlike
the other elements we've seen, `<text>` is a container element, and its content is the text we want to display. Figure 1-14 (see additional color insert)
shows the final result.

Figure 1-14. Stage seven—text and finished image

Example 1-8. Text

```
<svg width="140" height="170">
<title>Cat</title>
<desc>Stick Figure of a Cat</desc>

<circle cx="70" cy="95" r="50" style="stroke: black; fill: none;"/>
<circle cx="55" cy="80" r="5" stroke="black" fill="#339933"/>
<circle cx="85" cy="80" r="5" stroke="black" fill="#339933"/>
<g id="whiskers">
    <line x1="75" y1="95" x2="135" y2="85" style="stroke: black;"/>
    <line x1="75" y1="95" x2="135" y2="105" style="stroke: black;"/>
</g>
<use xlink:href="#whiskers" transform="scale(-1 1) translate(-140 0)"/>
<!-- ears -->
<polyline points="108 62,  90 10,  70 45,  50, 10,  32, 62"
    style="stroke: black; fill: none;" />
<!-- mouth -->
<polyline points="35 110, 45 120, 95 120, 105, 110"
    style="stroke: black; fill: none;" />
```

Example 1-8. Text (continued)

```
<!-- nose -->
<path d="M 75 90 L 65 90 A 5 10 0  0 0 75 90"
   style="stroke: black; fill: #ffcccc"/>
<text x="60" y="165" style="font-family: sans-serif; font-size: 14pt;
   stroke: none; fill: black;">Cat</text>
</svg>
```

That concludes our brief overview of SVG; in the following chapters we'll examine these concepts in depth.

2

Coordinates

The world of SVG is an infinite canvas. In this chapter, we'll discuss how you tell a viewer program which part of this canvas you're interested in, what its dimensions are, and how you locate points within that area.

The Viewport

The area of the canvas that your document intends to use is called the viewport. You establish the size of this viewport with the width and height attributes on the <svg> element. The values of these attributes can be simply a number, which is presumed to be in pixels; this is said to be specified in user coordinates. You may also specify width and height as a number followed by a unit identifier, which can be one of the following:

em The font size of the default font, usually equivalent to the height of a character

ex The height of the letter x

px Pixels

pt Points ($1/72$ of an inch)

pc Picas ($1/6$ of an inch)

cm Centimeters

mm Millimeters

in Inches

Examples:

```
<svg width="200" height="150">
<svg width="200px" height="200px">
```
Both of these specify an area 200 pixels wide and 150 pixels tall.

```
<svg width="2cm" height="3cm">
```
Specifies an area two centimeters wide and three centimeters high.

```
<svg width="2cm" height="36pt">
```
It is possible, though unusual, to mix units; this element specifies an area two centimeters wide and thirty-six points high.

If you have one `<svg>` element nested within another `<svg>` element, the nested tag may also specify its `width` and `height` as a percentage, measured in terms of the enclosing element. We will see nested `<svg>` elements in the section "Nested Systems of Coordinates."

Using Default User Coordinates

When you do not use unit specifiers on your `<svg>` element, the viewer sets up a coordinate system where the horizontal, or x-coordinate, increases as you go to the right, and the vertical, or y-coordinate, increases as you move vertically downward. The upper left corner of the viewport is defined to have an x- and y-coordinate of zero.* This point, written as (0, 0) is also called the origin. The coordinate system is a pure geometric system; points have neither width nor height, and the grid lines are considered infinitely thin. We'll return to this subject in Chapter 3.

Example 2-1 establishes a viewport two hundred pixels wide and two hundred pixels high, then draws a rectangle whose upper left corner is at coordinate (10, 10) with a width of 50 pixels and a height of 30 pixels.†
Figure 2-1 shows the result, with rulers and a grid to show the coordinate system.

Example 2-1. Using default coordinates

```
<svg width="200" height="200">
    <rect x="10" y="10" width="50" height="30"
        style="stroke: black; fill: none;"/>
</svg>
```

---

* In this book, we will specify a pair of x- and y-coordinates in parentheses, with the x-coordinate first. Thus, (10, 30) represents an x-coordinate of 10 and a y-coordinate of 30.

† To save space, we are leaving out the `<?xml ...?>` and `<!DOCTYPE ...>` lines. These are set in stone, so you can take them for granite.

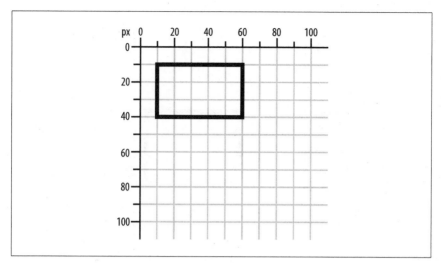

Figure 2-1. Rectangle using default coordinates

Even if you don't specify units in the viewport, you may still use them in some SVG shape elements, as we do in Example 2-2. Figure 2-2 shows the result, with rulers and a grid to show the coordinate system.

Example 2-2. Explicit use of units

```
<svg width="200" height="200">
    <rect x="10mm" y="10mm" width="15mm" height="10mm"
        style="stroke:black; fill:none;"/>
</svg>
```

Specifying units in the <svg> element does not affect coordinates given without units in other elements. Example 2-3 shows a viewport set up in millimeters, but the rectangle is still drawn at pixel (user) coordinates, as you see in Figure 2-3.

Example 2-3. Units on the svg element

```
<svg width="70mm" height="70mm">
    <rect x="10" y="10" width="50" height="30"
        style="fill: none; stroke: black;"/>
</svg>
```

Specifying User Coordinates for a Viewport

In the examples so far, numbers without units have been considered to be pixels. Sometimes this is not what you want. For example, you might want to set up a system where each user coordinate represents one-sixteenth of

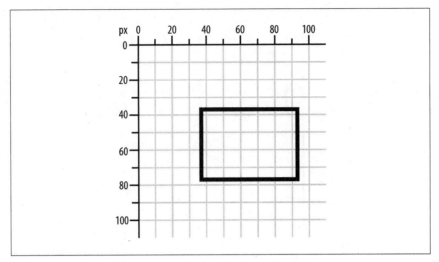

Figure 2-2. Rectangle using explicit units

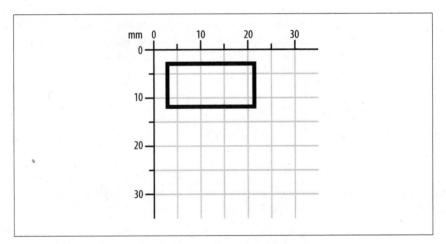

Figure 2-3. Viewport with units; rectangle without units

a centimeter. (We're using this coordinate system to prove a point, not to show a paragon of good design.) In this system, a square that is 40 units by 40 units will display as 2.5 centimeters on a side.

To accomplish this effect, you set the viewBox attribute on the <svg> element. The value of this attribute consists of four numbers that represent the minimum *x*-coordinate, minimum *y*-coordinate, width, and height of the user coordinate system that you want to superimpose on the viewport.

So, to set up the sixteen-units-per-centimeter coordinate system for a four centimeter by five centimeter drawing, you'd use this starting tag:

```
<svg width="4cm" height="5cm" viewBox="0 0 64 80">
```

Example 2-4 lists the SVG for a picture of a house, displayed using the new coordinate system.

Example 2-4. Using a viewBox

```
<svg width="4cm" height="5cm" viewBox="0 0 64 80">
   <rect x="10" y="35" width="40" height="40"
      style="stroke: black; fill: none;"/>
   <!-- roof -->
   <polyline points="10 35, 30 7.68, 50 35"
      style="stroke:black; fill: none;"/>
   <!-- door -->
   <polyline points="30 75, 30 55, 40 55, 40 75"
      style="stroke:black; fill: none;"/>
</svg>
```

Figure 2-4 shows the result. The grid and darker numbers show the new user coordinate system; the lighter numbers are positioned at one-centimeter intervals.

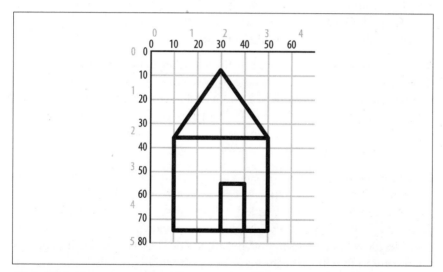

Figure 2-4. New user coordinates

The numbers you specify for the value of the viewBox attribute may be separated by commas or whitespace. If either the width or height is zero, none of your graphic will display. It is an error to specify a negative value for the viewBox width or height.

Preserving Aspect Ratio

In the previous example, the aspect ratio, or ratio of width to height, of the viewport and the viewBox were identical (4/5 = 64/80). What happens, though, if the aspect ratio of the viewport and the viewBox are not the same, as in this example, where viewBox has an aspect ratio of one to one, but the viewport has an aspect ratio of one to three?

```
<svg width="45px" height="135px" viewBox="0 0 90 90">
```

There are three things that SVG can do in this situation:

- Scale the graphic uniformly according to the smaller dimension so the graphic will fit entirely into the viewport. In the example, the picture would become half its original width and height. We'll show you examples of this in the section "Using the meet Specifier."

- Scale the graphic uniformly according to the larger dimension and cut off the parts that lie outside the viewport. In the example, the picture would become one and a half times its original width and height. We'll show you examples in the section "Using the slice Specifier."

- Stretch and squash the drawing so that it fits precisely into the new viewport. (That is, don't preserve the aspect ratio at all.) We will cover this in the section "Using the none Specifier."

In the first case, since the image will be smaller than the viewport in one dimension, you must specify where to position it. In the example, the picture will be scaled uniformly to a width and height of 45 pixels. The width of the reduced graphic fits the width of the viewport perfectly, but you must now decide whether the image meets (is aligned with) the top, middle, or bottom of the 135-pixel viewport height.

In the second case, since the image will be larger than the viewport in one dimension, you must specify which area is to be sliced away. In the example, the picture will be scaled uniformly to a width and height of 135 pixels. Now the height of the graphic fits the viewport perfectly, but you must decide whether to slice off the right side, left side, or both edges of the picture to fit within the 45-pixel viewport width.

Specifying Alignment for preserveAspectRatio

The preserveAspectRatio attribute lets you specify the alignment of the scaled image with respect to the viewport, and whether you want it to meet the edges or be sliced off. The model for this attribute is:

```
preserveAspectRatio="alignment [meet | slice]"
```

where *alignment* specifies the axis and location, and is one of xMinYMin, xMinYMid, xMinYMax, xMidYMin, xMidYMid, xMidYMax, xMaxYMin, xMaxYMid, or xMaxYMax. This alignment specifier is formed by concatenating an *x*-alignment and a *y*-alignment as shown in Table 2-1. The default value for preserveAspectRatio is xMidYMid meet.

> The *y*-alignment begins with a capital letter, since the *x*- and *y*-alignments are concatenated into a single word.

Table 2-1. Values for alignment portion of preserveAspectRatio

X alignment

Value	Action
xMin	Align minimum *x* of viewBox with left corner of viewport.
xMid	Align midpoint *x* value of viewBox with midpoint *x* value of viewport.
xMax	Align maximum *x* value of viewBox with right corner of viewport.

Y alignment

Value	Action
YMin	Align minimum *y* of viewBox with top edge of viewport.
YMid	Align midpoint *y* value of viewBox with midpoint *y* value of viewport.
YMax	Align maximum *y* value of viewBox with bottom edge of viewport.

So, if you want to have the picture with a viewBox="0 0 90 90" fit entirely within a viewport that is 45 pixels wide and 135 pixels high, aligned at the top of the viewport, you would write:

```
<svg width="45px" height="135px" viewBox="0 0 90 90"
     preserveAspectRatio="xMinYMin meet">
```

> In this case, since the width fits precisely, the *x*-alignment is irrelevant; you could equally well use xMidYmin or xMaxYMin. However, in the interests of consistency, it's usually best to make both specifiers the same when only one axis is affected.

This is all fairly abstract; here are some concrete examples that show you how the combinations of alignment and meet and slice interact with one another.

Using the meet Specifier

The starting <svg> tags in Example 2-5 all use the meet specifier.

Example 2-5. Use of meet specifier

```
<!-- tall viewports -->
<svg preserveAspectRatio="xMinYMin meet" viewBox="0 0 90 90"
    width="45" height="135">

<svg preserveAspectRatio="xMidYMid meet" viewBox="0 0 90 90"
    width="45" height="135">

<svg preserveAspectRatio="xMaxYMax meet" viewBox="0 0 90 90"
    width="45" height="135">

<!-- wide viewports -->
<svg preserveAspectRatio="xMinYMin meet" viewBox="0 0 90 90"
    width="135" height="45">

<svg preserveAspectRatio="xMidYMid meet" viewBox="0 0 90 90"
    width="135" height="45">

<svg preserveAspectRatio="xMaxYMax meet" viewBox="0 0 90 90"
    width="135" height="45">
```

Figure 2-5 shows where the reduced image fits into the enclosing viewBox.

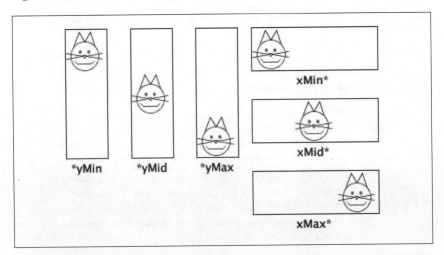

Figure 2-5. meet—viewBox fits in viewport

Using the slice Specifier

Figure 2-6 shows the use of the `slice` specifier to eliminate parts of the picture that do not fit in the viewport. They were created with the `<svg>` tags in Example 2-6.

Example 2-6. Use of slice specifier

```
<!-- tall viewports -->
<svg preserveAspectRatio="xMinYMin slice" viewBox="0 0 90 90"
    width="45" height="135">

<svg preserveAspectRatio="xMidYMid slice" viewBox="0 0 90 90"
    width="45" height="135">

<svg preserveAspectRatio="xMaxYMax slice" viewBox="0 0 90 90"
    width="45" height="135">

<!-- wide viewports -->
<svg preserveAspectRatio="xMinYMin slice" viewBox="0 0 90 90"
    width="135" height="45">

<svg preserveAspectRatio="xMidYMid slice" viewBox="0 0 90 90"
    width="135" height="45">

<svg preserveAspectRatio="xMaxYMax slice" viewBox="0 0 90 90"
    width="135" height="45">
```

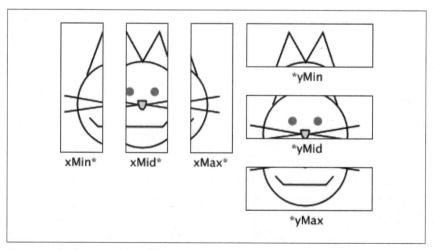

Figure 2-6. slice—graphic fills viewport

Using the none Specifier

Finally, there is the third option for scaling a graphic when the `viewBox` and `viewPort` don't have the same aspect ratio. If you specify `preserveAspectRatio="none"`, then the graphic will be scaled non-uniformly so that its user coordinates fit the viewport. Figure 2-7 shows such a "fun-house mirror" effect produced with the `<svg>` tags in Example 2-7.

Example 2-7. Aspect ratio not preserved

```
<!-- tall viewport -->
<svg preserveAspectRatio="none" viewBox="0 0 90 90"
   width="45" height="135">

<!-- wide viewport -->
<svg preserveAspectRatio="none" viewBox="0 0 90 90"
   width="135" height="45">
```

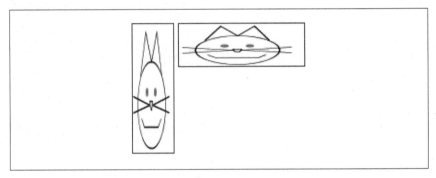

Figure 2-7. Aspect ratio not preserved

Nested Systems of Coordinates

You can establish a new viewport and system of coordinates at any time by putting another `<svg>` element into your document. The effect is to create a "mini-canvas" upon which you can draw. We used this technique to create illustrations such as Figure 2-5. Rather than drawing the rectangles, then rescaling and positioning the cat inside each one (the brute force approach), we took these steps:

- Draw the blue rectangles on the main canvas

- For each rectangle, define a new `<svg>` element with the appropriate `preserveAspectRatio` attribute

- Draw the cat into that new canvas (with `<use>`), and let SVG do the heavy lifting

Here's a simplified example that shows a circle on the main canvas, then inside a new canvas that's outlined by a blue rectangle that's also on the main canvas. Figure 2-8 is the result we wish to achieve.

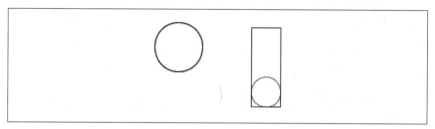

Figure 2-8. Nested viewport example

First, generate the SVG for the main coordinate system and the circle. Note that we've established the user coordinates to coincide exactly with the viewport in this document.

```
<svg width="200px" height="200px" viewBox="0 0 200 200">
    <circle cx="25" cy="25" r="25" style="stroke: black; fill: none;"/>
</svg>
```

The result is in Figure 2-9.

Figure 2-9. Circle in main viewport

Now, draw the boundary of the box showing where we want the new viewport to be:

```
<svg width="200px" height="200px" viewBox="0 0 200 200">
    <circle cx="25" cy="25" r="25" style="stroke: black; fill: none;"/>
    <rect x="100" y="5" width="30" height="80"
        style="stroke: blue; fill: none;"/>
</svg>
```

This produces Figure 2-10.

Now, add another <svg> element for the new viewport. In addition to specifying the viewBox, width, height, and preserveAspectRatio specification, you may also specify the x and y attributes—in terms of the enclosing <svg> element—where the new viewport is to be established. (If you don't give values for x and y, they are presumed to be zero.)

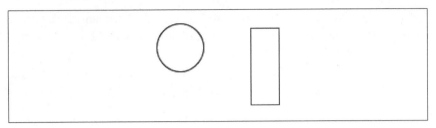

Figure 2-10. Circle and boundary box in main viewport

```
<svgwidth="200px" height="200px" viewBox="0 0 200 200">
   <circle cx="25" cy="25" r="25" style="stroke: black; fill: none;"/>
   <rect x="100" y="5" width="30" height="80"
      style="stroke: blue; fill: none;"/>

   <svg x="100px" y="5px" width="30px" height="80px" viewBox="0 0 50 50"
      preserveAspectRatio="xMaxYMax meet">
   </svg>
</svg>
```

Setting up the new coordinates with this nested <svg> element doesn't change the visual display, but it does permit you to add the circle in that new system, producing the result shown in Figure 2-8.

```
<svg width="200px" height="200px" viewBox="0 0 200 200">
   <circle cx="25" cy="25" r="25" style="stroke: black; fill: none;"/>
   <rect x="100" y="5" width="30" height="80" style="stroke: blue;
      fill: none;"/>

   <svg x="100px" y="5px" width="30px" height="80px" viewBox="0 0 50 50"
      preserveAspectRatio="xMaxYMax meet">
      <circle cx="25" cy="25" r="25" style="stroke: black;
         fill: none;"/>
   </svg>
</svg>
```

3

Basic Shapes

Once a coordinate system is established in the `<svg>` tag, you are ready to begin drawing. In this chapter, we will show the basic shapes you can use to create the major elements of most drawings: lines, rectangles, polygons, circles, and ellipses.

Lines

SVG lets you draw a straight line with the `<line>` element. Just specify the *x*- and *y*-coordinates of the line's endpoints. Coordinates may be specified without units, in which case they are considered to be user coordinates, or with units such as em, in, etc. as described in Chapter 2, in the section "The Viewport." The SVG in Example 3-1 draws several lines; the reference grid in Figure 3-1 is not part of the SVG that you see here.

```
<line x1="start-x" y1="start-y"
x2="end-x" y2="end-y">
```

Example 3-1. Basic lines

```
<svg width="200px" height="200px" viewBox="0 0 200 200">
    <!-- horizontal line -->
    <line x1="40" y1="20" x2="80" y2="20" style="stroke: black;"/>
    <!-- vertical line -->
    <line x1="0.7cm" y1="1cm" x2="0.7cm" y2="2.0cm" style="stroke: black;"/>
    <!-- diagonal line -->
    <line x1="30" y1="30" x2="85" y2="85" style="stroke: black;"/>
</svg>
```

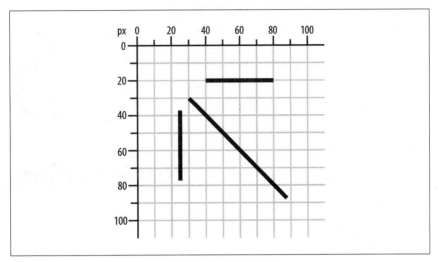

Figure 3-1. Basic lines

Stroke Characteristics

Lines are considered to be strokes of a pen that draws on the canvas. The size, color, and style of the pen stroke are part of the line's presentation. Thus, these characteristics will go into the `style` attribute.

stroke-width

As mentioned in Chapter 2, the canvas grid lines are infinitely thin. Where, then, does a line or stroke fall in relation to the grid line? The answer is that the grid line falls in the center of a stroke. Example 3-2 draws some lines where the stroke width has been set to ten user coordinates to make the effect obvious. The result, in Figure 3-2, has the grid lines drawn in so you can see the effect clearly.

Example 3-2. Demonstration of stroke-width

```
<svg width="200px" height="200px" viewBox="0 0 200 200">
    <!-- horizontal line -->
    <line x1="30" y1="10" x2="80" y2="10"
        style="stroke-width: 10; stroke: black;"/>
    <!-- vertical line -->
    <line x1="10" y1="30" x2="10" y2="80"
        style="stroke-width: 10; stroke: black;"/>
    <!-- diagonal line -->
    <line x1="25" y1="25" x2="75" y2="75"
        style="stroke-width: 10; stroke: black;"/>
</svg>
```

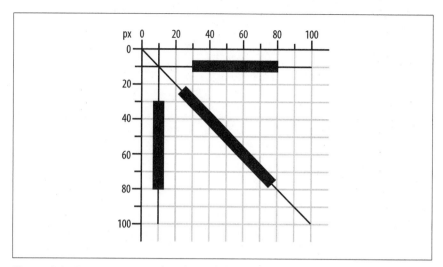

Figure 3-2. Demonstration of stroke-width

stroke Color

You can specify the stroke color in a variety of ways:

- One of the color keyword names: aqua, black, blue, fuchsia, gray, green, lime, maroon, navy, olive, purple, red, silver, teal, white, and yellow.

- A six-digit hexadecimal specifier in the form #*rrggbb*, where *rr* is the red component, *gg* is the green component, and *bb* is the blue component in the range 0-ff.

- A three-digit hexadecimal specifier in the form #*rgb*, where *r* is the red component, *g* is the green component, and *b* is the blue component in the range 0-f. This is a shorthand form of the previous method of specifying color. To produce the six-digit equivalent, each digit of the short form is duplicated; thus #d6e is the same as #dd66ee.

- An rgb specifier in the form rgb(*red-value*, *green-value*, *blue-value*), where each value is in the range 0-255 or a percentage in the range 0% to 100%. Example 3-3 uses all of these methods, with the colorful results of Figure 3-3 (see additional color insert).

Example 3-3. Demonstration of stroke color

```
<svg width="200px" height="200px" viewBox="0 0 200 200">
    <!-- red -->
    <line x1="10" y1="10" x2="50" y2="10"
        style="stroke: red; stroke-width: 5;"/>
```

Example 3-3. Demonstration of stroke color (continued)

```
<!-- light green -->
<line x1="10" y1="20" x2="50" y2="20"
    style="stroke: #9f9; stroke-width: 5;"/>

<!-- light blue -->
<line x1="10" y1="30" x2="50" y2="30"
    style="stroke: #9999ff; stroke-width: 5;"/>

<!-- medium orange -->
<line x1="10" y1="40" x2="50" y2="40"
    style="stroke: rgb(255, 128, 64); stroke-width: 5;"/>

<!-- deep purple -->
<line x1="10" y1="50" x2="50" y2="50"
    style="stroke: rgb(60%, 20%, 60%); stroke-width: 5;"/>
</svg>
```

Figure 3-3. Demonstration of stroke color

stroke-opacity

Up to this point, all the lines in the example have been solid, obscuring anything beneath them. You control the opacity (which is the opposite of transparency) of a line by giving the `stroke-opacity` a value from 0.0 to 1.0, where zero is completely transparent and one is completely opaque. A value less than zero will be changed to zero; a value greater than one will be changed to one. Example 3-4 varies the opacity from 0.2 to 1 in steps of 0.2, with the result in Figure 3-4.

Example 3-4. Demonstration of stroke-opacity

```
<svg width="200px" height="200px" viewBox="0 0 200 200">
    <line x1="10" y1="10" x2="50" y2="10"
        style="stroke-opacity: 0.2; stroke: black; stroke-width: 5;"/>
    <line x1="10" y1="20" x2="50" y2="20"
        style="stroke-opacity: 0.4; stroke: black; stroke-width: 5;"/>
    <line x1="10" y1="30" x2="50" y2="30"
        style="stroke-opacity: 0.6; stroke: black; stroke-width: 5;"/>
    <line x1="10" y1="40" x2="50" y2="40"
        style="stroke-opacity: 0.8; stroke: black; stroke-width: 5;"/>
    <line x1="10" y1="50" x2="50" y2="50"
        style="stroke-opacity: 1.0; stroke: black; stroke-width: 5;"/>
</svg>
```

Figure 3-4. Demonstration of stroke-opacity

stroke-dasharray attribute

If you need dotted or dashed lines, use the `stroke-dasharray` attribute, whose value consists of a list of numbers, separated by commas or white-space, specifying dash length and gaps. The list should have an even number of entries, but if you give an odd number of entries, SVG will repeat the list so the total number of entries is even. (See the last instance in Example 3-5.)

Example 3-5. Demonstration of stroke-dasharray

```
<svg width="200px" height="200px" viewBox="0 0 200 200">
    <!-- nine-pixel dash, five-pixel gap -->
    <line x1="10" y1="10" x2="100" y2="10"
        style="stroke-dasharray: 9, 5;
        stroke: black; stroke-width: 2;"/>

    <!-- five-pixel dash, three-pixel gap, nine-pixel dash, two-pixel gap -->
    <line x1="10" y1="20" x2="100" y2="20"
        style="stroke-dasharray: 5, 3, 9, 2;
        stroke: black; stroke-width: 2;"/>

    <!-- Odd number of entries is duplicated; this is equivalent to:
         nine-pixel dash, three-pixel gap,  five-pixel dash,
         nine-pixel gap,  three-pixel dash, five-pixel gap -->
    <line x1="10" y1="30" x2="100" y2="30"
        style="stroke-dasharray: 9, 3, 5;
        stroke: black; stroke-width: 2;"/>
</svg>
```

Figure 3-5 shows the results, zoomed in for clarity.

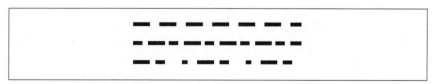

Figure 3-5. Demonstration of stroke-dasharray

Rectangles

The rectangle is the simplest of the basic shapes. You specify the *x*- and
y-coordinates of the upper left corner of the rectangle,* its width, and its
height. The interior of the rectangle is filled with the fill color you specify. If you do not specify a fill color, the interior of the shape is filled with
black. The fill color may be·specified in any of the ways described in the
section "stroke Color," or it may take the value none to leave the interior
unfilled and thus transparent. You may also specify a fill-opacity in the
same format as you did in the section "stroke-opacity." Both fill and
fill-opacity are presentation properties, and belong in the style
attribute.

After the interior is filled (if necessary), the outline of the rectangle is
drawn with strokes, whose characteristics you may specify as you did for
lines. If you do not specify a stroke, the value none is presumed, and no
outline is drawn. Example 3-6 draws several variations of the <rect> element. Figure 3-6 (see additional color insert) shows the result, with a grid
for reference.

Example 3-6. Demonstration of the rectangle element

```
<svg width="200px" height="200px" viewBox="0 0 200 200">
    <!-- black interior, no outline -->
    <rect x="10" y="10" width="30" height="50"/>

    <!-- no interior, black outline -->
    <rect x="50" y="10" width="20" height="40"
       style="fill: none; stroke: black;"/>

    <!-- blue interior, thick semi-transparent red outline -->
    <rect x="10" y="70" width="25" height="30"
       style="fill: #0000ff;
          stroke: red; stroke-width: 7; stroke-opacity: 0.5;"/>

    <!-- semi-transparent yellow interior, dashed green outline -->
    <rect x="50" y="70" width="35" height="20"
       style="fill: yellow; fill-opacity: 0.5;
          stroke: green; stroke-width: 2; stroke-dasharray: 5 2"/>
</svg>
```

---

* Technically, the x value is the smaller of the *x*-coordinate values and the y is the smaller of
  the *y*-coordinate values of the rectangle's sides in the current user coordinate system.
  Since we are not yet using transformations, which we will cover in Chapter 5, this is the
  moral equivalent of the upper left corner.

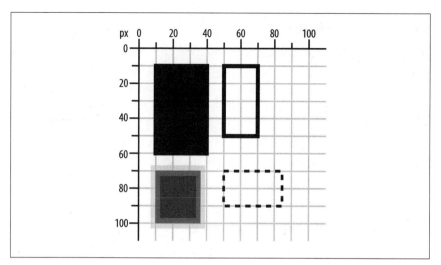

Figure 3-6. Demonstration of the rect element

 Since the strokes that form the outline "straddle" the abstract grid lines, the strokes will be half inside the shape and half outside the shape. Figure 3-7 (see additional color insert), a closeup of the semi-transparent red outline drawn in Example 3-6, shows this clearly.

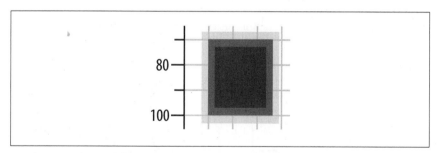

Figure 3-7. Closeup of transparent border

If you do not specify a starting x or y value, it is presumed to be zero. If you specify a width or height of zero, then the rectangle is not displayed. It is an error to provide negative values for either width or height.

Rounded Rectangles

If you wish to have rectangles with rounded corners, specify the *x*- and *y*-radius of the corner curvature. The maximum number you may specify for rx (the *x*-radius) is one-half the width of the rectangle; the maximum value of ry (the *y*-radius) is one-half the height of the rectangle. If you specify only one of rx or ry, they are presumed to be equal. Example 3-7 shows various combinations of rx and ry.

Example 3-7. Demonstration of rounded rectangles

```
<svg width="200px" height="200px" viewBox="0 0 200 200">
    <!-- rx and ry equal, increasing -->
    <rect x="10" y="10" width="20" height="40" rx="2" ry="2"
        style="stroke: black; fill: none;"/>

    <rect x="40" y="10" width="20" height="40" rx="5"
        style="stroke: black; fill: none;"/>

    <rect x="70" y="10" width="20" height="40" ry="10"
        style="stroke: black; fill: none;"/>

    <!-- rx and ry unequal -->
    <rect x="10" y="60" width="20" height="40" rx="10" ry="5"
        style="stroke: black; fill: none;"/>

    <rect x="40" y="60" width="20" height="40" rx="5" ry="10"
        style="stroke: black; fill: none;"/>
</svg>
```

Figure 3-8 shows the result, with a grid in the background for reference.

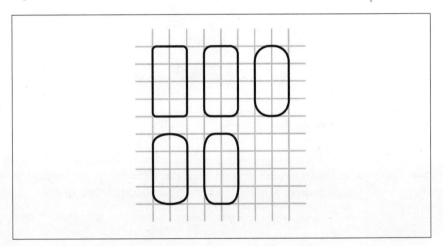

Figure 3-8. Demonstration of rounded rectangles

Circles and Ellipses

To draw a circle, use the `<circle>` element and specify the center *x*-coordinate, center *y*-coordinate, and radius with the `cx`, `cy`, and `r` attributes. As with a rectangle, the default is to fill the circle with black and draw no outline unless you specify some other combination of `fill` and `stroke`.

An ellipse also needs an *x*-radius and a *y*-radius in addition to a center *x*- and *y*-coordinate. The attributes for these radii are named `rx` and `ry`.

In both circles and ellipses, if the `cx` or `cy` is omitted, it is presumed to be zero. If the radius is zero, no shape will be displayed; it is an error to provide a negative radius. Example 3-8 draws some circles and ellipses which are shown in Figure 3-9.

Example 3-8. Demonstration of circles and ellipses

```
<svg width="200px" height="200px" viewBox="0 0 200 200">
   <circle cx="30" cy="30" r="20" style="stroke: black; fill: none;"/>
   <circle cx="80" cy="30" r="20"
      style="stroke-width: 5; stroke: black; fill: none;"/>

   <ellipse cx="30" cy="80" rx="10" ry="20"
      style="stroke: black; fill: none;"/>
   <ellipse cx="80" cy="80" rx="20" ry="10"
      style="stroke: black; fill: none;"/>
</svg>
```

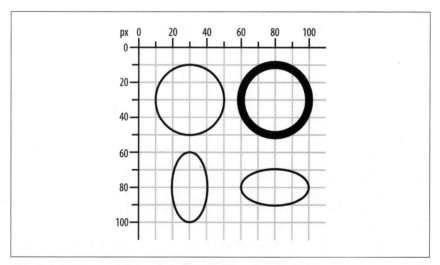

Figure 3-9. Demonstration of circle and ellipse elements

The polygon Element

In addition to rectangles, circles, and ellipses, you may want to draw hexagons, octagons, stars, or arbitrary closed shapes. The <polygon> element lets you specify a series of points that describe a geometric area to be filled and outlined as described earlier. The points attribute consists of a series of *x*- and *y*-coordinate pairs separated by commas or whitespace. You must give an even number of entries in the series of numbers. You don't have to return to the starting point; the shape will automatically be closed. Example 3-9 uses the <polygon> element to draw a parallelogram, a star, and an irregular shape.

Example 3-9. Demonstration of the polygon element

```
<svg width="200px" height="200px" viewBox="0 0 200 200">
    <!-- parallelogram -->
    <polygon points="15,10  55, 10  45, 20  5, 20"
        style="fill: red; stroke: black;"/>

    <!-- star -->
    <polygon
        points="35,37.5  37.9,46.1  46.9,46.1  39.7,51.5
                42.3,60.1  35,55  27.7,60.1  30.3,51.5
                23.1,46.1  32.1,46.1"
        style="fill: #ccffcc; stroke: green;"/>

    <!-- weird shape -->
    <polygon
        points="60 60,  65 72,  80 60,  90 90, 72 80, 72 85, 50 95"
        style="fill: yellow; fill-opacity: 0.5; stroke: black;
                stroke-width: 2;"/>
</svg>
```

The results, with a grid in the background for reference, are displayed in Figure 3-10.

Filling Polygons That Have Intersecting Lines

For the polygons shown so far, it's been easy to fill the shape. Since none of the lines forming the polygon cross over one another, the interior is easily distinguished from the exterior of the shape. However, when lines cross over one another, the determination of what is inside the polygon is not as easy. The SVG in Example 3-10 draws such a polygon. In Figure 3-11, is the middle section of the star considered to be inside or outside?

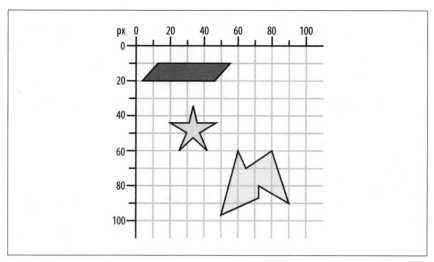

Figure 3-10. Demonstration of the polygon element

Example 3-10. Unfilled polygon with intersecting lines

```
<svg width="200px" height="200px" viewBox="0 0 200 200">

<polygon points="48,16  16,96  96,48  0,48  80,96"
    style="stroke: black; fill: none;"/>

</svg>
```

Figure 3-11. Unfilled polygon with intersecting lines

SVG has two different rules for determining whether a point is inside a polygon or outside it. The fill-rule (which is part of presentation) has a value of either nonzero or evenodd. Depending on the rule you choose, you get a different effect. Example 3-11 uses the rules to fill two diagrams of the star, as shown in Figure 3-12.

Example 3-11. Effect of different fill-rules

```
<svg width="200px" height="200px" viewBox="0 0 200 200">

<polygon style="fill-rule: nonzero; fill: yellow; stroke: black;"
    points="48,16  16,96  96,48  0,48  80,96" />

<polygon style="fill-rule: evenodd;  fill: #00ff00; stroke: black;"
    points="148,16  116,96  196,48  100,48  180,96" />

</svg>
```

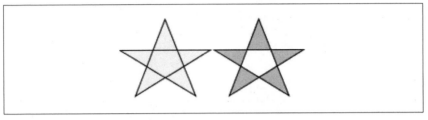

Figure 3-12. Effect of different fill-rules

Explanation of the Fill Rules

For the sake of completeness, we are describing how these fill-rules work, but you don't need to know the details in order to use them. The nonzero rule determines whether a point is inside or outside a polygon by drawing a line from the point in question to infinity. It counts how many times that line crosses the polygon's lines, adding one if the polygon line is going right to left, and subtracting one if the polygon line is going left to right. If the total comes out to zero, the point is outside the polygon. If the total is nonzero (hence the name) the point is inside the polygon.

The evenodd rule also draws a line from the point in question to infinity, but it simply counts how many times that line crosses your polygon's lines. If the total number of crossings is odd, then the point is inside; if even, then the point is outside.

The polyline Element

Finally, to round out our discussion of basic shapes, we'll return to straight lines. Sometimes you want a series of lines that does not make a closed shape. You can use multiple <line> elements, but if there are many lines it might be easier to use the <polyline> element. It has the same attributes as <polygon>, except that the shape is not closed. Example 3-12 draws the symbol for an electrical resistor, shown in Figure 3-13.

Example 3-12. Example of the polyline element

```
<svg width="200px" height="200px" viewBox="0 0 200 200">

<polyline
    points="5 20, 20 20, 25 10, 35 30, 45 10,
        55 30, 65 10, 75 30, 80 20, 95 20"
    style="stroke: black; stroke-width: 3; fill: none;"/>

</svg>
```

Figure 3-13. Example of the polyline element

 It's best to set the fill property to none when using <polyline>; otherwise, the SVG viewer attempts to fill the shape, sometimes with startling results like those in Figure 3-14.

Figure 3-14. Example of filled polyline

Line Caps and Joins

When drawing a <line> or <polyline>, you may specify the shape of the endpoints of the lines by setting the stroke-linecap style property to one of the values butt, round, or square. Example 3-13 shows these three values, with gray guide lines showing the actual endpoints of the lines. You can see in Figure 3-15 that round and square extend beyond the end coordinates; butt, the default, ends exactly at the specified endpoint.

Example 3-13. Values of the stroke-linecap property

```
<line x1="10" y1="15" x2="50" y2="15"
    style="stroke-linecap: butt; stroke-width: 15;"/>

<line x1="10" y1="45" x2="50" y2="45"
    style="stroke-linecap: round; stroke-width: 15;"/>
```

Example 3-13. Values of the stroke-linecap property (continued)

```
<line x1="10" y1="75" x2="50" y2="75"
    style="stroke-linecap: square; stroke-width: 15;"/>

<!-- guide lines -->
<line x1="10" y1="0" x2="10" y2="100" style="stroke: #999;"/>
<line x1="50" y1="0" x2="50" y2="100" style="stroke: #999;"/>
```

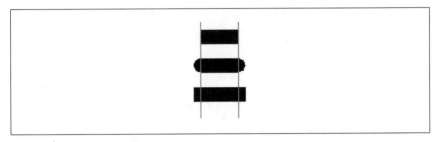

Figure 3-15. Values of the stroke-linecap attribute

You may specify the way lines connect at the corners of a shape with the stroke-linejoin style property, which may have the values miter (pointed), round (round—what did you expect?), or bevel (flat). Example 3-14 produces the result shown in Figure 3-16.

Example 3-14. Values of the stroke-linejoin attribute

```
<polyline
    style="stroke-linejoin: miter; stroke: black; stroke-width: 12;
    fill: none;"
    points="30 30, 45 15, 60 30"/>

<polyline
    style="stroke-linejoin: round; stroke: black; stroke-width: 12;
    fill: none;"
    points="90 30, 105 15, 120 30"/>

<polyline
    style="stroke-linejoin: bevel; stroke-width: 12; stroke: black;
    fill: none;"
    points="150 30, 165 15, 180 30"/>
```

Figure 3-16. Values of the stroke-linejoin attribute

If your lines meet at a sharp angle and have a mitered join, it's possible for the pointed part to extend beyond the lines' thickness. You may set the ratio of the miter to the thickness of the lines being joined with the stroke-miterlimit style property; its default value is 4.

Basic Shapes Reference Summary

The following tables summarize the basic shapes and presentation styles in SVG.

Shape Elements

Table 3-1 summarizes the basic shapes available in SVG.

Table 3-1. Table of shape elements

Shape	Description
`<line x1="start-x" y1="start-y" x2="end-x" y2="end-y"/>`	Draws a line from the starting point at coordinates (*start-x, start-y*) to the ending point at coordinates (*end-x, end-y*).
`<rect x="left-x" y="top-y" width="width" height="height"/>`	Draws a rectangle whose upper left corner is at (*left-x, top-y*) with the given *width* and *height*.
`<circle cx="center-x" cy="center-y" r="radius"/>`	Draws a circle with the given *radius*, centered at (*center-x, center-y*).
`<ellipse cx="center-x" cy="center-y" rx="x-radius" ry="y-radius"/>`	Draws an ellipse with the given *x-radius* and *y-radius* centered at (*center-x, center-y*).
`<polygon points="points-specifications"/>`	Draws an arbitrary closed polygon whose outline is described by the *points-specification*. The points are specified as pairs of *x-* and *y*-coordinates. These are user coordinates only; you may not add a length unit specifier.

Table 3-1. Table of shape elements (continued)

Shape	Description
`<polyline` `points="points-specifications"/>`	Draws an arbitrary series of connected lines as described by the *points-specification*. The points are specified as pairs of *x*- and *y*-coordinates. These are user coordinates only; you may not add a length unit specifier.

In all but the last two elements of Table 3-1, you may specify the attributes as simple numbers, in which case they will be presumed to be measured in user coordinates, or you may add a length unit specifier such as mm, pt, etc. For example:

```
<line x1="1cm" y1="30" width="50" height="10pt"/>
```

Specifying Colors

You may specify the color for filling or outlining a shape in one of the following ways:

- none, indicating that no outline is to be drawn or that the shape is not to be filled.

- A color name, which is one of aqua, black, blue, fuchsia, gray, green, lime, maroon, navy, olive, purple, red, silver, teal, white, or yellow.

- Six hexadecimal digits #*rrggbb*, each pair describing red, green, and blue values.

- Three hexadecimal digits #*rgb*, describing the red, green, and blue values. This is a shorthand for the previous method; digits are replicated so that #*rgb* is equivalent to #*rrggbb*.

- rgb(*r, g, b*), each value ranging from 0–255 or from 0% to 100%.

Stroke and Fill Characteristics

In order to see a line or the outline of a shape, you must specify the stroke characteristics, using the following attributes. A shape's outline is drawn after its interior is filled. All of these characteristics, summarized in Table 3-2, are presentation properties, and go in a style attribute.

Table 3-2. Stroke characteristics

Attribute	Values
stroke	The stroke color, as described in the section "Specifying Colors."
stroke-width	Width of stroke; may be given as user coordinates or with a length specifier. The stroke width is centered along the abstract grid lines.
stroke-opacity	A number ranging from 0.0 to 1.0; 0.0 is entirely transparent, 1.0 is entirely opaque.
stroke-dasharray	A series of numbers that tell the length of dashes and gaps with which a line is to be drawn. These numbers are in user coordinates only.
stroke-linecap	Shape of the ends of a line; has one of the values butt (the default), round, or square.
stroke-linejoin	The shape of the corners of a polygon or series of lines; has one of the values miter (pointed; the default), round, or bevel (flat).
stroke-miterlimit	Maximum ratio of length of the miter point to the width of the lines being drawn; the default value is 4.

You can control the way in which the interior of a shape is to be filled by using one of the fill attributes shown in Table 3-3. A shape is filled before its outline is drawn.

Table 3-3. Fill characteristics

Attribute	Values
fill	The fill color, as described in the section "Specifying Colors."
fill-opacity	A number ranging from 0.0 to 1.0; 0.0 is entirely transparent, 1.0 is entirely opaque.
fill-rule	This attribute can have the values nonzero or evenodd, which apply different rules for determining whether a point is inside or outside a shape. These rules generate different effects only when a shape has intersecting lines or "holes" in it. Details are in the section "Filling Polygons That Have Intersecting Lines" earlier in this chapter.

4

Document Structure

We've casually mentioned that SVG lets you separate a document's structure from its presentation. In this chapter, we're going to compare and contrast the two, discuss the presentational aspects of a document in more detail, and then show some of the SVG elements that you can use to make your document's structure clearer, more readable, and easier to maintain.

Structure and Presentation

As we mentioned in Chapter 1, in the section "Basic Shapes," one of XML's goals is provide a way to structure data and separate this structure from its visual presentation. Consider the drawing of the cat from that chapter; you recognize it as a cat because of its structure—the position and size of the geometric shapes that make up the drawing. If we were to make structural changes, such as shortening the whiskers, rounding the nose, and making the ears longer and rounding their ends, the drawing would become one of a rabbit, no matter what the surface presentation might be. The structure, therefore, tells you what a graphic *is*.

This is not to say that information about visual style isn't important; had we drawn the cat with thick purple lines and a gray interior, it would have been recognizable as a cat, but its appearance would have been far less pleasing. These differences are shown in Figure 4-1, albeit without the color differences. XML encourages you to separate structure and presentation; unfortunately, many discussions of XML emphasize structure at the expense of presentation. We'll right this wrong by going into detail about how you specify presentation in SVG.

Figure 4-1. Structure versus presentation

Using Styles with SVG

SVG lets you specify presentational aspects of a graphic in four ways; with inline styles, internal stylesheets, external stylesheets, and presentation attributes. Let's examine each of these in turn.

Inline Styles

Example 4-1 uses inline styles. This is exactly the way we've been using presentation information so far; we set the value of the `<style>` attribute to a series of visual properties and their values as described in Appendix B, in the section "Anatomy of a Style."

Example 4-1. Use of inline styles

```
<circle cx="20" cy="20" r="10"
    style="stroke: black; stroke-width: 1.5; fill: blue; fill-opacity: 0.6"/>
```

Internal Stylesheets

You don't need to place your styles inside each SVG element; you can create an internal stylesheet to collect commonly-used styles that you can apply to all occurrences of a particular element, or use as named classes to apply to individual elements. Example 4-2 sets up an internal stylesheet that will draw all circles in a blue double-thick dashed line with a light yellow interior. We have placed the stylesheet within a `<defs>` element, which we will discuss later in this chapter.

The example then draws several circles. The circles in the second row of Figure 4-2 have inline styles that override the specification in the internal stylesheet.

Example 4-2. Use of internal stylesheet

```
<svg width="200px" height="200px" viewBox="0 0 200 200">
<defs>
<style type="text/css"><![CDATA[
    circle {
        fill: #ffc;
        stroke: blue;
        stroke-width: 2;
        stroke-dasharray: 5 3
    }
    ]]></style>
</defs>

<circle cx="20" cy="20" r="10"/>
<circle cx="60" cy="20" r="15"/>
<circle cx="20" cy="60" r="10" style="fill: #cfc"/>
<circle cx="60" cy="60" r="15" style="stroke-width: 1;
    stroke-dasharray: none;"/>
</svg>
```

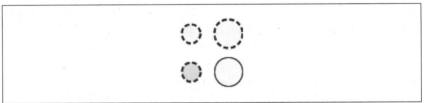

Figure 4-2. Internal stylesheet with SVG

External Stylesheets

If you want to apply a set of styles to multiple SVG documents, you could copy and paste the internal stylesheet into each of them. This, of course, is impractical for a large volume of documents if you ever need to make a global change to all the documents. Instead, you should take all the information between the beginning and ending <style> tags (excluding the <![CDATA[and]]>) and save it in an external file, which becomes an external stylesheet. Example 4-3 shows an external stylesheet that has been saved in a file named ext_style.css This stylesheet uses a variety of selectors, including *, which sets a default for all elements that don't have any other style, and it, together with the SVG, produces Figure 4-3.

Example 4-3. External stylesheet

```
* { fill:none; stroke: black; } /* default for all elements */

rect { stroke-dasharray: 7 3; }

circle.yellow { fill: yellow; }

.thick { stroke-width: 5; }

.semiblue { fill:blue; fill-opacity: 0.5; }
```

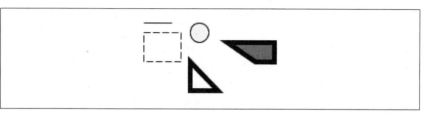

Figure 4-3. External stylesheet with SVG

Example 4-4 shows a complete SVG document (including `<?xml ...?>`, `<?xml-stylesheet ...?>`, and the `<!DOCTYPE>`) that references the external stylesheet.

Example 4-4. SVG file that references an external stylesheet

```
<?xml version="1.0"?>
<?xml-stylesheet href="ext_style.css" type="text/css"?>
<!DOCTYPE svg PUBLIC "-//W3C//DTD SVG 1.0//EN"
    "http://www.w3.org/TR/2001/REC-SVG-20010904/DTD/svg10.dtd">
<svg width="200px" height="200px" viewBox="0 0 200 200"
    preserveAspectRatio="xMinYMin meet">

<line x1="10" y1="10" x2="40" y2="10"/>
<rect x="10" y="20" width="40" height="30"/>
<circle class="yellow" cx="70" cy="20" r="10"/>
<polygon class="thick" points="60 50, 60 80,  90 80"/>
<polygon class="thick semiblue"
    points="100 30, 150 30, 150 50, 130 50"/>
</svg>
```

 Inline styles will almost always render more quickly than styles in an internal or external stylesheet; stylesheets and classes add rendering time due to look up and parsing.

Presentation Attributes

Although the overwhelming majority of your SVG documents will use styles for presentation information, SVG does permit you to specify this information in the form of presentation attributes. Instead of saying:

```
<circle cx="10" cy="10" r="5"
    style="fill: red; stroke:black; stroke-width: 2;"/>
```

You may write each of the properties as an attribute:

```
<circle cx="10" cy="10" r="5"
    fill="red" stroke="black" stroke-width="2"/>
```

If you are thinking that this is mixing structure and presentation, you are right. Presentation attributes do come in handy, though, when you are creating SVG documents by converting an XML data source to SVG, as you will see in Chapter 12. In these cases it can be easier to create individual attributes for each presentation property than to create the contents of a single `style` attribute. You may also need to use presentation attributes if the environment in which you will be placing your SVG cannot support stylesheets.

Presentation attributes are at the very bottom of the priority list. Any style specification coming from an inline, internal, or external stylesheet will override a presentation attribute. In the following SVG document, the circle will be filled in red, not green.

```
<svg width="200" height="200">
    <defs>
    <style type="text/css"><![CDATA[
        circle { fill: red; }
    ]]></style>
    </defs>
    <circle cx="20" cy="20" r="15" fill="green"/>
</svg>
```

Again, we emphasize that using `style` attributes or stylesheets should always be your first choice. Stylesheets let you apply a complex series of fill and stroke characteristics to all occurrences of certain elements within a document without having to duplicate the information into each element, as presentation attributes would require. The power and flexibility of stylesheets allow you to make significant changes in the look and feel of multiple documents with a minimum of effort.

Document Structure — Grouping and Referencing Objects

While it is certainly possible to define any drawing as an undifferentiated list of shapes and lines, most non-abstract art consists of groups of shapes and lines that form recognizable named objects. SVG has elements that let you do this sort of grouping to make your documents more structured and understandable.

The g Element

The <g> element gathers all of its child elements as a group, and often has an id attribute to give that group a unique name. Furthermore, each group may have its own <title> and <desc> to identify it for text-based XML applications or to aid in accessibility for visually-impaired users. In addition to the conceptual clarity that comes from the ability to group and document objects, the <g> element also provides notational convenience. Any styles you specify in the starting <g> tag will apply to all the child elements in the group. In Example 4-5, this saves us from having to duplicate the style="fill:none; stroke:black;" on every element shown in Figure 4-4. It is also possible to nest groups within one another, although we won't show any examples of this until Chapter 5.

You may think of the <g> element as analogous to the *Group Objects* function in programs such as Adobe Illustrator. It also serves a similar function to the concept of *layers* in such programs; a layer is also a grouping of related objects.

Example 4-5. Simple use of the g element

```
<svg width="240px" height="240px" viewBox="0 0 240 240">
<title>Grouped Drawing</title>
<desc>Stick-figure drawings of a house and people</desc>

<g id="house" style="fill: none; stroke: black;">
    <desc>House with door</desc>
    <rect x="6" y="50" width="60" height="60"/>
    <polyline points="6 50, 36 9, 66 50"/>
    <polyline points="36 110, 36 80, 50 80, 50 110"/>
</g>

<g id="man" style="fill: none; stroke: black;">
    <desc>Male human</desc>
    <circle cx="85" cy="56" r="10"/>
    <line x1="85" y1="66" x2="85" y2="80"/>
    <polyline points="76 104, 85 80, 94 104" />
```

Example 4-5. Simple use of the g element (continued)

```
    <polyline points="76 70, 85 76, 94 70" />
</g>

<g id="woman" style="fill: none; stroke: black;">
    <desc>Female human</desc>
    <circle cx="110" cy="56" r="10"/>
    <polyline points="110 66, 110 80, 100 90, 120 90, 110 80"/>
    <line x1="104" y1="104" x2="108" y2="90"/>
    <line x1="112" y1="90" x2="116" y2="104"/>
    <polyline points="101 70, 110 76, 119 70" />
</g>
</svg>
```

Figure 4-4. Grouped stick figure drawing

The use Element

Complex graphics often have repeated elements. For example, a product brochure may have the company logo at the upper left and lower right of each page. If you were drawing the brochure with a graphic design program, you'd draw the logo once, group all its elements together, then copy and paste them to the other location. The SVG <use> element gives you an analogous copy-and-paste ability with a group that you've defined with <g>.

Once you have defined a group of graphic objects, you can display them again with the <use> tag. To specify the group you wish to reuse, give its URI in an xlink:href attribute, and specify the x and y location where the group's (0, 0) point should be moved to. (We will see another way to achieve this effect in Chapter 5, in the section "The translate Transformation.") So, to create another house and set of people as shown in Figure 4-5, you'd put these lines just before the closing </svg> tag:

```
    <use xlink:href="#house" x="70" y="100"/>
    <use xlink:href="#woman" x="-80" y="100"/>
    <use xlink:href="#man" x="-30" y="100"/>
```

Figure 4-5. Re-use of grouped stick figures

The defs Element

You may have noticed some drawbacks with the preceding example:

- The math for deciding where to place the re-used man and woman requires you to know the positions of the originals and use that as your base, rather than using a simple number like zero.

- The fill and stroke color for the house were established by the original, and can't be overriden by the <use>. This means you can't make a row of multi-colored houses.

- The document draws all three groups: the woman, the man, and the house. You can't "store them away" and draw only a set of houses or only a set of people.

The <defs> element solves these problems. By putting the grouped objects between the beginning and ending <defs> tags, you instruct SVG to define them without displaying them. The SVG specification, in fact, recommends that you put all objects that you wish to re-use within a <defs> element so that SVG viewers working in a streaming environment can process data more efficiently. In Example 4-6, the house, man, and woman are defined so that their upper left corner is at (0, 0), and the house is not given any fill color. Since the groups will be within the <defs> element, they will not be drawn on the screen right away, and will serve as a "template" for future use. We have also constructed another group named couple, which, in turn, <use>s the man and woman groups. (Note that the bottom half of Figure 4-6 can't use couple, since the woman is to the left of the man.)

Example 4-6. Example of the defs element

```
<svg width="240px" height="240px" viewBox="0 0 240 240">
<title>Grouped Drawing</title>
<desc>Stick-figure drawings of a house and people</desc>

<defs>
<g id="house" style="stroke: black;">
    <desc>House with door</desc>
    <rect x="0" y="41" width="60" height="60"/>
    <polyline points="0 41, 30 0, 60 41"/>
    <polyline points="30 101, 30 71, 44 71, 44 101"/>
</g>

<g id="man" style="fill: none; stroke: black;">
    <desc>Male human</desc>
    <circle cx="10" cy="10" r="10"/>
    <line x1="10" y1="20" x2="10" y2="44"/>
    <polyline points="1 58, 10 44, 19 58"/>
    <polyline points="1 24, 10 30, 19 24"/>
</g>

<g id="woman" style="fill: none; stroke: black;">
    <desc>Female human</desc>
    <circle cx="10" cy="10" r="10"/>
    <polyline points="10 20, 10 34, 0 44, 20 44, 10 34"/>
    <line x1="4" y1="58" x2="8" y2="44"/>
    <line x1="12" y1="44" x2="16" y2="58"/>
    <polyline points="1 24, 10 30, 19 24" />
</g>

<g id="couple">
    <desc>Male and female human</desc>
    <use xlink:href="#man" x="0" y="0"/>
    <use xlink:href="#woman" x="25" y="0"/>
</g>
</defs>

<!-- make use of the defined groups -->
<use xlink:href="#house" x="0" y="0" style="fill: #cfc;"/>
<use xlink:href="#couple" x="70" y="40"/>

<use xlink:href="#house" x="120" y="0" style="fill: #99f;"/>
<use xlink:href="#couple" x="190" y="40"/>

<use xlink:href="#woman" x="0" y="145"/>
<use xlink:href="#man" x="25" y="145"/>
<use xlink:href="#house" x="65" y="105" style="fill: #c00;"/>
</svg>
```

The <use> element is not restricted to using objects from the same file in which it occurs; the xlink:href attribute may specify any valid file or URI. This makes it possible to collect a set of common elements in one SVG

Figure 4-6. Result of using groups within defs

file and use them selectively from other files. For example, you could create a file named identity.svg that contains all of the identity graphics that your organization uses:

```
<g id="company_mascot">
  <!-- drawing of company mascot -->
</g>

<g id="company_logo" style="stroke: none;">
  <polygon points="0 20, 20 0, 40 20, 20 40"
    style="fill: #696;"/>
  <rect x="7" y="7" width="26" height="26"
    style="fill: #c9c;"/>
</g>

<g id="partner_logo">
  <!-- drawing of company partner's logo -->
</g>
```

and then refer to it with:

```
<use xlink:href="identity.svg#company_logo" x="200" y="200"/>
```

The symbol Element

The <symbol> element provides another way of grouping elements. Unlike the <g> element, a <symbol> is never displayed, so you don't have to enclose it in a <defs> specification. However, it is customary to do so, since a symbol really is something you're defining for later use. Additionally, symbols can specify viewBox and preserveAspectRatio attributes, so that a symbol can fit into the viewport established by the use element.

Example 4-7 shows that the width and height are ignored for a simple group (the top two octagons), but are used when displaying a symbol. The edges of the lower right octagon in Figure 4-7 are cut off because the preserveAspectRatio has been set to slice.

Example 4-7. Groups versus symbols

```
<svg width="200px" height="200px" viewBox="0 0 200 200">
<title>Symbols vs. groups</title>
<desc>Use</desc>

<defs>
<g id="octagon" style="stroke: black;">
    <desc>Octagon as group</desc>
    <polygon points="
        36 25, 25 36, 11 36, 0 25,
        0 11, 11 0, 25 0, 36 11"/>
</g>

<symbol id="sym-octagon" style="stroke: black;"
    preserveAspectRatio="xMidYMid slice" viewBox="0 0 40 40">
    <desc>Octagon as symbol</desc>
    <polygon points="
        36 25, 25 36, 11 36, 0 25,
        0 11, 11 0, 25 0, 36 11"/>
</symbol>
</defs>

<use xlink:href="#octagon" x="40" y="40" width="30" height="30"
        style="fill: #c00;"/>
<use xlink:href="#octagon" x="80" y="40" width="40" height="60"
        style="fill: #cc0;"/>
<use xlink:href="#sym-octagon" x="40" y="80" width="30" height="30"
        style="fill: #cfc;"/>
<use xlink:href="#sym-octagon" x="80" y="80" width="40" height="60"
        style="fill: #699;"/>
</svg>
```

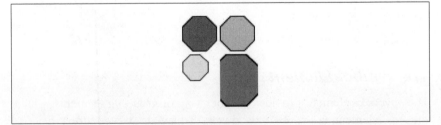

Figure 4-7. Groups versus symbols

The image Element

While <use> lets you re-use a portion of an SVG file, the <image> element includes an entire SVG or raster file. If you are including an SVG file, the x, y, width, and height attributes establish the viewport in which the referenced file will be drawn; if you're including a raster file, it will be scaled to fit the rectangle that the attributes specify. You can currently include either JPEG or PNG raster files. Example 4-8 shows how to include a JPEG image with SVG; the result is in Figure 4-8 (see additional color insert).

Figure 4-8. JPEG image included in an SVG file

Example 4-8. Use of the image element

```
<svg width="310px" height="310px" viewBox="0 0 310 310">

<ellipse cx="154" cy="154" rx="150" ry="120" style="fill: #999999;"/> ❶
<ellipse cx="152" cy="152" rx="150" ry="120" style="fill: #cceeff;"/> ❷

<image xlink:href="kwanghwamun.jpg" ❸
    x="72" y="92" ❹
    width="160" height="120"/> ❺

</svg>
```

❶ Create a gray ellipse to simulate a drop shadow.*

❷ Create the main blue ellipse. Since it occurs after the gray ellipse, it is displayed above that object.

❸ Specify the URI of the file to include.

❹ Specify the upper left corner of the image.

❺ Specify the width and height to which the image should be scaled. If these aren't in the same aspect ratio as the original picture, it will appear stretched or squashed.

---

* We'll see another way to create a drop shadow in Chapter 10 in the section "Creating a Drop Shadow."

5

Transforming the
Coordinate System

Up to this point, all graphics have been displayed "as is." There will be times when you have a graphic that you would like to move to a new location, rotate, or scale. To accomplish these tasks, you add the trans- form attribute to the appropriate SVG elements. This chapter examines the details of these transformations.

The translate Transformation

In Chapter 4, you saw that you can use x and y attributes with the <use> element to place a group of graphic objects at a specific place. Look at the SVG in Example 5-1, which defines a square and draws it at the upper left corner of the grid, then re-draws it with the upper left corner at coordi- nates (50, 50). The dotted lines in Figure 5-1 aren't part of the SVG, but serve to show the part of the canvas that we're interested in.

Example 5-1. Moving a graphic with use

```
<svg width="200px" height="200px" viewBox="0 0 200 200">
    <g id="square">
        <rect x="0" y="0" width="20" height="20"
            style="fill: black; stroke-width: 2;"/>
    </g>
    <use xlink:href="#square" x="50" y="50"/>
</svg>
```

As it turns out, the x and y values are really a shorthand for one form of the more general and more powerful transform attribute. Specifically, the x and y values are converted to an attribute like transform="translate(*x- value, y-value*)", where translate is a fancy technical term for "move."

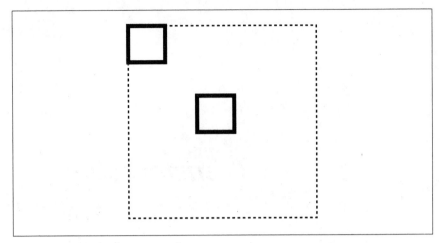

Figure 5-1. Result of moving with use

The *x-value* and *y-value* are measured in the current user coordinate system. Let's use `transform` to get the same effect of making a second square with its upper left corner at (50, 50). Example 5-2 lists the SVG.

Example 5-2. Moving the coordinate system with translation

```
<svg width="200px" height="200px" viewBox="0 0 200 200">
    <g id="square">
        <rect x="0" y="0" width="20" height="20"
            style="fill: none; stroke:black; stroke-width: 2;"/>
    </g>
    <use xlink:href="#square" transform="translate(50,50)"/>
</svg>
```

The resulting display will look exactly like that in Figure 5-1. You might think this was accomplished by moving the square to a different place on the grid, as shown conceptually in Figure 5-2, but you would be wrong.

What is really going on behind the scenes is an entirely different story. Rather than moving the square, the `translate` specification picks up the *entire grid* and moves it to a new location on the canvas. As far as the square is concerned, it's still being drawn with its upper left corner at (0, 0), as depicted in Figure 5-3.

A translation transformation *never* changes a graphic object's grid coordinates; rather, it changes the position of the grid on the canvas.

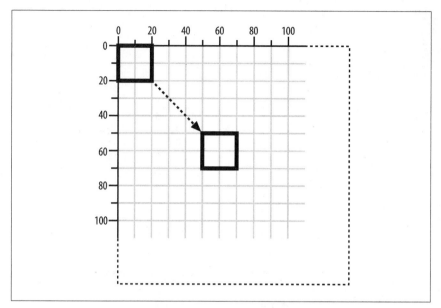

Figure 5-2. How moving appears to work (but really doesn't)

At first glance, using translate seems as ridiculous and inefficient as moving your couch further away from the outside wall of the house by moving the entire living room, walls and all, to a new position. Indeed, if translation were the only transformation available, moving the entire coordinate system would be wasteful. However, we will soon see other transformations, and combinations of a sequence of transformations, which are more mathematically and conceptually convenient if they apply to the entire coordinate system.

The scale Transformation

It is possible to make an object appear larger or smaller than the size at which it was defined by scaling the coordinate system. Such a transformation is specified either as:

transform="scale(*value*)"

Multiplies all *x*- and *y*-coordinates by the given *value*.

transform="scale(*x-value*, *y-value*)"

Multiplies all *x*-coordinates by the given *x-value* and all *y*-coordinates by the given *y-value*.

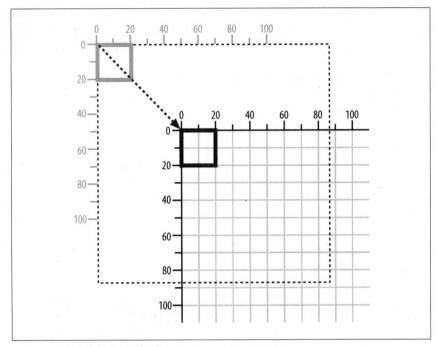

Figure 5-3. How moving with translate really works

Example 5-3 is an example of the first kind of scaling transformation, which uniformly doubles the scale of both axes. Once again, the dotted lines in Figure 5-4 aren't in the SVG; they simply show the area of the canvas that we're interested in. Note that the square's upper left corner is at (10, 10).

Example 5-3. Uniformly scaling a graphic

```
<svg width="200px" height="200px" viewBox="0 0 200 200">
    <g id="square">
        <rect x="10" y="10" width="20" height="20"
            style="fill: none; stroke: black;"/>
    </g>
    <use xlink:href="#square" transform="scale(2)"/>
</svg>
```

You might be thinking, "Wait a minute—I can understand why the square got larger. But I didn't ask for a translate, so why is the square in a different place?" Everything becomes clear when you look at Figure 5-5 to see what has actually occurred. The grid hasn't moved; the (0, 0) point of the coordinate system is still in the same place, but each user coordinate is now twice as large as it used to be. You can see from the grid lines that the upper left corner of the rectangle is still at (10, 10) on the new, larger

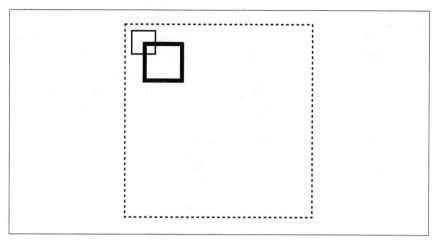

Figure 5-4. Result of using scale transformation

grid, since objects *never* move. This also explains why the outline of the larger square is thicker. The `stroke-width` is still one user unit, but that unit has now become twice as large, so the stroke thickens.

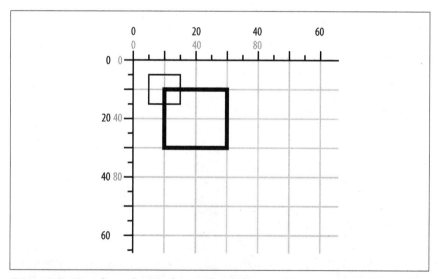

Figure 5-5. How the scale transformation works

 A scaling transformation *never* changes a graphic object's grid coordinates or its stroke width; rather, it changes the size of the coordinate system (grid) with respect to the canvas.

It is possible to specify a different scale factor for the *x*-axis and *y*-axis of the coordinate system by using the second form of the `scale` transformation. Example 5-4 draws the square with the *x*-axis scaled by a factor of three and the *y*-axis scaled by a factor of one and a half. As you can see in Figure 5-6, the one-unit stroke width is also non-uniformly scaled.

Example 5-4. Non-uniform scaling of a graphic

```
<svg width="200px" height="200px" viewBox="0 0 200 200">
    <g id="square">
        <rect x="10" y="10" width="20" height="20"
            style="fill: none; stroke: black;"/>
    </g>
    <use xlink:href="#square" transform="scale(3, 1.5)"/>
</svg>
```

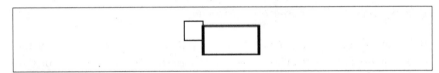

Figure 5-6. Result of using non-uniform scale transformation

To this point, we have only applied the `transform` attribute to the `<use>` element. You can apply a transformation to a series of elements by grouping them and transforming the group:

```
<g id="group1" transform="translate(3, 5)">
    <line x1="10" y1="10" x1="30" y2="30"/>
    <circle cx="20" cy="20" r="10"/>
</g>
```

You may also apply a transformation to a single object or basic shape. For example, here is a rectangle whose coordinate system is scaled by a factor of three:

```
<rect x="15" y="20" width="10" height="5"
    transform="scale(3)"
    style="fill: none; stroke: black;"/>
```

It's fairly clear that the width and height of the scaled rectangle should be three times as large as the unscaled rectangle. However, you may wonder if the *x*- and *y*-coordinates are evaluated before or after the rectangle is scaled. The answer is that SVG applies transformations to the coordinate system before it evaluates any of the shape's coordinates. Example 5-5 is the SVG for the scaled rectangle, shown in Figure 5-7 with grid lines that are drawn in the unscaled coordinate system.

Example 5-5. Transforming a single graphic

```
<!-- grid guide lines in non-scaled coordinate system -->
<line x1="0" y1="0" x2="100" y2="0" style="stroke: black;"/>
<line x1="0" y1="0" x2="0" y2="100" style="stroke: black;"/>
<line x1="45" y1="0" x2="45" y2="100" style="stroke: gray;"/>
<line x1="0" y1="60" x2="100" y2="60" style="stroke: gray;"/>

<!-- rectangle to be transformed -->
<rect x="15" y="20" width="10" height="5"
    transform="scale(3)"
    style="fill: none; stroke: black;"/>
```

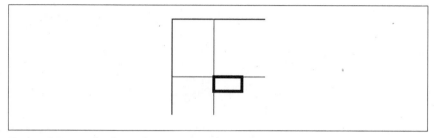

Figure 5-7. Result of transforming a single graphic

The effect of applying a transformation to a shape is the same as if the shape were enclosed in a transformed group. In the preceding example, the scaled rectangle is equivalent to this SVG:

```
<g transform="scale(3)">
    <rect x="15" y="20" width="10" height="5"
        style="fill: none; stroke: black;"/>
</g>
```

Sequences of Transformations

It is possible to do more than one transformation on a graphic object. You just put the transformations, separated by whitespace, in the value of the transform attribute. Here is a rectangle that undergoes two transformations, a translation followed by a scaling. (The axes are drawn to show that the rectangle has, indeed, moved.)

```
<!-- draw axes -->
<line x1="0" y1="0" x2="0" y2="100" style="stroke: gray;"/>
<line x1="0" y1="0" x2="100" y2="0" style="stroke: gray;"/>
```

```
<rect x="10" y="10" height="20" width="15"
    transform="translate(30, 20) scale(2)"
    style="fill: gray;"/>
```

This is the equivalent of the following sequence of nested groups, and both will produce what you see in Figure 5-8.

```
<g transform="translate(30, 20)">
    <g transform="scale(2)">
    <rect x="10" y="10" height="20" width="15"
        style="fill: gray;"/>
    </g>
</g>
```

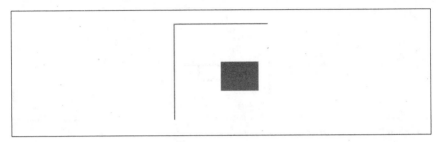

Figure 5-8. Result of translate followed by scale

Figure 5-9 shows what is happening at each stage of the transformation.

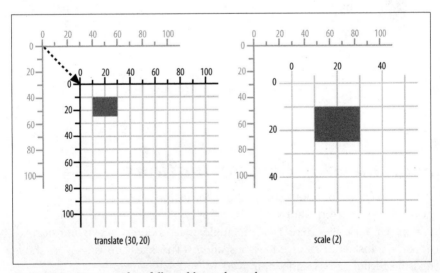

Figure 5-9. How translate followed by scale works

The order in which you do a sequence of transformations affects the result. In general, transformation A followed by transformation B will not give the same result as transformation B followed by transformation A.

Example 5-6 draws the same rectangle as in the previous example, only in a light gray color. Then it draws the rectangle again, but does the `scale` before the `translate`. As you can see from the result in Figure 5-10, the rectangles end up in very different places on the canvas.

Example 5-6. Sequence of transformations—scale followed by translate

```
<!-- draw axes -->
<line x1="0" y1="0" x2="0" y2="100" style="stroke: gray;"/>
<line x1="0" y1="0" x2="100" y2="0" style="stroke: gray;"/>

<rect x="10" y="10" width="20" height="15"
    transform="translate(30, 20) scale(2)" style="fill: #ccc;"/>

<rect x="10" y="10" width="20" height="15"
    transform="scale(2) translate(30, 20)"
    style="fill: black;"/>
```

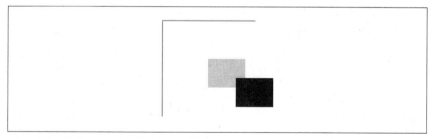

Figure 5-10. Result of scale followed by translate

The reason that the black rectangle ends up farther away from the origin is that the scaling is applied first, so that the translate of 20 units in the *x*-direction and 10 units in the *y*-direction is done with units that are now twice as large, as shown in Figure 5-11.

Technique: Converting from Cartesian Coordinates

If you are transferring data from other systems to SVG, you may have to deal with vector drawings that use Cartesian coordinates (the ones you

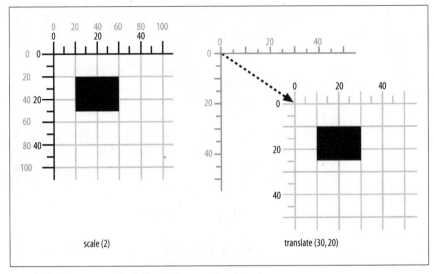

Figure 5-11. How scale followed by translate works

learned about in high school algebra) to represent data. In this system, the (0, 0) point is at the lower left of the canvas, and *y*-coordinates increase as you move upwards. Figure 5-12 shows the coordinates of a trapezoid drawn with Cartesian coordinates.

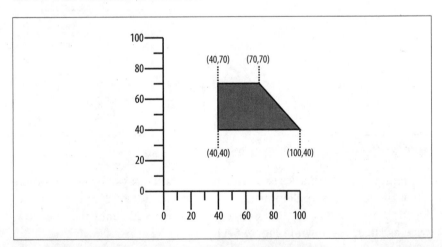

Figure 5-12. Trapezoid drawn with Cartesian coordinates

Since the *y*-axis is "upside-down" relative to the SVG default, the coordinates have to be recalculated. Rather than do it by hand, you can use a sequence of transformations to have SVG do all the work for you. First, translate the picture into SVG, with the coordinates exactly as shown in Example 5-7. (We'll also include the axes as a guide.) To nobody's surprise, the picture will come out upside-down. Note that the image in Figure 5-13 is *not* left-to-right reversed, since the *x*-axis points the same direction in both Cartesian coordinates and the default SVG coordinate system.

Example 5-7. Direct use of Cartesian coordinates

```
<svg width="200px" height="200px" viewBox="0 0 200 200">
    <!-- axes -->
    <line x1="0" y1="0" x2="100" y2="0" style="stroke: black;"/>
    <line x1="0" y1="0" x2="0" y2="100" style="stroke: black;"/>

    <!-- trapezoid -->
    <polygon points="40 40, 100 40, 70 70, 40 70"
        style="fill: gray; stroke: black;"/>
</svg>
```

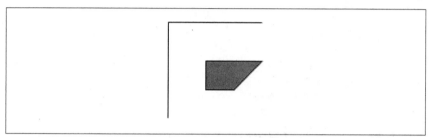

Figure 5-13. Result of using original Cartesian coordinates

To finish the conversion, follow these steps:

1. Find the maximum *y*-coordinate in the original drawing. In this case, it turns out to be 100, the endpoint of the *y*-axis in the original.

2. Enclose the entire drawing in a `<g>` element.

3. Enter a translate that moves the coordinate system downwards by the maximum y value.

    ```
    transform="translate(0, max-y)"
    ```

4. The next transform will be to scale the *y*-axis by a factor of –1, flipping it upside-down.

    ```
    transform="translate(0, max-y) scale(1, -1)"
    ```

Example 5-8 incorporates this transformation, producing a right-side-up trapezoid in Figure 5-14.

Example 5-8. Transformed Cartesian coordinates

```
<svg width="200px" height="200px" viewBox="0 0 200 200">
  <g transform="translate(0,100) scale(1,-1)">
    <!-- axes -->
    <line x1="0" y1="0" x2="100" y2="0" style="stroke: black;"/>
    <line x1="0" y1="0" x2="0" y2="100" style="stroke: black;"/>

    <!-- trapezoid -->
    <polygon points="40 40, 100 40, 70 70, 40 70"
        style="fill: gray; stroke: black;"/>
  </g>
</svg>
```

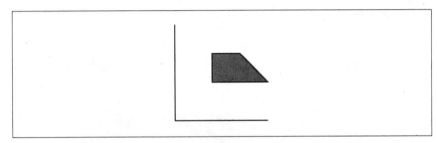

Figure 5-14. Transformed Cartesian coordinates

The rotate Transformation

It is also possible to rotate the coordinate system by a specified angle. In the default coordinate system, angle measure increases as you rotate clockwise, with a horizontal line having an angle of zero degrees, as shown in Figure 5-15.

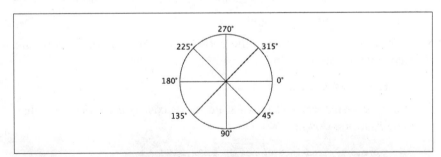

Figure 5-15. Default measurement of angles

Unless you specify otherwise, the center of rotation (a fancy term for the "pivot point") is presumed to be (0, 0). Example 5-9 shows a square drawn in gray, then drawn again in black after the coordinate system is rotated 45 degrees. The axes are also shown as a guide. Figure 5-16 shows the result. If you're surprised that the square has appeared to move, you shouldn't be. Remember, the entire coordinate system has been rotated, as shown in Figure 5-17.*

Example 5-9. Rotation around the origin

```
<!-- axes -->
<polyline points="100 0, 0 0, 0 100" style="stroke: black; fill: none;"/>

<!-- normal and rotated square -->
<rect x="70" y="30" width="20" height="20" style="fill: gray;"/>
<rect x="70" y="30" width="20" height="20"
    transform="rotate(45)" style="fill: black;"/>
```

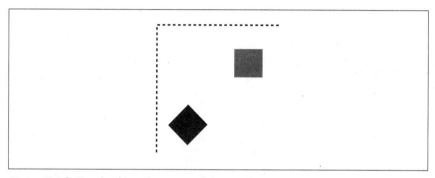

Figure 5-16. Result of rotation around the origin

Most of the time, you will not want to rotate the entire coordinate system around the origin; you'll want to rotate a single object around a point other than the origin. You can do that via this series of transformations: translate(*centerX, centerY*) rotate(*angle*) translate(-*centerX, -centerY*). SVG provides another version of rotate to make this common task easier. In this second form of the rotate transformation, you specify the angle and the center point around which you want to rotate:

```
rotate(angle, centerX, centerY)
```

This has the effect of temporarily establishing a new system of coordinates with the origin at the specified center *x* and *y* points, doing the rotation, and then re-establishing the original coordinates. Example 5-10 shows this form of rotate to create multiple copies of an arrow, shown in Figure 5-18.

---

* All the figures in this chapter are static pictures. This one shows two squares; one rotated and one unrotated. To show an animation of a rotating square, use <animateTransform>, which we will discuss in Chapter 11, in the section "The animateTransform Element."

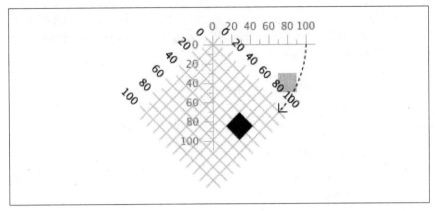

Figure 5-17. How rotation around the origin works

Example 5-10. Rotation around a center point

```
<!-- center of rotation -->
<circle cx="50" cy="50" r="3" style="fill: black;"/>

<!-- non-rotated arrow -->
<g id="arrow" style="stroke: black;">
    <line x1="60" y1="50" x2="90" y2="50"/>
    <polygon points="90 50, 85 45, 85 55"/>
</g>

<!-- rotated around center point -->
<use xlink:href="#arrow" transform="rotate(60, 50, 50)"/>
<use xlink:href="#arrow" transform="rotate(-90, 50, 50)"/>
<use xlink:href="#arrow" transform="rotate(-150, 50 50)"/>
```

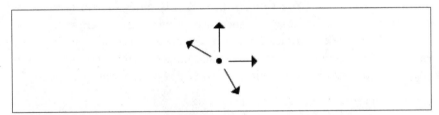

Figure 5-18. Result of rotation around a center point

Technique: Scaling Around a Center Point

While it's possible to rotate around a point other than the origin, there is no corresponding capability to scale around a point. You can, however, make concentric symbols with a simple series of transformations. To scale an object by a given factor around a center point, do this:

```
translate(-centerX*(factor-1), -centerY*(factor-1))
scale(factor)
```

You may also want to divide the stroke-width by the scaling factor so the outline stays the same width while the object becomes larger. Example 5-11 draws the set of concentric rectangles shown in Figure 5-19.*

Example 5-11. Scaling around a center point

```
<!-- center of scaling -->
<circle cx="50" cy="50" r="2" style="fill: black;"/>

<!-- non-scaled rectangle -->
<g id="box" style="stroke: black; fill: none;">
    <rect x="35" y="40" width="30" height="20"/>
</g>

<use xlink:href="#box" transform="translate(-50,-50) scale(2)"
    style="stroke-width: 0.5;"/>
<use xlink:href="#box" transform="translate(-75,-75) scale(2.5)"
    style="stroke-width: 0.4;"/>
<use xlink:href="#box" transform="translate(-100,-100) scale(3)"
    style="stroke-width: 0.33;"/>
```

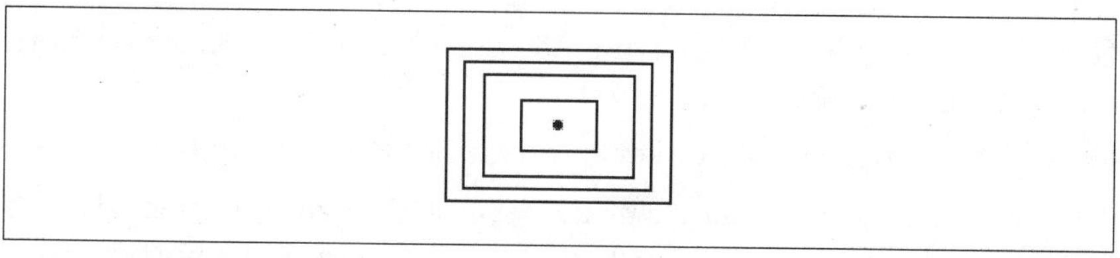

Figure 5-19. Result of scaling around a center point

The skewX and skewY Transformations

SVG also has two other transformations: skewX and skewY, which let you skew one of the axes. The general form is skewX(*angle*) and skewY(*angle*) The skewX transformation "pushes" all *x*-coordinates by the specified angle, leaving *y*-coordinates unchanged. skewY skews the *y*-coordinates, leaving *x*-coordinates unchanged, as shown in Example 5-12.

---

* This is also a static picture, a "square bullseye." If you want to show an animation of an expanding square, you'll use <animateTransform>, which we will discuss in Chapter 11, in the section "The animateTransform Element."

Example 5-12. skewX and skewY

❶
```
<g style="stroke: gray; stroke-dasharray: 4 4;">
    <line x1="0" y1="0" x2="200" y2="0"/>
    <line x1="20" y1="0" x2="20" y2="90"/>
    <line x1="120" y1="0" x2="120" y2="90"/>
</g>

<g transform="translate(20, 0)"> ❷
    <g transform="skewX(30)"> ❸
        <polyline points="50 0, 0 0, 0 50" ❹
            style="fill: none; stroke: black; stroke-width: 2;"/>
        <text x="0" y="60">skewX</text> ❺
    </g>
</g>

<g transform="translate(120, 0)"> ❻
    <g transform="skewY(30)">
        <polyline points="50 0, 0 0, 0 50"
            style="fill: none; stroke: black; stroke-width: 2;"/>
        <text x="0" y="60">skewY</text>
    </g>
</g>
```

❶ These dashed lines are drawn in the default coordinate system, before any transformation has occurred.

❷ This will move the entire skewed "package" to the desired location.

❸ Skew the *x*-coordinates 30 degrees. This transformation doesn't change the origin, which will still be at (0, 0) in the new coordinate system.

❹ To make things easier, we draw the object at the origin.

❺ Text will be covered in more detail in Chapter 8.

❻ These elements are organized exactly like the preceding ones, except the *y*-coordinates are skewed.

Notice that skewX leaves the horizontal lines in Figure 5-20 horizontal, and skewY leaves the vertical lines untouched. Go figure.

Transformation Reference Summary

Table 5-1 gives a quick summary of the transformations available in SVG.

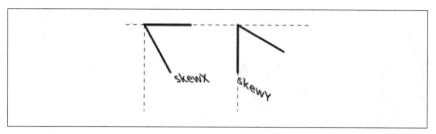

Figure 5-20. Result of skewX and skewY transformations

Table 5-1. SVG transformations

Transformation	Description
translate(*x*, *y*)	Moves the user coordinate system by the specified *x* and *y* amounts. Note: If you don't specify a *y* value, zero is assumed.
scale(*xFactor*, *yFactor*)	Multiplies all user coordinate systems by the specified *xFactor* and *yFactor*. The factors may be fractional or negative.
scale(*factor*)	Same as scale(*factor, factor*).
rotate(*angle*)	Rotates the user coordinate by the specified *angle*. The center of rotation is the origin (0, 0). In the default coordinate system, angle measure increases as you rotate clockwise, with a horizontal line having an angle of zero degrees.
rotate(*angle*, *centerX*, *centerY*)	Rotates the user coordinate by the specified *angle*. *centerX* and *centerY* specify the center of rotation.
skewX(*angle*)	Skews all *x*-coordinates by the specified *angle*. Visually, this makes vertical lines appear at an angle.
skewY(*angle*)	Skews all *y*-coordinates by the specified *angle*. Visually, this makes horizontal lines appear at an angle.

6

Paths

All of the basic shapes described in Chapter 3 are really shorthand forms
for the more general <path> element. You are well advised to use these
shortcuts; they help make your SVG more readable and more structured.
The <path> element is more general; it draws the outline of any arbitrary
shape by specifying a series of connected lines, arcs, and curves. This outline can be filled and drawn with a stroke, just as the basic shapes are.
Additionally, these paths (as well as the shorthand basic shapes) may be
used to define the outline of a clipping area or a transparency mask, as
you will see in Chapter 9.

All of the data describing an outline is in the <path> element's d attribute
(the d stands for *data*). The path data consists of one-letter commands,
such as M for *moveto* or L for *lineto*, followed by the coordinate information for that particular command.

moveto, lineto, and closepath

Every path must begin with a *moveto* command. The command letter is a
capital M followed by an *x*- and *y*-coordinate, separated by commas or
whitespace. This command sets the current location of the "pen" that's
drawing the outline.

This is followed by one or more *lineto* commands, denoted by a capital L,
also followed by *x*- and *y*-coordinates, and separated by commas or
whitespace. Example 6-1 has three paths. The first draws a single line, the
second draws a right angle, and the third draws two thirty-degree angles.
When you "pick up" the pen with another *moveto*, you are starting a new
subpath. Notice that the use of commas and whitespace as separators is
different, but perfectly legal, in all three paths. The result is Figure 6-1.

Example 6-1. Using moveto and lineto

```
<g style="stroke: black; fill: none;">
    <!-- single line -->
    <path d="M 10 10 L 100 10"/>

    <!-- a right angle -->
    <path d="M 10, 20  L 100, 20  L  100,50"/>

    <!-- two thirty-degree angles -->
    <path d="M 40 60, L 10 60, L 40 42.68,
        M 60 60, L 90 60, L 60 42.68"/>
</g>
```

Examining the last path more closely:

Value	Action
M 40 60	Move pen to (40, 60)
L 10 60	Draw a line to (10, 60)
L 40 42.68	Draw a line to (40, 42.68)
M 60 60	Start a new subpath; move pen to (60, 60)—no line is drawn
L 90 60	Draw a line to (90, 60)
L 60 42.68	Draw a line to (60, 42.68)

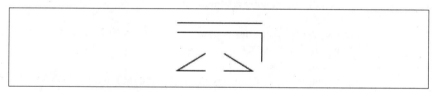

Figure 6-1. Result of using moveto and lineto

You may have noticed that the path data doesn't look very much like the typical values for XML attributes. Because the entire path data is contained in one attribute rather than an individual element for each point or line segment, a path takes up less memory when read into a Document Object Model structure by an XML parser. Additionally, a path's compact notation allows a complex graphic to be transmitted without requiring a great deal of bandwidth.

If you want to use a <path> to draw a rectangle, you can draw all four lines, or you can draw the first three lines and then use the *closepath* command, denoted by a capital Z, to draw a straight line back to the beginning point of the current subpath. Example 6-2 is the SVG for Figure 6-2, which shows a rectangle drawn the hard way, a rectangle drawn with *closepath*, and a path that draws two triangles by opening and closing two subpaths.

Example 6-2. Using closepath

```
<g style="stroke: black; fill: none;">
    <!-- rectangle; all four lines -->
    <path d="M 10 10, L 40 10, L 40 30, L 10 30, L 10 10"/>

    <!-- rectangle with closepath -->
    <path d="M 60 10, L 90 10, L 90 30, L 60 30, Z"/>

    <!-- two thirty-degree triangles -->
    <path d="M 40 60, L 10 60, L 40 42.68, Z
        M 60 60, L 90 60, L 60 42.68, Z"/>
</g>
```

Examining the last path more closely:

Value	Action
M 40 60	Move pen to (40, 50)
L 10 60	Draw a line to (10, 60)
L 40 42.68	Draw a line to (40, 42.68)
Z	Close path by drawing a straight line to (40, 60), where this sub-path began
M 60 60	Start a new subpath; move pen to (60, 60)—no line is drawn
L 90 60	Draw a line to (90, 60)
L 60 42.68	Draw a line to (60, 42.68)
Z	Close path by drawing a straight line to (60, 60), where this sub-path began

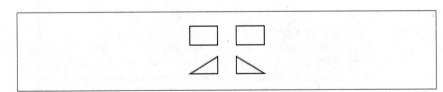

Figure 6-2. Result of using closepath

Relative moveto and lineto

The preceding commands are all represented by uppercase letters, and the coordinates are presumed to be *absolute* coordinates. If you use a lower-case command letter, the coordinates are interpreted as being *relative* to the current pen position. Thus, the following two paths are equivalent:

```
<path d="M 10 10 L 20 10 L 20 30  M 40 40 L 55 35"
    style="stroke: black;"/>
<path d="M 10 10 l 10  0 l  0 20  m 20 10 l 15 -5"
    style="stroke: black;"/>
```

If you start a path with a lowercase m (*moveto*), its coordinates will be interpreted as an absolute position since there's no previous pen position from which to calculate a relative position. All the other commands in this chapter also have the same upper- and lowercase distinction. An uppercase command's coordinates are absolute and a lowercase command's coordinates are relative. The *closepath* command, which has no coordinates, has the same effect in both upper- and lowercase.

Path Shortcuts

If content is king and design is queen, then bandwidth efficiency is the royal courtier who keeps the palace running smoothly. Since any non-trivial drawing will have paths with many tens of coordinate pairs, the <path> element has shortcuts that allow you to represent a path in as few bytes as possible.

The Horizontal lineto and Vertical lineto Commands

Since horizontal and vertical lines are so common, a path may specify a horizontal line with an H command followed by an absolute x-coordinate or an h command followed by a relative x-coordinate. Similarly, a vertical line is specified with a V command followed by an absolute y-coordinate or a v command followed by a relative y-coordinate.

Shortcut	Equivalent to	Effect
H 20	L 20 current_y	Draws a line to absolute location (20, current_y)
h 20	l 20 0	Draws a line to (current_x+20, current_y)
V 20	L current_x 20	Draws a line to absolute location (current_x, 20)
v 20	l current_x 20	Draws a line to location (current_x, current_y+20)

Thus, the following path draws a rectangle 15 units in width and 25 units in height, with the upper left corner at coordinates (12, 24).

```
<path d="M 12 24 h 15 v 25 h -15 z"/>
```

Notational Shortcuts for a Path

Paths can also be made shorter by applying the following two rules:

1. You may place multiple sets of coordinates after an `L` or `l`, just as you do in the `<polyline>` element. The following six paths all draw the same diamond that is shown in Figure 6-3; the first three are in absolute coordinates and the last three in relative coordinates. The third and sixth paths have an interesting twist—if you place multiple pairs of coordinates after a *moveto*, all the pairs after the first are presumed to be preceded by a *lineto*.*

    ```
    <path d="M 30 30 L 55 5 L 80 30 L 55 55 Z"/>
    <path d="M 30 30 L 55 5 80 30 55 55 Z"/>
    <path d="M 30 30 55 5 80 30 55 55 Z"/>
    <path d="m 30 30 l 25 -25 l 25 25 l -25 25 z"/>
    <path d="m 30 30 l 25 -25 25 25 -25 25 z"/>
    <path d="m 30 30 25 -25 25 25 -25 25 z"/>
    ```

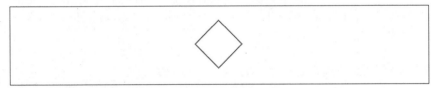

Figure 6-3. Result of drawing a diamond with a path

2. Any whitespace that is not necessary may be eliminated. You don't need a blank after a command letter since all commands are one letter only. You don't need a blank between a number and a command since the command letter can't be part of the number. You don't need a blank between a positive and a negative number since the leading minus sign of the negative number can't be a part of the positive number. This lets you reduce the third and sixth paths in the preceding listing even further:

    ```
    <path d="M30 30 55 5 80 30 55 55Z"/>
    <path d="m30 30 25-25 25 25-25 25z"/>
    ```

    Another example of the whitespace elimination rule in action is shown by the example that drew a rectangle 15 units in width and 25 units in height, with the upper left corner at coordinates (12, 24):

---

* You can also put multiple single coordinates after an *horizontal lineto* or *vertical lineto*, although it's rather pointless to do so. `H 25 35 45` is the same as `H 45`, and `v 11 13 15` is the same as `v 39`.

```
<path d="M 12 24 h 15 v 25 h -15 z"/> <!-- original -->
<path d="M12 24h15v25h-15z"/> <!-- shorter -->
```

Elliptical Arc

Lines are simple; two points on a path uniquely determine the line segment between them. Since an infinite number of curves can be drawn between two points, you must give additional information to draw a curved path between them. The simplest of the curves we will examine is the elliptical arc—that is, drawing a section of an ellipse that connects two points.

Although arcs are visually the simplest curves, specifying a unique arc requires the *most* information. The first pieces of information you need to specify are the *x*- and *y*-radii of the ellipse on which the points lie. This narrows it down to two possible ellipses, as you can see in section (a) of Figure 6-4. The two points divide the two ellipses into four arcs. Two of them, (b) and (c), are arcs that measure less than 180 degrees. The other two, (d) and (e) are greater than 180 degrees. If you look at (b) and (c), you will notice that they are differentiated by their direction; (b) is drawn in the direction of increasing negative angle, and (c) in the direction of increasing positive angle. The same relationship holds true between (d) and (e).

But wait—we still haven't uniquely specified the potential arcs! There's no law that says that the ellipse has to have its *x*-radius parallel to the *x*-axis. Part (f) of Figure 6-4 shows the two points with their candidate ellipses rotated thirty degrees with respect to the *x*-axis.

(Figure 6-4 is adapted from the one found in section 8.3.8 of the World Wide Web Consortium's SVG specification.)

Thus, an arc command begins with the A abbreviation for absolute coordinates or a for relative coordinates, and is followed by seven parameters:

- The *x*- and *y*-radius of the ellipse on which the points lie.
- The *x-axis-rotation* of the ellipse.
- The *large-arc-flag*, which is zero if the arc's measure is less than 180 degrees, or one if the arc's measure is greater than or equal to 180 degrees.
- The *sweep-flag*, which is zero if the arc is to be drawn in the negative angle direction, or one if the arc is to be drawn in the positive angle direction.

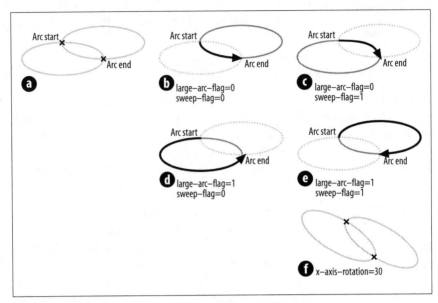

Figure 6-4. Variations of the elliptical arc command

- The ending *x*- and *y*- coordinates of the ending point. (The starting
  point is determined by the last point drawn or the last *moveto* command.)

Here are the paths used to draw the elliptical arcs in sections (b) through
(e) of Figure 6-4:

```
<path d="M 125,75 A100,50 0 0,0 225,125"/> <!-- b -->
<path d="M 125,75 A100,50 0 0,1 225,125"/> <!-- c -->
<path d="M 125,75 A100,50 0 1,0 225,125"/> <!-- d -->
<path d="M 125,75 A100,50 0 1,1 225,125"/> <!-- e -->
```

As a further example, let's enhance the background that we started in
Example 4-8 to complete the yin/yang symbol that is part of the Korean
flag. Example 6-3 keeps the full ellipses as <ellipse> elements, but creates
the semicircles that it needs with paths. The result is shown in Figure 6-5
(see additional color insert).

Example 6-3. Using elliptical arc

```
<!-- gray drop shadow -->
<ellipse cx="154" cy="154" rx="150" ry="120" style="fill: #999999;"/>

<!-- light blue ellipse -->
<ellipse cx="152" cy="152" rx="150" ry="120" style="fill: #cceeff;"/>

<!-- large light red semicircle fills upper half,
     followed by small light red semicircle that dips into
```

Example 6-3. Using elliptical arc (continued)

```
    lower left half of symbol -->
<path d="M 302 152 A 150 120, 0, 1, 0, 2 152
    A 75 60, 0, 1, 0, 152 152" style="fill: #ffcccc;"/>

<!-- light blue semicircle rises into upper right half of symbol -->
<path d="M 152 152 A 75 60, 0, 1, 1, 302 152" style="fill: #cceeff;"/>
```

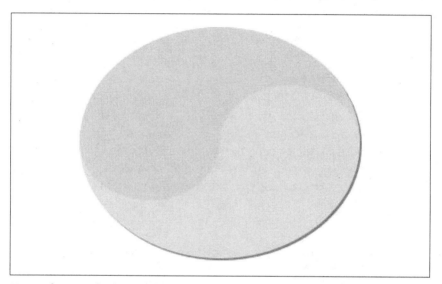

Figure 6-5. Result of using elliptical arc

Technique: Converting from Other Arc Formats

Some other vector graphics systems let you specify an arc by defining a center point for the ellipse, its *x*- and *y*-radius, the starting angle, and the extent of the angle's arc. This is a straightforward method of specification, and is excellent for drawing arcs as single objects. This, paradoxically, is exactly why SVG instead chooses such a seemingly eccentric method to specify arcs. In SVG, an arc is not presumed to be living in lonely splendor; it is intended to be part of a connected path of lines and curves. (For example, a rounded rectangle is precisely that—a series of lines and elliptical arcs.) Thus, it makes sense to specify an arc by its endpoints.

Sometimes, though, you do want an isolated semicircle (or, more accurately, semi-ellipse). Presume that you have an ellipse specified as:

```
<ellipse cx="cx" cy="cy" rx="rx" ry="ry"/>
```

Here are the paths to draw the four possible semi-ellipses:

```
<!-- northern hemisphere -->
<path d="M cx-rx cy A rx ry 0 1 1 cx+rx cy"/>
<!-- southern hemipshere -->
<path d="M cx-rx cy A rx ry 0 1 0 cx+rx cy"/>
<!-- eastern hemisphere -->
<path d="M cx cy-ry A rx ry 0 1 1 cx cy+ry"/>
<!-- western hemisphere -->
<path d="M cx cy-ry A rx ry 0 1 0 cx cy+ry"/>
```

For the more general case, when you wish to draw an arbitrary arc that has been specified in "center-and-angles" notation and wish to convert it to SVG's "endpoint-and-sweep" format, use the following Perl script. It prompts you for center coordinates, radii, starting angle, and angle extent. The output is a <path> tag that you can insert into your SVG files.

```perl
#!/usr/bin/perl

#
#    Convert an elliptical arc based around a central point
#    to an elliptical arc parameterized for SVG.
#
#    Input is a list containing:
#        center x coordinate
#        center y coordinate
#        x-radius of ellipse
#        y-radius of ellipse
#        beginning angle of arc in degrees
#        arc extent in degrees
#        x-axis rotation angle in degrees
#
#    Output is a list containing:
#
#        x-coordinate of beginning of arc
#        y-coordinate of beginning of arc
#        x-radius of ellipse
#        y-radius of ellipse
#        large-arc-flag as defined in SVG specification
#        sweep-flag  as defined in SVG specification
#        x-coordinate of endpoint of arc
#        y-coordinate of endpoint of arc
#
sub convert_to_svg
{
    my ($cx, $cy, $rx, $ry, $theta1, $delta, $phi) = @_;
    my ($theta2, $pi);
```

```perl
    my ($x0, $y0, $x1, $y1, $large_arc, $sweep);

    #
    #   Convert angles to radians
    #
    $pi = atan2(1,1) * 4;          # approximation of pi

    $theta2 = $delta + $theta1;
    $theta1 = $theta1 * $pi / 180.0;
    $theta2 = $theta2 * $pi / 180.0;
    $phi_r = $phi * $pi / 180.0;

    #
    #   Figure out the coordinates of the beginning and
    #   ending points
    #
    $x0 = $cx + cos($phi_r) * $rx * cos($theta1) +
        sin(-$phi_r) * $ry * sin($theta1);
    $y0 = $cy + sin($phi_r) * $rx * cos($theta1) +
        cos($phi_r) * $ry * sin($theta1);

    $x1 = $cx + cos($phi_r) * $rx * cos($theta2) +
        sin(-$phi_r) * $ry * sin($theta2);
    $y1 = $cy + sin($phi_r) * $rx * cos($theta2) +
        cos($phi_r) * $ry * sin($theta2);

    $large_arc = ($delta > 180) ? 1 : 0;
    $sweep = ($delta > 0) ? 1 : 0;

    return ($x0, $y0, $rx, $ry, $phi, $large_arc, $sweep, $x1, $y1);
}

#
#   Request input
#
print "Enter center x,y coordinates > ";
$data = <>;
$data =~ s/,/ /g;
($cx, $cy) = split /\s+/, $data;

print "Enter x and y radii > ";
$data = <>;
$data =~ s/,/ /g;
($rx, $ry) = split/\s+/, $data;

print "Enter starting angle in degrees > ";
$theta = <>;
chomp $theta;

print "Enter angle extent in degrees > ";
$delta = <>;
chomp $delta;

print "Enter angle of rotation in degrees > ";
```

```
$phi = <>;
chomp $phi;


#
#   Echo original data
#
print "(cx,cy)=($cx,$cy)   rx=$rx ry=$ry ",
    "start angle=$theta extent=$delta rotate=$phi\n";

($x0, $y0, $rx, $ry, $phi, $large_arc_flag, $sweep_flag, $x1, $y1) =
    convert_to_svg( $cx, $cy, $rx, $ry, $theta, $delta, $phi);


#
#   Produce a <path> element that fits the
#   specifications
#
print "<path d=\"M $x0 $y0 ",       # Moveto initial point
    "A $rx $ry ",                   # Arc command and radii,
    "$phi ",                        # angle of rotation,
    "$large_arc_flag ",             # the "large-arc" flag,
    "$sweep_flag ",                 # the "sweep" flag,
    "$x1 $y1\"/>\n";                # and the endpoint
```

If you wish to convert from the SVG format to a "center-and-angles" format, the mathematics is considerably more complex. You can see the formulas in detail in the SVG specification. This Perl script was adapted from the code in the Apache XML Batik project.

```
#!/usr/bin/perl

sub acos
{
    atan2( sqrt(1 - $_[0] * $_[0]), $_[0] );
}


#
#   Convert an elliptical arc based around a central point
#   to an elliptical arc parameterized for SVG.
#
#   Input is a list containing:
#
#       x-coordinate of beginning of arc
#       y-coordinate of beginning of arc
#       x-radius of ellipse
#       y-radius of ellipse
#       large-arc-flag as defined in SVG specification
#       sweep-flag  as defined in SVG specification
#       x-coordinate of endpoint of arc
#       y-coordinate of endpoint of arc
#
#   Output is a list containing:
#       center x coordinate
#       center y coordinate
```

```perl
#       x-radius of ellipse
#       y-radius of ellipse
#       beginning angle of arc in degrees
#       arc extent in degrees
#       x-axis rotation angle in degrees
#

sub convert_from_svg
{
    my ($x0, $y0, $rx, $ry, $phi, $large_arc, $sweep, $x, $y) = @_;
    my ($cx, $cy, $theta, $delta, $phi);

    # a plethora of temporary variables
    my (
        $dx2, $dy2, $phi_r, $x1, $y1,
        $rx_sq, $ry_sq,
        $x1_sq, $y1_sq,
        $sign, $sq, $coef,
        $cx1, $cy1, $sx2, $sy2,
        $p, $n,
        $ux, $uy, $vx, $vy
    );

    # Compute 1/2 distance between current and final point
    $dx2 = ($x0 - $x) / 2.0;
    $dy2 = ($y0 - $y) / 2.0;

    # Convert from degrees to radians
    $pi = atan2(1, 1) * 4.0;
    $phi %= 360;
    $phi_r = $phi * $pi / 180.0;

    # Compute (x1, y1)
    $x1 = cos($phi_r) * $dx2 + sin($phi_r) * $dy2;
    $y1 = -sin($phi_r) * $dx2 + cos($phi_r) * $dy2;

    # Make sure radii are large enough
    $rx = abs($rx); $ry = abs($ry);
    $rx_sq = $rx * $rx;
    $ry_sq = $ry * $ry;
    $x1_sq = $x1 * $x1;
    $y1_sq = $y1 * $y1;

    $radius_check = ($x1_sq / $rx_sq) + ($y1_sq / $ry_sq);
    if ($radius_check > 1)
    {
        $rx *= sqrt($radius_check);
        $ry *= sqrt($adius_check);
        $rx_sq = $rx * $rx;
        $ry_sq = $ry * $ry;
    }

    # Step 2: Compute (cx1, cy1)
```

```perl
$sign = ($large_arc == $sweep) ? -1 : 1;
$sq = (($rx_sq * $ry_sq) - ($rx_sq * $y1_sq) - ($ry_sq * $x1_sq)) /
      (($rx_sq * $y1_sq) + ($ry_sq * $x1_sq));
$sq = ($sq < 0) ? 0 : $sq;
$coef = ($sign * sqrt($sq));
$cx1 = $coef * (($rx * $y1) / $ry);
$cy1 = $coef * -(($ry * $x1) / $rx);

#   Step 3: Compute (cx, cy) from (cx1, cy1)

$sx2 = ($x0 + $x) / 2.0;
$sy2 = ($y0 + $y) / 2.0;

$cx = $sx2 + (cos($phi_r) * $cx1 - sin($phi_r) * $cy1);
$cy = $sy2 + (sin($phi_r) * $cx1 + cos($phi_r) * $cy1);

#   Step 4: Compute angle start and angle extent

$ux = ($x1 - $cx1) / $rx;
$uy = ($y1 - $cy1) / $ry;
$vx = (-$x1 - $cx1) / $rx;
$vy = (-$y1 - $cy1) / $ry;
$n = sqrt( ($ux * $ux) + ($uy * $uy) );
$p = $ux; # 1 * ux + 0 * uy
$sign = ($uy < 0) ? -1 : 1;

$theta = $sign * acos( $p / $n );
$theta = $theta * 180 / $pi;

$n = sqrt(($ux * $ux + $uy * $uy) * ($vx * $vx + $vy * $vy));
$p = $ux * $vx + $uy * $vy;
$sign = (($ux * $vy - $uy * $vx) < 0) ? -1 : 1;
$delta = $sign * acos( $p / $n );
$delta = $delta * 180 / $pi;

if ($sweep == 0 && $delta > 0)
{
    $delta -= 360;
}
elsif ($sweep == 1 && $delta < 0)
{
    $delta += 360;
}

$delta %= 360;
$theta %= 360;

return ($cx, $cy, $rx, $ry, $theta, $delta, $phi);
}


#
#   Request input
#
print "Enter starting x,y coordinates > ";
```

```
$data = <>;
$data =~ s/,/ /g;
($x0, $y0) = split /\s+/, $data;

print "Enter ending x,y coordinates > ";
$data = <>;
$data =~ s/,/ /g;
($x, $y) = split /\s+/, $data;

print "Enter x and y radii > ";
$data = <>;
$data =~ s/,/ /g;
($rx, $ry) = split/\s+/, $data;

print "Enter rotation angle in degrees ";
$phi = <>;
chomp $phi;

print "Large arc flag (0=no, 1=yes) > ";
$large_arc = <>;
chomp $large_arc;

print "Sweep flag (0=negative, 1=positive) > ";
$sweep = <>;
chomp $sweep;

print "From ($x0,$y0) to ($x,$y) rotate $phi",
    " large arc=$large_arc sweep=$sweep\n";

($cx, $cy, $rx, $ry, $theta, $delta, $phi) =
    convert_from_svg( $x0, $y0, $rx, $ry, $phi, $large_arc, $sweep,
        $x, $y );

print "Ellipse center = ($cx, $cy)\n";
print "Start angle = $theta\n";
print "Angle extent = $delta\n";
```

Bézier Curves

Arcs can be characterized as clean and functional, but one would rarely use the word "graceful" to describe them. If you want graceful, you need to use curves which are produced by graphing quadratic and cubic equations. Mathematicians have known about these curves for literally hundreds of years, but drawing them was always a computationally demanding task. This changed when Pierre Bézier, working for French car manufacturer Rénault and Paul de Casteljau, an engineer for Citroën, independently discovered a computationally convenient way to generate these curves.

If you have used graphics programs like Adobe Illustrator, you draw these Bézier curves by specifying two points and then moving a "handle" as shown in the following diagram. The end of this handle is called the control point, because it controls the shape of the curve. As you move the handle, the curve changes in a way that, to the uninitiated, is completely mystifying. Mike Woodburn, a graphic designer at Key Point Software, suggests Figure 6-6 as a way to visualize how the control point and the curve interact: imagine that the line is made of flexible metal. Inside the control point is a magnet; the closer a point is to the control point, the more strongly it is attracted.

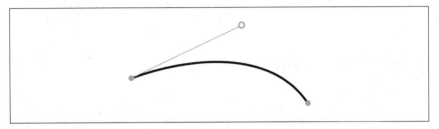

Figure 6-6. How graphics programs draw Bézier curves

Another way to visualize the role of the control point is based on the de Casteljau method of constructing the curves. We will use this approach in the following sections. For further details on the underlying mathematics, presented in a remarkably lucid fashion, see this web site: *http://graphics. cs.ucdavis.edu/GraphicsNotes/Bezier-Curves/Bezier-Curves.html.*

Quadratic Bézier Curves

The simplest of the Bézier curves is the quadratic curve. You specify a beginning point, an ending point, and a control point. Imagine two tent poles placed at the endpoints of the line. These tent poles meet at the control point. Stretched between the centers of the tent poles is a rubber band. The place where the curve bends is tied to the exact center of that rubber band. This situation is shown in Figure 6-7.

Programs like Adobe Illustrator show you only one of the "tent poles." The next time you're using such a program, mentally add in the second pole and the resulting curves will be far less mysterious.

That's the concept; now for the practical matter of actually producing such a curve in SVG. You specify a quadratic curve in a <path> data with the Q or q command. The command is followed by two sets of coordinates that specify a control point and an endpoint. The uppercase command implies

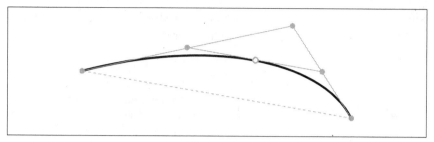

Figure 6-7. Visualizing a quadratic Bézier curve

absolute coordinates; lowercase implies relative coordinates. The curve in Figure 6-7 was drawn from (30, 75) to (300, 120) with the control point at (240, 30), and was specified in SVG as follows:

```
<path d="M30 75 Q 240 30, 300 120" style="stroke: black; fill: none;"/>
```

You may specify several sets of coordinates after a quadratic curve command. This will generate a polybézier curve. Presume you want a <path> that draws a curve from (30, 100) to (100, 100) with a control point at (80, 30) and then continues with a curve to (200, 80) with a control point at (130, 65). Here is the SVG for this path, with control point coordinates in bold. The result is shown in the left half of Figure 6-8; the control points and lines are shown in the right half of the figure.

```
<path d="M30 100 Q 80 30, 100 100, 130 65, 200 80"/>
```

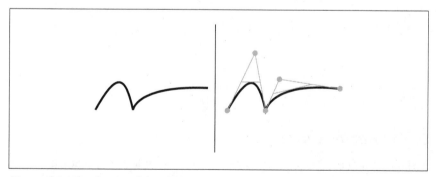

Figure 6-8. Quadratic polybézier curve

You are probably wondering, "What happened to 'graceful?' That curve is just lumpy." This is an accurate assessment. Just because curves are connected doesn't mean that they will look good together. That's why SVG provides the *smooth quadratic curve* command, which is denoted by the letter T (or t if you want to use relative coordinates). The command is followed by the next endpoint of the curve; the control point is calculated automatically, as the specification says, by "reflection of the control point on the previous command relative to the current point."

 For the mathematically inclined, the new control point *x2*, *y2* is calculated from the curve's starting point *x*, *y* and the previous control point *x1*, *y1* with these formulas:

```
x2 = 2 * x - x1
y2 = 2 * y - y1
```

Here is a quadratic Bézier curve drawn from (30, 100) to (100, 100) with a control point at (80, 30) and then smoothly continued to (200, 80). The left half of Figure 6-9 shows the curve; the right half shows the control points. The reflected control point is shown with a dashed line. Gracefulness has returned!

```
<path d="M30 100 Q 80 30, 100 100 T 200 80"/>
```

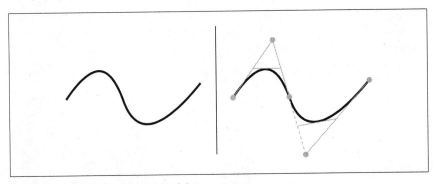

Figure 6-9. Smooth quadratic polybézier curve

Cubic Bézier Curves

A single quadratic Bézier curve has exactly one inflection point (the point where the curve changes direction). While these curves are more versatile than simple arcs, we can do even better by using cubic Bézier curves, which can have one or two inflection points.

The difference between the quadratic and cubic curves is that the cubic curve has two control points, one for each endpoint. The technique for generating the cubic curve is similar to that for generating the quadratic curve. You draw three lines that connect the endpoints and control points (a), and connect their midpoints. That produces two lines (b). You connect *their* midpoints, and that produces one line (c), whose midpoint determines one of the points on the final curve.* See Figure 6-10.

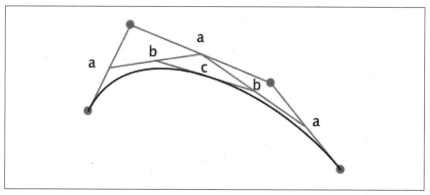

Figure 6-10. Visualizing a cubic Bézier curve

To specify such a cubic curve, use the C or c command. The command is followed by three sets of coordinates that specify the control point for the start point, the control point for the end point, and the end point. As with all the other path commands, an uppercase command implies absolute coordinates; lowercase implies relative coordinates. The curve in the preceding diagram was drawn from (20, 80) to (200, 120) with control points at (50, 20) and (150, 60). The SVG for the path was as follows:

```
<path d="M20 80 C 50 20, 150 60, 200 120"
      style="stroke: black; fill: none;"/>
```

There are many interesting curves you can draw, depending upon the relationship of the control points (see Figure 6-11). To make the graphic cleaner, we show only the lines from each endpoint to its control point.

As with quadratic curves, you can construct a cubic polybézier by specifying several sets of coordinates after a cubic curve command. The last point of the first curve becomes the first point of the next curve, and so on. Here is a <path> that draws a cubic curve from (30, 100) to (100, 100) with control points at (50, 50) and (70, 20); it is immediately followed by a curve that doubles back to (65, 100) with control points at (110, 130) and (45, 150). Here is the SVG for this path, with control point coordinates in bold. The result is shown in the left half of Figure 6-12; the control points and lines are shown in the right half of the diagram.

```
<path d="M30 100 C 50 50, 70 20, 100 100, 110, 130, 45, 150, 65, 100"/>
```

---

* We're dispensing with the tent analogy; it gets too unwieldy. Curves based on yurts and geodesic domes are left as exercises for the reader.

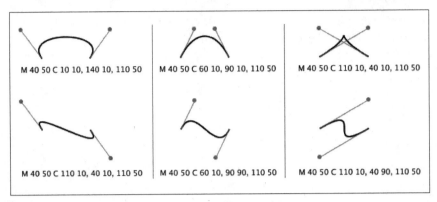

Figure 6-11. Result of cubic Bézier control point combinations

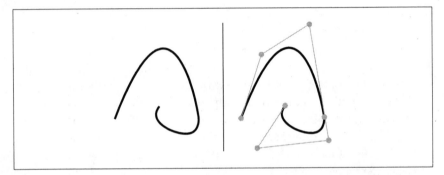

Figure 6-12. Cubic polybézier curve

If you want to guarantee a smooth join between curves, you can use the S command (or s if you want to use relative coordinates). In a manner analogous to that of the T command for quadratic curves, the new curve will take the previous curve's endpoint as its starting point, and the first control point will be the reflection of the previous ending control point. All you need to supply will be the control point for the next endpoint on the curve, followed by the next endpoint itself.

Here is a cubic Bézier curve drawn from (30, 100) to (100, 100) with control points at (50, 30) and (70, 50). It continues smoothly to (200, 80), using (150, 40) as its ending control point. The upper half shows the curve; the lower half shows the control points. The reflected control point is shown with a dashed line in Figure 6-13.

```
<path d="M30 100 C 50 30, 70 50, 100 100 S 150 40, 200 80"/>
```

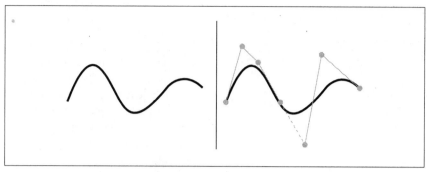

Figure 6-13. Smooth cubic polybézier curve

Path Reference Summary

In Table 6-1, uppercase commands use absolute coordinates and lower-case commands use relative coordinates.

Table 6-1. Path commands

Command	Arguments	Effect
M m	*x y*	Move to given coordinates.
L l	*x y*	Draw a line to the given coordinates. You may supply multiple sets of coordinates to draw a polyline.
H h	*x*	Draw a horizontal line to the given *x*-coordinate.
V v	*y*	Draw a vertical line to the given *x*-coordinate.
A a	*rx ry x-axis-rotation* *large-arc sweep x y*	Draw an elliptical arc from the current point to (*x*, *y*). The points are on an ellipse with *x*-radius *rx* and *y*-radius *ry*. The ellipse is rotated *x-axis-rotation* degrees. If the arc is less than 180 degrees, *large-arc* is zero; if greater than 180 degrees, *large-arc* is one. If the arc is to be drawn in the positive direction, *sweep* is one; otherwise it is zero.
Q q	*x1 y1 x y*	Draw a quadratic Bézier curve from the current point to (*x*, *y*) using control point (*x1*, *y1*).

Table 6-1. Path commands (continued)

Command	Arguments	Effect
T t	*x y*	Draw a quadratic Bézier curve from the current point to (*x*, *y*). The control point will be the reflection of the previous Q command's control point. If there is no previous curve, the current point will be used as the control point.
C c	*x1 y1 x2 y2 x y*	Draw a cubic Bézier curve from the current point to (*x*, *y*) using control point (*x1*, *y1*) as the control point for the beginning of the curve and (*x2*, *y2*) as the control point for the endpoint of the curve.
S s	*x2 y2 x y*	Draw a cubic Bézier curve from the current point to (*x*, *y*), using (*x2*, *y2*) as the control point for this new endpoint. The first control point will be the reflection of the previous C command's ending control point. If there is no previous curve, the current point will be used as the first control point.

Paths and Filling

The information described in Chapter 3 in the section "Filling Polygons That Have Intersecting Lines" is also applicable to paths, which can not only have intersecting lines, but can also have "holes" in them. Consider the paths in Example 6-4, both of which draw nested squares. In the first path, both squares are drawn clockwise; in the second path, the outer square is drawn clockwise and the inner square is drawn counterclockwise.

Example 6-4. Using different fill-rule values on paths

```
<!-- both paths clockwise -->
<path d="M 0 0, 60 0, 60 60, 0 60 Z
    M 15 15, 45 15, 45 45, 15 45Z"/>

<!-- outer path clockwise; inner path counterclockwise -->
<path d="M 0 0, 60 0, 60 60, 0 60 Z
    M 15 15, 15 45, 45 45, 45 15Z"/>
```

Figure 6-14 shows that there is a difference when you use a `fill-rule` of `nonzero`, which takes into account the direction of the lines when determining whether a point is inside or outside a path. Using a `fill-rule` of `evenodd` produces the same result for both paths; it uses total number of lines crossed and ignores their direction.

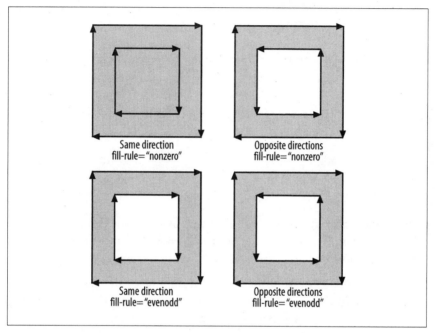

Figure 6-14. Result of using different fill-rule values

The marker element

Let us presume the following path, which uses a line, an elliptical arc, and another line to draw the rounded corner in Figure 6-15:

```
<path d="M 10 20 100 20 A 20 30 0 0 1 120 50 L 120 110"
    style="fill: none; stroke: black;"/>
```

We'd like to mark the direction of the path by putting a circle at the beginning, a solid triangle at the end, and arrowheads at the other vertices, as shown in Figure 6-16. To achieve this effect, we will construct three <marker> elements and tell the <path> to reference them.

Let's start with Example 6-5, which adds the circular marker. A marker is a "self-contained" graphic with its own private set of coordinates, so you have to specify its `markerWidth` and `markerHeight` height in the starting <marker> tag. That is followed by the SVG elements required to draw the

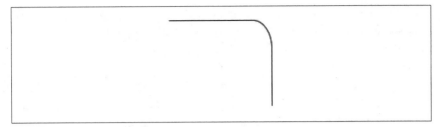

Figure 6-15. Lines and arc

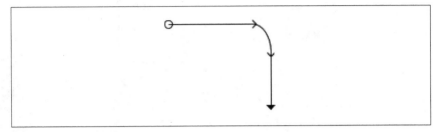

Figure 6-16. Lines and arc with markers

marker, and ends with a closing </marker>. A <marker> element does not display by itself, but we are putting it in a <defs> element because that's where reusable elements belong.

Since we want the circle to be at the beginning of the path, we add a marker-start to the style in the <path>.* The value of this property is a URL reference to the <marker> element we've just created.

Example 6-5. First attempt at circular marker

```
<defs>
<marker id="mCircle" markerWidth="10" markerHeight="10">
    <circle cx="5" cy="5" r="4" style="fill: none; stroke: black;"/>
</marker>
</defs>

<path  d="M 10 20 100 20 A 20 30 0 0 1 120 50 L 120 110"
    style="marker-start: url(#mCircle);
    fill: none; stroke: black;"/>
```

The result in Figure 6-17 is not quite what we planned...

The reason the circle appears in the wrong place is that, by default, the start marker's (0, 0) point is aligned with the beginning coordinate of the path. Example 6-6 adds refX and refY attributes that tell which

---

* Yes, markers are considered to be part of presentation rather than structure. This is one of those gray areas where you could argue either case.

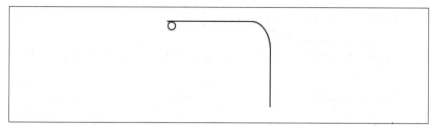

Figure 6-17. Misplaced circular marker

coordinates (in the marker's system) are to align with the beginning coordinate. Once these are added, the circular marker appears exactly where it is desired in Figure 6-18.

Example 6-6. Correctly placed circular marker

```
<marker id="mCircle" markerWidth="10" markerHeight="10" refX="5" refY="5">
    <circle cx="5" cy="5" r="4" style="fill: none; stroke: black;"/>
</marker>
```

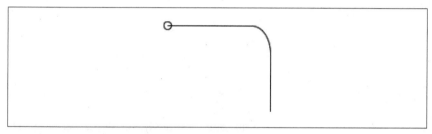

Figure 6-18. Correctly placed circular marker

Given this information, we can now write Example 6-7, which adds the triangular marker and references it as the marker-end for the path. Then we can add the arrowhead marker and reference it as the marker-mid. The marker-mid will be attached to every vertex except the beginning and end of the path. Notice that the refX and refY attributes have been set so the wide end of the arrowhead aligns with the intermediate vertices while the tip of the solid triangle aligns with the ending vertex. Figure 6-19 shows the result, which draws the first marker correctly but not the others.

Example 6-7. Attempt to use three markers

```
<defs>
    <marker id="mCircle" markerWidth="10" markerHeight="10"
        refX="5" refY="5">
        <circle cx="5" cy="5" r="4" style="fill: none; stroke: black;"/>
    </marker>

    <marker id="mArrow" markerWidth="6" markerHeight="10"
```

Example 6-7. Attempt to use three markers (continued)

```
     refX="0" refY="4">
        <path d="M 0 0 4 4 0 8" style="fill: none; stroke: black;"/>
     </marker>

     <marker id="mTriangle" markerWidth="5" markerHeight="10"
        refX="5" refY="5">
        <path d="M 0 0 5 5 0 10 Z" style="fill: black;"/>
     </marker>
</defs>

<path d="M 10 20 100 20 A 20 30 0 0 1 120 50 L 120 110"
    style="marker-start: url(#mCircle);
        marker-mid: url(#mArrow);
        marker-end: url(#mTriangle);
        fill: none; stroke: black;"/>
```

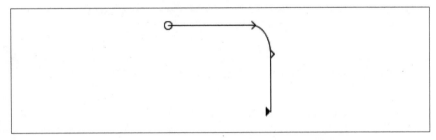

Figure 6-19. Incorrectly oriented markers

To get the effect you want, you must explicitly set a marker's orient attribute to auto. This makes it automatically rotate to match the direction of the path.* (You may also specify a number of degrees, in which case the marker will always be rotated by that amount.) Here in Example 6-8 are the markers, set to produce the effect shown in Figure 6-16. We don't need to orient the circle; it looks the same no matter how it's rotated.

Example 6-8. Correctly oriented markers

```
<defs>
    <marker id="mCircle" markerWidth="10" markerHeight="10"
        refX="5" refY="5">
        <circle cx="5" cy="5" r="4" style="fill: none; stroke: black;"/>
    </marker>

    <marker id="mArrow" markerWidth="6" markerHeight="10"
        refX="0" refY="4" orient="auto">
        <path d="M 0 0 4 4 0 8" style="fill: none; stroke: black;"/>
```

---

* To be exact, the rotation is the average of the angle of the direction of the line going into the vertex and the direction of the line going out of the vertex.

Example 6-8. Correctly oriented markers (continued)

```
    </marker>

    <marker id="mTriangle" markerWidth="5" markerHeight="10"
        refX="5" refY="5" orient="auto">
        <path d="M 0 0 5 5 0 10 Z" style="fill: black;"/>
    </marker>
</defs>

<path d="M 10 20 100 20 A 20 30 0 0 1 120 50 L 120 110"
    style="marker-start: url(#mCircle);
        marker-mid: url(#mArrow);
        marker-end: url(#mTriangle);
        fill: none; stroke: black;"/>
```

Another useful attribute is the markerUnits attribute. If set to strokeWidth, the marker's coordinate system is set so that one unit equals the stroke width. This makes your marker grow in proportion to the stroke width; it's the default behavior and it's usually what you want. If you set the attribute to userSpaceOnUse, the marker's coordinates are presumed to be the same as the coordinate system of the object that references the marker. The marker will remain the same size irrespective of the stroke width.

Marker Miscellanea

If you want the same marker at the beginning, middle, and end of a path, you don't need to specify all of the marker-start, marker-mid, and marker-end properties. Just use the marker property and have it reference the marker you want. Thus, if we wanted all the vertices to have a circular marker, as shown in Figure 6-20, we'd write the SVG in Example 6-9.

Example 6-9. Using a single marker for all vertices

```
<defs>
    <marker id="mCircle" markerWidth="10" markerHeight="10"
        refX="5" refY="5">
        <circle cx="5" cy="5" r="4" style="fill: none; stroke: black;"/>
    </marker>
</defs>

<path d="M 10 20 100 20 A 20 30 0 0 1 120 50 L 120 110"
    style="marker: url(#mCircle); fill: none; stroke: black;"/>
```

It is also possible to set the viewBox and preserveAspectRatio attributes on a <marker> element to gain even more control over its display. These work exactly as described in Chapter 2, in the section "Specifying User Coordinates for a Viewport" and in the section "Preserving Aspect Ratio."

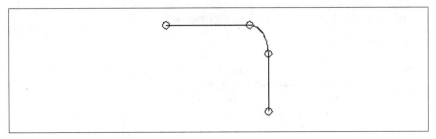

Figure 6-20. Using a single marker for all vertices

You may reference a <marker> in a <polygon>, <polyline>, or <line> element as well as in a <path>.

The following thought may have occurred to you: "If a marker can have a path in it, can *that* path have a marker attached to it as well?" The answer is yes, it can, but the second marker must fit into the rectangle established by the first marker's markerWidth and markerHeight. Please remember that just because a thing can be done does not mean that it should be done. If you need such an effect, you are probably better off to draw the secondary marker as a part of the primary marker rather than attempting to nest markers.

7

Patterns and Gradients

To this point, we have used only solid colors to fill and outline graphic objects. You are not restricted to using solid colors; you may also use a pattern or a gradient to fill or outline a graphic. That's what we'll examine in this chapter.

Patterns

To use a pattern, you define a graphic object that is replicated horizontally and vertically to fill another object (or stroke). This graphic object is called a tile, because the act of filling an object with a pattern is very much like covering an area of a floor with tiles. In this section, we will use the quadratic curve drawn by the SVG in Example 7-1 as our tile. It's outlined in gray to show its area (20 by 20 user units) clearly.

Example 7-1. Path for a pattern tile

```
<path d="M 0 0 Q 5 20 10 10 T 20 20"
    style="stroke: black; fill: none;"/>
<path d="M 0 0 h20 v20 h-20 z"
    style="stroke: gray; fill: none;"/>
```

Figure 7-1 is zoomed in so you can see it in detail.

patternUnits

To create a pattern tile, you must enclose the <path> elements that describe your tile in a <pattern> element, and then make several decisions. The first decision is how you wish to space the tiles, and this is reflected in the patternUnits attribute. Do you want the tiles spaced to fill

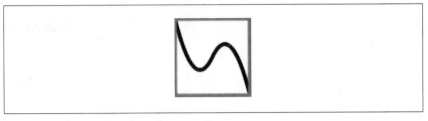

Figure 7-1. Zoomed-in view of pattern tile

a certain percentage of each object they're applied to, or you do want them spaced at equal intervals, no matter what the size of the object they're filling?

If you want the tile dimensions on an object-by-object basis, you specify the pattern's upper left x and y coordinates, and its width and height as percentages or decimals in the range zero to one, and set the patternUnits attribute to objectBoundingBox. An object's bounding box is the smallest rectangle that completely encloses a particular graphic object. Example 7-2 shows the sample tile replicated five times horizontally and five times vertically in any object that it fills.

Example 7-2. Tiles spaced with patternUnits set to objectBoundingBox

```
<defs>
<pattern id="tile" x="0" y="0" width="20%" height="20%"
    patternUnits="objectBoundingBox">
<path d="M 0 0 Q 5 20 10 10 T 20 20"
    style="stroke: black; fill: none;"/>
<path d="M 0 0 h 20 v 20 h -20 z"
    style="stroke: gray; fill: none;"/>
</pattern>
</defs>

<rect x="20" y="20" width="100" height="100"
    style="fill: url(#tile); stroke: black;"/>
<rect x="135" y="20" width="70" height="80"
    style="fill: url(#tile); stroke: black;"/>
<rect x="220" y="20" width="150" height="130"
    style="fill: url(#tile); stroke: black;"/>
```

In Figure 7-2, the leftmost rectangle, which is 100 user units wide and tall, provides an exact fit for five tiles that are each 20 user units wide and tall. In the middle rectangle, the width and height aren't great enough to show any one pattern tile completely, so they are truncated. In the rightmost rectangle, extra space is added since the rectangle's width and height exceeds five times the space required for a single tile. In all cases, since we set x and y, the upper left corner of the tile coincides with the upper left corner of the rectangle.

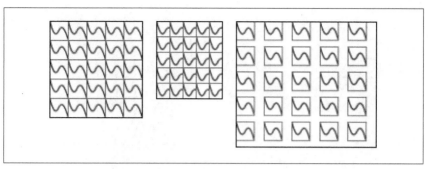

Figure 7-2. Tiles spaced by objectBoundingBox

If you're used to most graphics programs, this behavior comes as somewhat of a shock. Typical graphic editing programs put tiles directly next to
one another to fill the area, no matter what its size. There is never extra
padding between tiles, and tiles are cut off only by the edge of the object
they're filling. If this is the behavior that you want, you must set the patternUnits attribute to userSpaceOnUse, and specify the x and y coordinates, and the width and height of the tile in user units. Example 7-3 uses
the sample tile, set to its exact width and height of twenty user units.

Example 7-3. Tiles spaced with patternUnits set to userSpaceOnUse

```
<defs>
<pattern id="tile" x="0" y="0" width="20" height="20"
    patternUnits="userSpaceOnUse">
<path d="M 0 0 Q 5 20 10 10 T 20 20"
    style="stroke: black; fill: none;"/>
<path d="M 0 0 h 20 v 20 h -20 z"
    style="stroke: gray; fill: none;"/>
</pattern>
</defs>

<rect x="20" y="20" width="100" height="100"
    style="fill: url(#tile); stroke: black;"/>
<rect x="135" y="20" width="70" height="80"
    style="fill: url(#tile); stroke: black;"/>
<rect x="220" y="20" width="150" height="130"
    style="fill: url(#tile); stroke: black;"/>
```

In Figure 7-3, the tiles have constant size in all three rectangles. Their
alignment is, however, dependent upon the underlying coordinate system.
The middle rectangle, for example, has an *x*-coordinate that is not a multiple of twenty, so the rectangle's upper left corner doesn't coincide with a
tile's upper left corner. (The top edges do align, since the upper *y*-coordi-
nate of all three rectangles was carefully chosen to be a multiple of
twenty.)

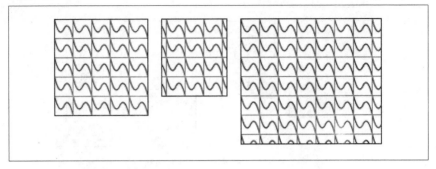

Figure 7-3. Tiles spaced by userSpaceOnUse

If you do not specify a value for patternUnits, the default is objectBoundingBox.

patternContentUnits

You must next decide what units are to be used to express the pattern data itself. By default, the patternContentUnits attribute is set to userSpaceOnUse. If you set the attributes to objectBoundingBox, the path data points are expressed in terms of the object being filled. Example 7-4 shows the SVG that produces Figure 7-4.

If you use the objectBoundingBox for your patternContentU-nits, you should draw any objects to be filled with the upper left corner of their bounding boxes at the origin (0, 0). Also, you will have to reduce the stroke-width of the pattern data to 0.01, since these units are percentages, not user units.

Example 7-4. patternContentUnits set to objectBoundingBox

```
<defs>
<pattern id="tile"
    patternUnits="objectBoundingBox"
    patternContentUnits="objectBoundingBox"
  x="0" y="0" width=".2" height=".2">
    <path d="M 0 0 Q .05 .20 .10 .10 T .20 .20"
        style="stroke: black; fill: none; stroke-width: 0.01;"/>
    <path d="M 0 0 h 0.2 v 0.2 h-0.2z"
        style="stroke: black; fill: none; stroke-width: 0.01;"/>
```

Example 7-4. patternContentUnits set to objectBoundingBox (continued)

```
</pattern>

</defs>

<g transform="translate(20,20)">
<rect x="0" y="0" width="100" height="100"
    style="fill: url(#tile); stroke: black;"/>
</g>

<g transform="translate(135,20)">
<rect x="0" y="0" width="70" height="80"
    style="fill: url(#tile); stroke: black;"/>
</g>

<g transform="translate(220,20)">
<rect x="0" y="0" width="150" height="130"
    style="fill: url(#tile); stroke: black;"/>
</g>
```

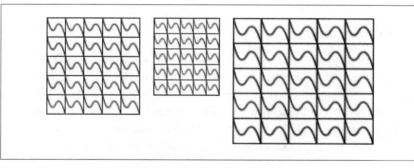

Figure 7-4. patternContentUnits set to objectBoundingBox

If you want to reduce an existing graphic object for use as a tile, it's easier to use the viewBox attribute to scale it. Specifying viewBox will override any patternContentUnits information. Another possible option is to use the preserveAspectRatio attribute, as described in Chapter 2, in the section "Preserving Aspect Ratio." Example 7-5 uses a scaled-down version of the cubic polybézier curve from Figure 6-12 as a tile. The stroke-width is set to 5; otherwise, when scaled down, the pattern you see in Figure 7-5 would not be visible.

Example 7-5. Using viewBox to scale a pattern

```
<defs>
<pattern id="tile"
    patternUnits="userSpaceOnUse"
    x="0" y="0" width="20" height="20"
    viewBox="0 0 150 150">
```

Example 7-5. Using viewBox to scale a pattern (continued)

```
    <path d="M30 100 C 50 50, 70 20, 100 100, 110, 130, 45, 150, 65, 100"
        style="stroke: black; stroke-width: 5; fill: none;"/>
</pattern>
</defs>

<rect x="20" y="20" width="100" height="100"
    style="fill: url(#tile); stroke: black;"/>
```

Figure 7-5. Pattern scaled with viewBox

Nested Patterns

Again, this may have occurred to you: "If an object can be filled with a pattern, can *that* pattern be filled with a pattern as well?" The answer is yes. As opposed to nested markers, which are rarely necessary, there are some effects you can't easily achieve without nested patterns. Example 7-6 creates a rectangle filled with circles, all filled with horizontal stripes. This produces the unusual, but valid, polka-dot effect shown in Figure 7-6.

Example 7-6. Nested patterns

```
<defs>
<pattern id="stripe"
    patternUnits="userSpaceOnUse"
    x="0" y="0" width="6" height="6">
    <path d="M 0 0 6 0"
        style="stroke: black; fill: none;"/>
</pattern>

<pattern id="polkadot"
    patternUnits="userSpaceOnUse"
    x="0" y="0" width="36" height="36">
    <circle cx="12" cy="12" r="12"
        style="fill: url(#stripe);  stroke: black;"/>
</pattern>
</defs>

<rect x="36" y="36" width="100" height="100"
    style="fill: url(#polkadot); stroke: black;"/>
```

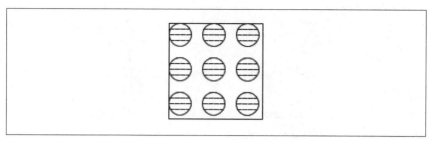

Figure 7-6. Patterns within patterns

Gradients

Rather than filling an object with a solid color, you can fill it with a gradient, a smooth color transition from one shade to another. Gradients can be linear, where the color transition occurs along a straight line, or radial, where the transition occurs along a circular path.

linearGradient

A linear gradient is a transition through a series of colors along a straight line. You specify the colors you want at specific locations, called gradient stops. The stops are part of the structure of the gradient; the colors are part of the presentation. Example 7-7 shows the SVG for a gradient that fills a rectangle with a smooth transition from gold to cyan, which you can see in Figure 7-7 (see additional color insert).

Example 7-7. Simple two-color gradient

```
<defs>
<linearGradient id="two_hues">
    <stop offset="0%" style="stop-color: #ffcc00;"/>
    <stop offset="100%" style="stop-color: #0099cc;"/>
</linearGradient>
</defs>

<rect x="20" y="20" width="200" height="100"
    style="fill: url(#two_hues);  stroke: black;"/>
```

The stop element

Let's examine the <stop> element more closely. It has two required attributes; the offset tells the point along the line at which the color should be equal to the stop-color. The offset is expressed as a percentage from 0 to 100% or as a decimal value from 0 to 1.0. While you don't need to place stops at 0% and 100%, you usually will. Example 7-8 is a

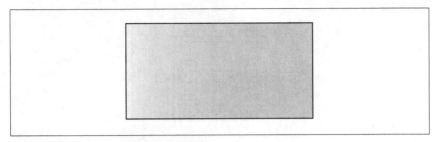

Figure 7-7. Simple two-color gradient

slightly more complex linear gradient, with stops for gold at 0%, reddish-purple at 33.3%, and light green at 100%; it is shown in Figure 7-8 (see additional color insert).

Example 7-8. Three-color gradient

```
<defs>
<linearGradient id="three_stops">
    <stop offset="0%" style="stop-color: #ffcc00;"/>
    <stop offset="33.3%" style="stop-color: #cc6699"/>
    <stop offset="100%" style="stop-color: #66cc99;"/>
</linearGradient>
</defs>

<rect x="20" y="20" width="200" height="100"
    style="fill: url(#three_stops); stroke: black;"/>
```

Figure 7-8. Three-stop gradient

Establishing a transition line for a linear gradient

The default behavior of a linear gradient is to transition along a horizontal line from the left side of an object to its right side. If you want the transition of colors to occur across a vertical line or a line at an angle, you must specify the line's starting point with the x1 and y1 attributes and its ending points with the x2 and y2 attributes. By default, these are also expressed as percentages from 0% to 100% or decimals from 0 to 1. In Example 7-9, we'll use the same color stops in a horizontal, vertical, and diagonal gradient. Rather than duplicate the stops into each <linearGradient> element, we'll use the xlink:href attribute to refer to the original left-to-right gradient. The stops will be inherited, but the *x*- and *y*-coordinates will be overriden by each individual gradient. The arrows in Figure 7-9 (see additional color insert) do not appear in the SVG of Example 7-9.

Example 7-9. Defining vectors for a linear gradient

```
<defs>
<linearGradient id="three_stops">
    <stop offset="0%" style="stop-color: #ffcc00;"/>
    <stop offset="33.3%" style="stop-color: #cc6699"/>
    <stop offset="100%" style="stop-color: #66cc99;"/>
</linearGradient>

<linearGradient id="right_to_left"
    xlink:href="#three_stops"
    x1="100%" y1="0%" x2="0%" y2="0%"/>

<linearGradient id="down"
    xlink:href="#three_stops"
    x1="0%" y1="0%" x2="0%" y2="100%"/>

<linearGradient id="up"
    xlink:href="#three_stops"
    x1="0%" y1="100%" x2="0%" y2="0%"/>

<linearGradient id="diagonal"
    xlink:href="#three_stops"
    x1="0%" y1="0%" x2="100%" y2="100%"/>
</defs>

<rect x="40" y="20" width="200" height="40"
    style="fill: url(#three_stops); stroke: black;"/>

<rect x="40" y="70" width="200" height="40"
    style="fill: url(#right_to_left); stroke: black;"/>

<rect x="250" y="20" width="40" height="200"
    style="fill: url(#down); stroke: black;"/>

<rect x="300" y="20" width="40" height="200"
    style="fill: url(#up); stroke: black;"/>

<rect x="40" y="120" width="200" height="100"
    style="fill: url(#diagonal); stroke: black;"/>
```

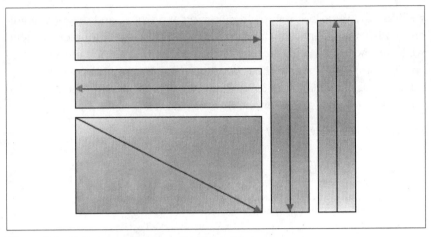

Figure 7-9. Defining vectors for a linear gradient

If you wish to establish the transition line using user space coordinates instead of percentages, set the gradientUnits to userSpaceOnUse instead of the default value, which is objectBoundingBox.

The spreadMethod attribute

The transition line does not have to go from one corner of an object to another. What happens if you say that the transition line goes from (20%, 30%) to (40%, 80%)? What happens to the part of the object outside that line? You can set the spreadMethod attribute to one of these values:

pad
> The beginning and ending stop colors will be extended to the edges of the object.

repeat
> The gradient will be repeated start-to-end until it reaches the edges of the object being filled.

reflect
> The gradient will be reflected end-to-start, start-to-end until it reaches the edges of the object being filled.

Figure 7-10 (see additional color insert) shows the leftmost square's gradient padded, the middle square's gradient repeated, and the right square's gradient reflected. The original transition line has been added to the SVG for each square in Example 7-10 to make the effect easier to detect.

Example 7-10. Effects of spreadMethod values on a linear gradient

```
<defs>
<linearGradient id="partial"
    x1="20%" y1="30%" x2="40%" y2="80%">
    <stop offset="0%" style="stop-color: #ffcc00;"/>
    <stop offset="33.3%" style="stop-color: #cc6699"/>
    <stop offset="100%" style="stop-color: #66cc99;"/>
</linearGradient>

<linearGradient id="padded"
    xlink:href="#partial"
    spreadMethod="pad"/>

<linearGradient id="repeated"
    xlink:href="#partial"
    spreadMethod="repeat"/>

<linearGradient id="reflected"
    xlink:href="#partial"
    spreadMethod="reflect"/>

<line id="show-line" x1="20" y1="30" x2="40" y2="80"
    style="stroke: white;"/>
</defs>

<rect x="20" y="20" width="100" height="100"
    style="fill: url(#padded); stroke: black;"/>
<use xlink:href="#show-line" transform="translate (20,20)"/>

<rect x="130" y="20" width="100" height="100"
    style="fill: url(#repeated); stroke: black;"/>
<use xlink:href="#show-line" transform="translate (130,20)"/>

<rect x="240" y="20" width="100" height="100"
    style="fill: url(#reflected); stroke: black;"/>
<use xlink:href="#show-line" transform="translate (240,20)"/>
```

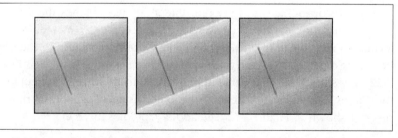

Figure 7-10. spreadMethod values pad, repeat, and reflect for a linear gradient

radialGradient

The other type of gradient you can use is the radial gradient, where the color transition occurs along a circular path.* It's set up in much the same way as a linear gradient. Example 7-11 sets three stops, which, as you see in Figure 7-11 (see additional color insert), are orange, green, and purple.

Example 7-11. Radial gradient with three stops

```
<defs>
<radialGradient id="three_stops">
    <stop offset="0%" style="stop-color: #f96;"/>
    <stop offset="50%" style="stop-color: #9c9;"/>
    <stop offset="100%" style="stop-color: #906;"/>
</radialGradient>
</defs>

<rect x="20" y="20" width="100" height="100"
    style="fill: url(#three_stops); stroke: black;"/>
```

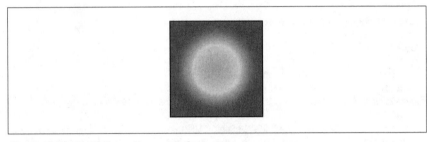

Figure 7-11. Radial gradient with three stops

Establishing transition limits for a radial gradient

Instead of using a line to determine where the 0% and 100% stop points should be, a radial gradient's limits are determined by a circle; the center is the 0% stop point, and the outer circumference defines the 100% stop point. You define the outer circle with the cx (center *x*), cy (center *y*), and r (radius) attributes. All of these are in terms of percentages of the object's bounding box. The default values for all these attributes is 50%. Example 7-12 draws a square with a radial gradient with the zero point centered at the upper left of the square and the outer edge at the lower right. The result is shown in Figure 7-12 (see additional color insert).

---

* If the bounding box of the object being filled is not square, the transition path will become elliptical to match the aspect ratio of the bounding box.

Example 7-12. Setting limits for a radial gradient

```
<defs>
<radialGradient id="center_origin"
    cx="0" cy="0" r="100%">
    <stop offset="0%" style="stop-color: #f96;"/>
    <stop offset="50%" style="stop-color: #9c9;"/>
    <stop offset="100%" style="stop-color: #906;"/>
</radialGradient>
</defs>


<rect x="20" y="20" width="100" height="100"
    style="fill: url(#center_origin); stroke: black;"/>
```

Figure 7-12. Setting limits for a radial gradient

The 0% stop point, also called the focal point, is by default placed at the center of the circle that defines the 100% stop point. If you wish to have the 0% stop point at some point other than the center of the limit circle, you must change the fx and fy attributes. The focal point should be within the circle established for the 100% stop point. If it's not, the SVG viewer program will automatically move the focal point to the outer circumference of the end circle.

In Example 7-13, the circle is centered at the origin with a radius of 100%, but the focal point is at (30%, 30%). As you see in Figure 7-13 (see additional color insert), this has the visual effect of moving the "center."

Example 7-13. Setting focal point for a radial gradient

```
<defs>
<radialGradient id="focal_set"
    cx="0" cy="0" fx="30%" fy="30%" r="100%">
    <stop offset="0%" style="stop-color: #f96;"/>
    <stop offset="50%" style="stop-color: #9c9;"/>
    <stop offset="100%" style="stop-color: #906;"/>
</radialGradient>
</defs>


<rect x="20" y="20" width="100" height="100"
    style="fill: url(#focal_set); stroke: black;"/>
```

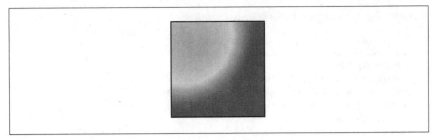

Figure 7-13. Setting focal point for a radial gradient

The default values for the limit-setting attributes of a `<radialGradient>` are as follows:

Attribute	Default value
cx	50% (horizontal center of object bounding box)
cy	50% (vertical center of object bounding box)
r	50% (half the width/height of object bounding box)
fx	same as cx
fy	same as cy

 If you wish to establish the circle limits using user space coordinates instead of percentages, set the `gradientUnits` to `userSpaceOnUse` instead of the default value, which is `objectBoundingBox`.

The spreadMethod attribute for radial gradients

In the event that the limits you've described don't reach to the edges of the object, you can set the `spreadMethod` attribute to one of the values `pad`, `repeat`, or `reflect` as described earlier in the section "The spreadMethod attribute" to fill up the remaining space as you wish. We've written all three effects in Example 7-14; Figure 7-14 (see additional color insert) shows the leftmost square's gradient padded, the middle square's gradient repeated, and the right square's gradient reflected.

Example 7-14. Effects of spreadMethod values on a radial gradient

```
<defs>
<radialGradient id="three_stops"
    cx="0%" cy="0%" r="70%">
    <stop offset="0%" style="stop-color: #f96;"/>
    <stop offset="50%" style="stop-color: #9c9;"/>
    <stop offset="100%" style="stop-color: #906;"/>
```

Example 7-14. Effects of spreadMethod values on a radial gradient (continued)

```
</radialGradient>

<radialGradient id="padded" xlink:href="#three_stops"
    spreadMethod="pad"/>
<radialGradient id="repeated" xlink:href="#three_stops"
    spreadMethod="repeat"/>
<radialGradient id="reflected" xlink:href="#three_stops"
    spreadMethod="reflect"/>
</defs>

<rect x="20" y="20" width="100" height="100"
    style="fill: url(#padded); stroke: black;"/>
<rect x="130" y="20" width="100" height="100"
    style="fill: url(#repeated); stroke: black;"/>
<rect x="240" y="20" width="100" height="100"
    style="fill: url(#reflected); stroke: black;"/>
```

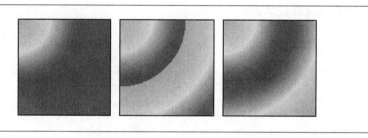

Figure 7-14. spreadMethod values pad, repeat, and reflect for a radial gradient

Gradient Reference Summary

Linear and radial gradients describe a smooth transition of colors used to fill an object. The object in question has a bounding box, defined as the smallest rectangle that entirely contains the object. The <linearGradient> and <radialGradient> elements are both containers for a series of <stop> elements. Each of these <stop> elements specifies a stop-color and an offset. For linear gradients, the offset is a percentage of the distance along the gradient's linear vector. For radial gradients, it is a percentage of the distance along the gradient's radius.

For a linear gradient, the starting point of the vector (which has the 0% stop color) is defined by the attributes x1 and y1; the ending point (which has the 100% stop color) by the attributes x2 and y2.

For a radial gradient, the focal point (which has the 0% stop color) is defined by the attributes fx and fy; the circle that has the 100% stop color is defined by its center coordinates cx and cy and its radius r.

If the gradientUnits attribute has the value objectBoundingBox, the coordinates are taken as a percentage of bounding box's dimensions (this is the default). If the value is set to userSpaceOnuse, the coordinates are taken to be in the coordinate system used by the object that is being filled.

If the vector for a linear gradient or the circle for a radial gradient does not reach to the boundaries of the object being filled, the remaining space will be colored as determined by the value of the spreadMethod attribute: pad, the default, extends the start and end colors to the boundaries; repeat repeats the gradient start-to-end until it reaches the boundaries; and reflect replicates the gradient end-to-start and start-to-end until it reaches the object boundaries.

Transforming Gradients and Patterns

Sometimes you may need to skew, stretch, or rotate a pattern or gradient. You're not transforming the object being filled; you're transforming the pattern or the color spectrum used to fill the object. The gradientTransform and patternTransform attributes let you do just that, as written in Example 7-15 and shown in Figure 7-15 (see additional color insert):

Example 7-15. Transforming patterns and gradients

```
<defs>
<linearGradient id="plain">
    <stop offset="0%" style="stop-color: #ffcc00;"/>
    <stop offset="33.3%" style="stop-color: #cc6699"/>
    <stop offset="100%" style="stop-color: #66cc99;"/>
</linearGradient>

<linearGradient id="skewed-gradient"
  gradientTransform="skewX(10)"
  xlink:href="#plain"/>

<pattern id="tile" x="0" y="0" width="20%" height="20%"
    patternUnits="objectBoundingBox">
<path d="M 0 0 Q 5 20 10 10 T 20 20"
    style="stroke: black; fill: none;"/>
<path d="M 0 0 h 20 v 20 h -20 z"
    style="stroke: gray; fill: none;"/>
</pattern>

<pattern id="skewed-tile"
    patternTransform="skewY(15)"
    xlink:href="#tile"/>
</defs>
```

Example 7-15. Transforming patterns and gradients (continued)

```
<rect x="20" y="10" width="100" height="100"
    style="fill: url(#tile); stroke: black;"/>
<rect x="135" y="10" width="100" height="100"
    style="fill: url(#skewed-tile); stroke: black;"/>

<rect x="20" y="120" width="200" height="50"
    style="fill: url(#plain); stroke: black;"/>
<rect x="20" y="190" width="200" height="50"
    style="fill: url(#skewed-gradient); stroke: black;"/>
```

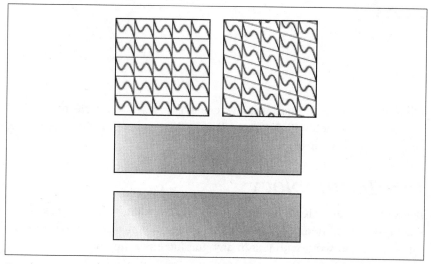

Figure 7-15. Transformation of a pattern and gradient

One final note about gradients and patterns—although we've only
applied them to the filled area of a shape, you may also apply them to the
stroke. This lets you produce a multicolored or patterned outline for an
object. You'll usually set the stroke-width to a number greater than one
so that the effect is more clearly visible.

8

Text

While it may be true that every picture tells a story, it's perfectly all right to use words to help tell the story. Thus, SVG has several elements that let you add text to your graphics.

Text Terminology

Before we investigate the primary method of adding text, the `<text>` element, we should define some terms you'll see if you read the SVG specification or if you work with text in any graphic environment:

Character
>   A character, as far as an XML document is concerned, is a byte or bytes with a numeric value according to the Unicode standard. For example, what we call the letter "g" is the character with Unicode value 103.

Glyph
>   A glyph is the visible representation of a character or characters. A single character can have many different glyphs to represent it. Figure 8-1 shows the word "glyphs" written with two different sets of glyphs—look particularly at the initial "g"—it's the same character, but the glyphs are markedly different.

>   Multiple characters can reduce to a single glyph; some fonts have separate glyphs for the letter combinations "fl" and "ff" to make their spacing look better (these are called ligatures). Other times, a single character can be composed of multiple glyphs; a print program might create the character é (which has Unicode value 233) by combining the "e" glyph with a non-spacing accent mark " ´ ".

glyphs glyphs

Figure 8-1. Two sets of glyphs

Font

A collection of glyphs representing a certain set of characters. All the glyphs in a font will normally have the following characteristics in common:

Baseline, ascent, and descent

All the glyphs in a font line up on the baseline. The distance from the baseline to the top of the character is the ascent; the distance from the baseline to the bottom of the character is the descent. The total height of the character is also called the em-height. The em-box is a square that has a width as large as an em-height.

The upper dotted line in Figure 8-2 is used to determine the cap-height, which is the height of a capital letter above the baseline. The lower dotted line is used to determine the ex-height, which, logically enough, is the distance from the baseline to the top of a lower case letter "x."

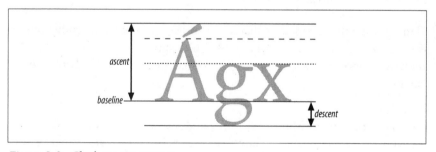

Figure 8-2. Glyph measurements

Simple Attributes and Properties of the text Element

The simplest form of the `<text>` element requires only two attributes, x and y, which define the point where the baseline of the first character of the element's content is placed. The default style for text, as with all objects, is to have a fill color of black and no outline. This, as it turns out, is precisely what you want for text. If you set the outline as well as the fill, the text looks uncomfortably thick. If you set only the outline, you can get a fairly pleasant set of outlined glyphs, especially if you lower the stroke width. Example 8-1 uses the placement and stroke/fill characteristics for <text>; the result is Figure 8-3.

Example 8-1. Text placement and outlining

```
<!-- guide lines -->
<path d="M 20 10, 20 120 M 10 30 100 30 M 10 70 100 70
    M 10 110 100 110" style="stroke: gray;"/>

<text x="20" y="30">Simplest Text</text>
<text x="20" y="70" style="stroke: black;">Outlined/filled</text>
<text x="20" y="110" style="stroke: black; stroke-width: 0.5;
    fill: none;">Outlined only</text>
```

Figure 8-3. Text placement and outlining

Many of the other properties that apply to text are the same as they are in the Cascading Style Sheets standard. The following is a list of the CSS properties and values that are implemented in the Apache Batik viewer version 1.0:

font-family

The value is a whitespace-separated list of font family names or generic family names. The generic family names are serif, sans-serif, and monospace. Serif fonts have little "hooks" at the ends of the strokes; sans-serif fonts don't. In Figure 8-1, the word at the left is in a serif font and the word on the right is in a sans-serif font. Both serif and sans-serif fonts are proportional; the width of a capital M is not the same as the width of a capital I. A monospace font, which may or may not have serifs, is one where all the glyphs have the same width, like the letters of a typewriter.

font-size

The value is the baseline-to-baseline distance of glyphs if you were to have more than one line of text. (In SVG, you can't have multi-line <text> content, so the concept is somewhat abstract.) If you use units on this attribute, as in `style="font-size: 18pt"`, the eighteen-point size will be converted to user units before being rendered, so it can be affected by transformations.

font-weight

The two most commonly used values of this property are bold and normal. You need the normal value in case you want to place non-bold text in a group that has been set to `style="font-weight: bold"`.

font-style

The two most commonly used values of this property are italic and normal.

text-decoration

Possible values of this property are none, underline, overline, and line-through.

word-spacing

The value of this property is a length, either in explicit units such as pt or in user units. Make this a positive number to increase the space between words, set it to normal to keep normal space, or make it negative to tighten up the space between words. The length you specify is *added* to the normal spacing.

letter-spacing

The value of this property is a length, either in explicit units such as pt or in user units. Make this a positive number to increase the space between individual letters, set it to normal to keep normal space, or make it negative to tighten up the space between letters. The length you specify is *added* to the normal spacing.

Example 8-2 uses these styles to produce Figure 8-4, with effects you'd expect from any competent text application.

Example 8-2. Text weight, style, decoration, and spacing attributes

```
<g style="font-size: 18pt">
<text x="20" y="20" style="font-weight:bold;">bold</text>
<text x="120" y="20" style="font-style:italic;">italic</text>
<text x="20" y="60" style="text-decoration:underline;">under</text>
<text x="120" y="60" style="text-decoration:overline;">over</text>
<text x="200" y="60"
    style="text-decoration:line-through;">through</text>
<text x="20" y="90" style="word-spacing: 10pt;">more word space</text>
<text x="20" y="120" style="word-spacing: -3pt;">less word space</text>
<text x="20" y="150" style="letter-spacing: 5pt;">wide letter space</text>
<text x="20" y="180" style="letter-spacing: -2pt;">narrow letter space</text>
</g>
```

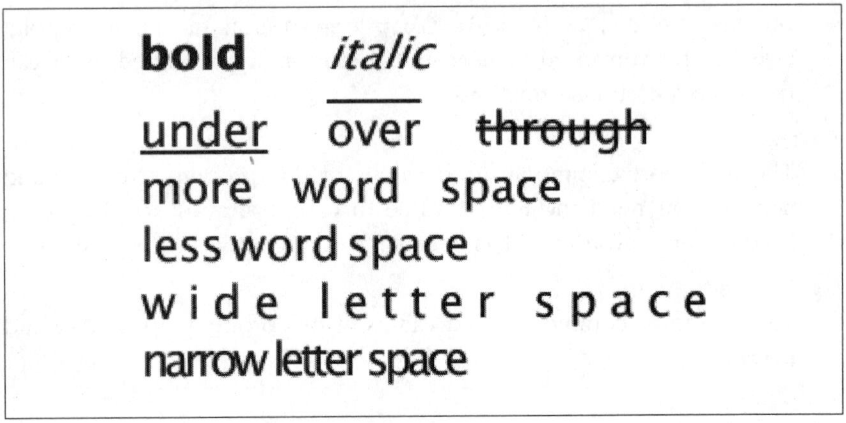

bold   *italic*

<u>under</u>   over   ~~through~~
more word space
less word space
w i d e   l e t t e r   s p a c e
narrow letter space

Figure 8-4. Text weight, style, decoration, and spacing

Text Alignment

The <text> element lets you specify the starting point, but you don't know, *a priori*, its ending point. This would make it difficult to center or right-align text, were it not for the text-anchor property. You set it to a value of start, middle, or end. For fonts that are drawn left-to-right, these are equivalent to left, center, and right alignment. For fonts that are drawn in other directions (see the section "Internationalization and Text") these have a different effect. Example 8-3 shows three text strings, all starting at an *x*-location of 100, but with differing values of text-anchor. A guide line is drawn to show the effect more clearly in the result, Figure 8-5.

Example 8-3. Use of text-anchor

```
<g style="font-size: 14pt;">
<path d="M 100 10 100 100" style="stroke: gray; fill: none;"/>
<text x="100" y="30" style="text-anchor: start">Start</text>
<text x="100" y="60" style="text-anchor: middle">Middle</text>
<text x="100" y="90" style="text-anchor: end">End</text>
</g>
```

The tspan element

Another consequence of not knowing a text string's length in advance is that it is difficult to construct a string with varying text attributes, such as this sentence, which switches among *italic*, normal, and **bold** text. If you had only the <text> element, you'd need to experiment to find where each differently styled segment of text ended in order to space them properly. To solve this problem, SVG provides the <tspan>, or text span element. Analogous to the XHTML <span> element, <tspan> is a *tabula rasa*

Figure 8-5. Result of using text-anchor

that may be embedded in text content, and upon which you may impose style changes. The `<tspan>` remembers the text position, so you don't have to. Thus, Example 8-4, which produces the display in Figure 8-6.

Example 8-4. Using tspan to change styles

```
<text x="10" y="30" style="font-size:12pt;">
    Switch among
    <tspan style="font-style:italic">italic</tspan>, normal,
    and <tspan style="font-weight:bold">bold</tspan> text.
</text>
```

Switch among *italic*, normal, and **bold** text.

Figure 8-6. Styles changed with tspan

In addition to changing presentation properties such as font size, color, weight, etc., you can also use attributes with `<tspan>` to change the positioning of individual letters or sets of letters. If, for example, you want superscripts or subscripts, you can use the dy attribute to offset characters within a span. The value you assign to this attribute is added to the vertical position of the characters, and continues to affect text even outside the span. Negative values are allowed. A similar attribute, dx, offsets characters horizontally. Example 8-5 uses vertical offsets to create the "falling letters" in Figure 8-7.

Example 8-5. Using dy to change vertical positioning within text

```
<text x="10" y="30" style="font-size:12pt;">
    F <tspan dy="4">a</tspan>
    <tspan dy="8">l</tspan>
    <tspan dy="12">l</tspan>
</text>
```

If you wish to express the offsets in absolute terms rather than relative terms, you use the x and y attributes. This is handy for doing multi-line runs of text. In fact, you must do it this way, since, as you will see in the

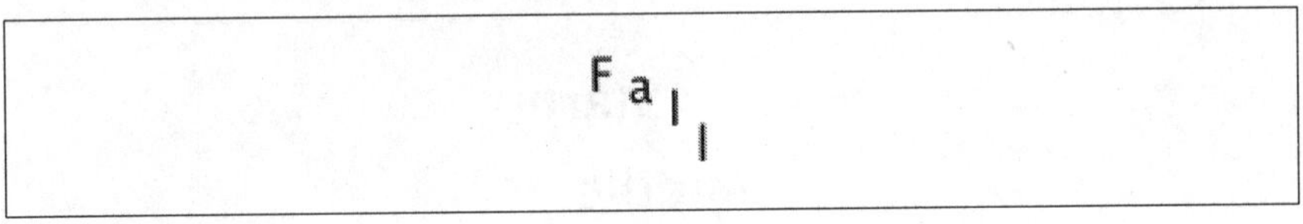

F a l
l

Figure 8-7. Vertical positioning with dy

section "Whitespace and Text," SVG never displays newline characters in text. (The lack of a newline will be remedied in SVG 1.1.) If your SVG viewer allows text selection, putting multiple lines into a single <text> element, as we have done in Example 8-6 will allow the selection to include all the lines. You should always use <tspan>s within a <text> element to group related lines, not only to allow them to be selected as a unit, but also because it adds structure to your document.

Example 8-6. Use of absolute positioning with tspan

```
<text x="10" y="30" style="font-size:12pt;">
    They dined on mince, and slices of quince,
    <tspan x="20" y="50">Which they ate with a
        runcible spoon;</tspan>
    <tspan x="10" y="70">And hand in hand, on the edge
        of the sand,</tspan>
    <tspan x="20" y="90">They danced by the light of the moon.</tspan>
</text>
```

There's no visual evidence in Figure 8-8 that all the text is in one <text> element, but trust us—they're all connected.

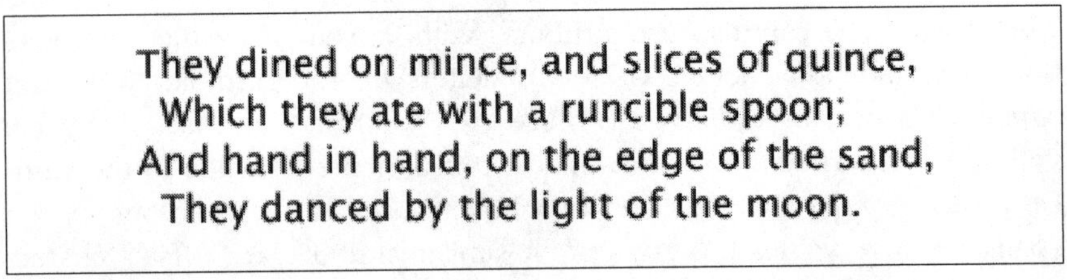

They dined on mince, and slices of quince,
Which they ate with a runcible spoon;
And hand in hand, on the edge of the sand,
They danced by the light of the moon.

Figure 8-8. Absolutely positioned poetry

You may also rotate a letter or series of letters within a <tspan> by using the rotate attribute, whose value is an angle in degrees.

If you have to modify the positions of several characters, you can do it easily by specifying a series of numbers for any of the x, y, dx, dy, and rotate attributes. The numbers you specified will be applied, one after another, to the characters within the <tspan>. This is shown in Example 8-7.

Example 8-7. Use of multiple values for dx and dy in a text span

```
<text x="30" y="30" style="font-size:14pt">
<tspan dx="0 4 -3 5 -4 6" dy="0 -3 7 3 -2 -8">Shaken</tspan>
</text>
```

Although Figure 8-9 doesn't show it, the effects of dx and dy persist after the <tspan> ends. If more text were placed after the closing </tspan>, it would be at the same offsets as the letter n. It would not return to the baseline established by the first capital S.

Figure 8-9. Multiple horizontal and vertical offsets

If you have nested <tspan> elements, the x, y, dx, dy, and rotate attribute values are *not* inherited by the inner elements.

Although you can use the dy attribute to produce superscripts and subscripts, it's easier to use the baseline-shift style, as we have done in Example 8-8. This style property has values of super and sub. You may also specify a length, such as 0.5em, or a percentage, which is calculated in terms of the font size. baseline-shift's effects are restricted to the span in which it occurs.

Example 8-8. Use of baseline-shift

```
<text x="20" y="25" style="font-size: 12pt;">
C<tspan style="baseline-shift: sub;">12</tspan>
H<tspan style="baseline-shift: sub;">22</tspan>
O<tspan style="baseline-shift: sub;">11</tspan> (sugar)
</text>

<text x="20" y="70" style="font-size: 12pt;">
6.02 x 10<tspan baseline-shift="super">23</tspan>
(Avogadro's number)
</text>
```

In Figure 8-10, the subscripted numbers appear too large. In an ideal case we'd set the font-size as well, but we wanted this example to concentrate on only one concept.

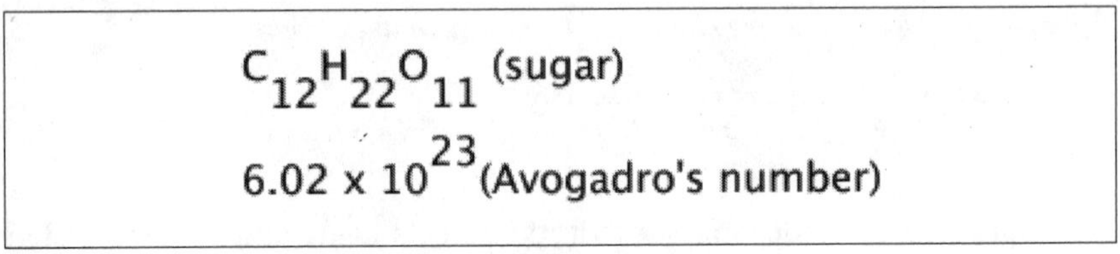

$$C_{12}H_{22}O_{11} \text{ (sugar)}$$

$$6.02 \times 10^{23}\text{(Avogadro's number)}$$

Figure 8-10. Subscripts and superscripts

Setting *textLength*

Although we said that there's no *a priori* way to determine the endpoint of a segment of text, you can explicitly specify the length of text as the value of the textLength attribute. SVG will then fit the text into the given space. It does so by adjusting the space between glyphs and leaving the glyphs themselves untouched, or it can fit the words by adjusting both the spacing and glyph size. If you want to adjust space only, set the value of the lengthAdjust to spacing (this is the default). If you want SVG to fit the words into a given length by adjusting both spacing and glyph size, set lengthAdjust to spacingAndGlyphs. Example 8-9 uses these attributes to achieve the results of Figure 8-11.

Example 8-9. Use of textLength and lengthAdjust

```
<g style="font-size: 14pt;">
<path d="M 20 10 20 70 M 220 10 220 70" style="stroke: gray;"/>
<text x="20" y="30"
    textLength="200" lengthAdjust="spacing">Two words</text>
<text x="20" y="60"
    textLength="200" lengthAdjust="spacingAndGlyphs">Two words</text>

<text x="20" y="90">Two words
    <tspan style="font-size: 10pt;">(normal length)</tspan></text>

<path d="M 20 100 20 170 M 100 100 100 170" style="stroke: gray;"/>
<text x="20" y="120"
    textLength="80" lengthAdjust="spacing">Two words</text>
<text x="20" y="160"
    textLength="80" lengthAdjust="spacingAndGlyphs">Two words</text>
</g>
```

Vertical Text

When you use SVG to create charts, graphs, or tables, you will often want labels running down the vertical axes. One way to achieve vertically-oriented text is to use a transformation to rotate the text 90 degrees. Another way to achieve the same effect is to change the value of the writing-mode style property to the value tb (meaning *top* to *bottom*).

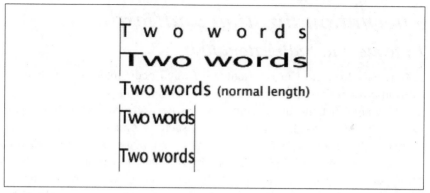

Figure 8-11. Effects of varying textLength and lengthAdjust

Sometimes, though, you want the letters to appear in a vertical column with no rotation. Example 8-10 does this by setting the glyph-orientation-vertical property with a value of zero. (Its default value is 90, which is what rotates top-to-bottom text 90 degrees.) In Figure 8-12, this setting tends displays the inter-letter spacing as unnaturally large. Setting a small negative value for letter-spacing solves this problem.

Example 8-10. Producing vertical text

```
<text x="10" y="20" transform="rotate(90,10,20)">Rotated 90</text>
<text x="50" y="20" style="writing-mode: tb;">Writing Mode tb</text>
<text x="90" y="20" style="writing-mode: tb;
    glyph-orientation-vertical: 0;">Vertical zero</text>
```

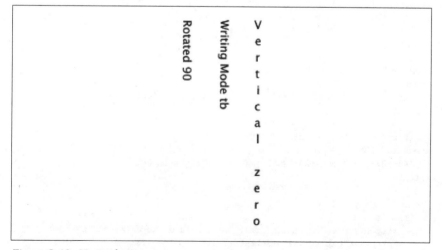

Figure 8-12. Vertical text

Internationalization and Text

Unicode and Bidirectionality

XML is based on the Unicode standard (fully documented at the Unicode Consortium's web site, *http://www.unicode.org*). This lets text display in any language that the underlying viewer software can displaying, as you can see in Figure 8-13. Some languages such as Arabic and Hebrew are written right to left, so when text in these languages is mixed with text written left to right, as English is, the text is bidirectional, or bidi for short. The system software knows which characters go in which direction and works out their positions accordingly. Example 8-11 also overrides the implicit directionality of a segment of text by setting its direction style property to rtl, which stands for *right-to-left*. If you wish to change the direction of Hebrew or Arabic text, set it to ltr, which is *left-to-right*. You must also explicity override the underlying Unicode bidirectionality algorithm by setting the unicode-bidi style property to bidi-override.

Example 8-11. International text using Unicode

```
<g style="font-size: 14pt;">

<text x="10" y="30">Greek: </text>
<text x="100" y="30">
   &#x3b1;&#x3b2;&#x3b3;&#x3b4;&#x3b5;
</text>

<text x="10" y="50">Russian:</text>
<text x="100" y="50">
   &#x430;&#x431;&#x432;&#x433;&#x434;
</text>

<text x="10" y="70">Hebrew:</text>
<text x="100" y="70">
    &#x5d0;&#x5d1;&#x5d2;&#x5d3;&#x5d4; (written right to left)
</text>

<text x="10" y="90">Arabic:</text>
<text x="100" y="90">
    &#x627;&#x628;&#x629;&#x62a; (written right to left)
</text>

<text x="10" y="130">
   This is
       <tspan style="direction: rtl; unicode-bidi: bidi-override;
         font-weight: bold;">right-to-left</tspan>
   text.
</text>
</g>
```

Greek: αβγδε
Russian: абвгд
Hebrew: אבגדה (written right to left)
Arabic: ابةت (written right to left)

This is **tfel-ot-thgir** writing.

Figure 8-13. Multilingual text

The switch Element

The ability to display multiple languages in a single document is useful for such things as a brochure for an event that receives international visitors. Sometimes, though, you would like to create one document with content in two languages, say, Spanish and Russian. People viewing the document with Spanish system software would see the Spanish text, and Russians would see Russian text.

SVG provides this capability with the <switch> element. This element searches through all its children until it finds one whose systemLanguage attribute has a value that matches the language the user has chosen in the viewer software's preferences. The value of systemLanguage is a single value or comma-separated list of language names. A language name is either a two-letter language code, such as ru for Russian, or a language code followed by a country code, which specifies a sublanguage. For instance, fr-CA denotes Canadian French, while fr-CH denotes Swiss French.

Once a matching child element is found, all its children will be displayed. All the other children of the <switch> will be bypassed. Example 8-12 shows text in UK English, US English, Spanish, and Russian. Since a match of language code alone is considered a match, and country codes are used only to "break a tie," the text for UK English must come first.

Example 8-12. Use of the switch element

```
<circle cx="40" cy="60" r="20" style="fill: none; stroke: black;"/>
<g font-size="12pt">
<switch>
    <g systemLanguage="en-UK">
        <text x="10" y="30">A circle</text>
        <text x="10" y="100">without colour.</text>
    </g>
    <g systemLanguage="en">
```

Example 8-12. Use of the switch element (continued)

```
        <text x="10" y="30">A circle</text>
        <text x="10" y="100">without color.</text>
  </g>
  <g systemLanguage="es">
        <text x="10" y="30">Un c&#xed;rculo</text>
        <text x="10" y="100">sin color.</text>
  </g>
  <g systemLanguage="ru">
        <text x="10" y="30">
        &#x41a;&#x440;&#x443;&#x433;
        </text>
        <text x="10" y="100">&#x431;&#x435;&#x437;
        &#x441;&#x432;&#x435;&#x442;&#x430;;.</text>
  </g>
</switch>
</g>
```

Figure 8-14 is a combination of screenshots taken with the language set to
each of the choices in Example 8-12.

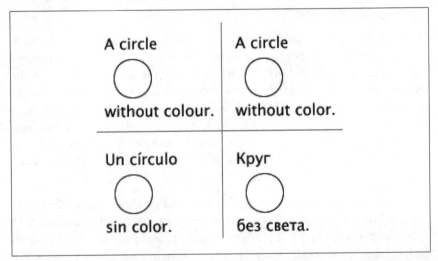

Figure 8-14. Combined screenshots as seen with different language preferences

Using a Custom Font

Sometimes you need special symbols that are not represented in Unicode,
or you want a subset of the Unicode characters without having to install
an entire font. An example is Figure 8-15, which needs only a few of the
over 2,000 Korean syllables. You can create a custom font as described in
Appendix E and give its starting <font> tag a unique id. Here is the rele-

vant portion of a file that contains six of the Korean syllables exported from the Batang TrueType font. The file is called *kfont.svg*:

```
<font id="kfont-defn" horiz-adv-x="989" vert-adv-y="1200"
    vert-origin-y="0">
    <font-face font-family="bakbatn"
        units-per-em="1000"
        panose-1="2 3 6 0 0 1 1 1 1 1"
        ascent="800" descent="-200" baseline="0" />
        <missing-glyph horiz-adv-x="500" />
        <!-- glyph definitions go here -->
    </font-face>
</font>
```

Figure 8-15. Korean syllables from an external font

Once that is done, Example 8-13 can reference the font in that external file. For the sake of consistency, the value of the font-family that you use in this SVG file should match the value in the external file.

Example 8-13. Use of an external font

```
<defs>
    <font-face font-family="bakbatn">
        <font-face-src>
            <font-face-uri xlink:href="kfont.svg#kfont-defn"/>
        </font-face-src>
    </font-face>
</defs>

<text font-size="28" x="20" y="40" style="font-family: bakbatn;">
    &#xc11c;&#xc6b8; - &#xb300;&#xd55c;&#xbbfc;&#xad6d;
</text>
```

Text on a Path

Text does not have to go in a straight horizontal or vertical line. It can follow any arbitrary path; simply enclose the text in a <textPath> element that uses an xlink:href attribute to refer to a previously defined <path> element. Letters will be rotated to stand "perpendicular" to the curve (that is, the letter's baseline will be tangent to the curve). Text along a gently curving and continuous path is easier to read than text that follows a sharply angled or discontinuous path.

The path you reference in the <textPath> element will *not* be displayed. That's why Example 8-14 has to draw the paths with <use> elements.

Example 8-14. Examples of textPath

```
<defs>
<path id="curvepath"
    d="M30 40 C 50 10, 70 10, 120 40 S 150 0, 200 40"
    style="stroke: gray; fill: none;"/>

<path id="round-corner"
    d="M250 30 L 300 30 A 30 30 0 0 1 330 60 L 330 110"
    style="stroke: gray; fill: none;"/>

<path id="sharp-corner"
    d="M 30 110 100 110 100 160"
    style="stroke: gray; fill: none;"/>

<path id="discontinuous"
    d="M 150 110 A 40 30 0 1 0 230 110 M 250 110 270 140"
    style="stroke: gray; fill: none;"/>
</defs>


<use xlink:href="#curvepath"/>
<text style="font-size: 12;">
    <textPath xlink:href="#curvepath">
    Following a cubic Bézier curve.
    </textPath>
</text>

<use xlink:href="#round-corner"/>
<text style="font-size: 12;">
    <textPath xlink:href="#round-corner">
    Going 'round the bend
    </textPath>
</text>

<use xlink:href="#sharp-corner"/>
<text style="font-size: 12;">
    <textPath xlink:href="#sharp-corner">
    Making a quick turn
    </textPath>
</text>

<use xlink:href="#discontinuous"/>
<text style="font-size: 12;">
    <textPath xlink:href="#discontinuous">
    Text along a broken path
```

Example 8-14. Examples of textPath (continued)

```
    </textPath>
</text>
```

Example 8-14 produces Figure 8-16; Figure 8-17 shows you what it looks like if we draw the text without the underlying paths.

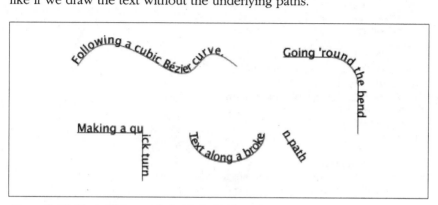

Figure 8-16. Text along a path (with paths shown)

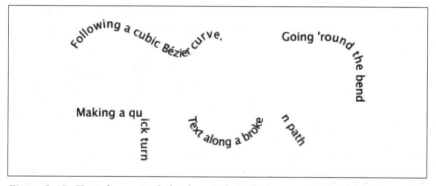

Figure 8-17. Text along a path (paths not shown)

You may adjust the beginning point of the text along its path by setting the startOffset attribute to a percentage or to a length. For example, startOffset="25%" will start the text one-fourth of the distance along the path, and startOffset="30" will start the text at a distance of thirty user units from the beginning of the path. If you wish to center text on a path, as in Example 8-15, set textanchor="middle" on the <text> element and startOffset="50%" on the <textPath> element. Text that falls beyond the ends of the path will not be displayed, as shown in the left half of Figure 8-18.

Example 8-15. Text Length and startOffset

```
<defs>
<path id="short-corner" transform="translate(40,40)"
    d="M0 0 L 30 0 A 30 30 0 0 1 60 30 L 60 60"
    style="stroke: gray; fill: none;"/>

<path id="long-corner" transform="translate(140,40)"
    d="M0 0 L 50 0 A 30 30 0 0 1 80 30 L 80 80"
    style="stroke: gray; fill: none;"/>
</defs>

<use xlink:href="#short-corner"/>
<text style="font-size: 12;">
    <textPath xlink:href="#short-corner">
    This text is too long for the path.
    </textPath>
</text>

<use xlink:href="#long-corner"/>
<text style="font-size: 12; text-anchor: middle;">
    <textPath xlink:href="#long-corner" startOffset="50%">
    centered
    </textPath>
</text>
```

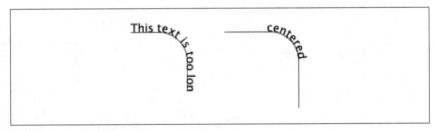

Figure 8-18. Effects of long text and startOffset

Whitespace and Text

You may change the way that SVG handles whitespace (blanks, tabs, and newline characters) within text by changing the value of the xml:space attribute. If you specify a value of default (which, coincidentally, is the default value), SVG will handle whitespace as follows:

- Remove all newline characters
- Change all tabs to blanks
- Remove all leading and trailing blanks
- Change any run of intermediate blanks to a single blank

Thus, this string, where \t represents a tab and \n represents a newline, and an underscore represents a blank, this text:

```
\n\n___abc_\t\t_def_\n\n__ghi
```

will render as:

```
abc_def_ghi
```

The other setting of xml:space is preserve. With this setting, SVG will simply convert all newline and tab characters to blanks, and then display the result, including leading and trailing blanks. the same text:

```
\n\n___abc_\t\t_def_\n\n__ghi
```

then renders as:

```
_____abc____def_____ghi
```

 SVG's handling of whitespace is not like that of HTML. SVG's default handling eliminates all newlines; HTML changes internal newlines to a space. SVG's preserve method converts newlines to blanks; HTML's <pre> element does not. There is no newline in SVG 1.0; this bothers people until they realize that SVG text is oriented towards graphic display, not textual content (as in XHTML).

Case Study—Adding Text to a Graphic

Figure 8-19 (see additional color insert) adds Korean and English text to the Korean national symbol shown in Figure 6-5. The text is centered along an elliptical path. The additional SVG in Example 8-16 is shown in boldface.

Example 8-16. Text case study

```
<defs>
    <font-face font-family="bakbatn">
        <font-face-src>
            <font-face-uri xlink:href="kfont.svg#kfont-defn"/>
        </font-face-src>
    </font-face>

    <path id="upper-curve" d="M -8 154 A 162 130 0 1 1 316 154"/>
    <path id="lower-curve" d="M -21 154 A 175 140 0 1 0 329 154"/>
</defs>

<ellipse cx="154" cy="154" rx="150" ry="120" style="fill: #999999;"/>
<ellipse cx="152" cy="152" rx="150" ry="120" style="fill: #cceeff;"/>
```

Example 8-16. Text case study (continued)

```
<!-- large light red semicircle fills upper half,
     followed by small light red semicircle that dips into
     lower left half of symbol -->
<path d="M 302 152 A 150 120, 0, 1, 0, 2 152
   A 75 60, 0, 1, 0, 152 152" style="fill: #ffcccc;"/>

<!-- light blue semicircle rises into upper right half of symbol -->
<path d="M 152 152 A 75 60, 0, 1, 1, 302 152" style="fill: #cceeff;"/>

<text font-family="bakbatn" style="font-size: 28; text-anchor: middle;">
   <textPath xlink:href="#upper-curve" startOffset="50%">
   &#xc11c;&#xc6b8; - &#xb300;&#xd55c;&#xbbfc;&#xad6d;
   </textPath>
</text>

<text style="font-size: 14pt; text-anchor: middle;">
   <textPath xlink:href="#lower-curve" startOffset="50%">
   Seoul - Republic of Korea
   </textPath>
</text>
```

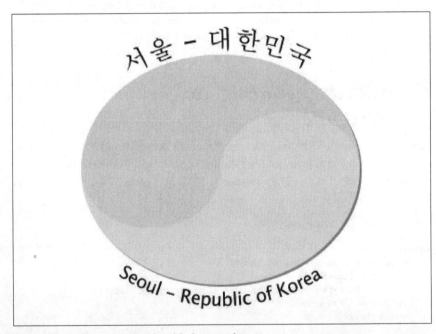

Figure 8-19. Text along path added to graphic

9

Clipping and Masking

Sometimes you don't want to see an entire picture; for example, you might wish to draw a picture as though it were seen through binoculars or a keyhole; everything outside the boundary of the eyepieces or keyhole will be invisible. Or, you might want to set a mood by showing an image as though viewed through a translucent curtain. SVG accomplishes such effects with clipping and masking.

Clipping to a Path

When you create an SVG document, you establish its viewport by specifying the width and height of the area you're interested in. This automatically becomes your clipping area; anything drawn outside these limits will not be displayed. You can establish a clipping area of your own with the `<clipPath>` element. Here's the simplest case: establishing a rectangular clip path. Inside the `<clipPath>` element will be the `<rect>` we wish to clip to. The rectangle itself is not displayed; we only love it for its coordinates. Thus, we are free to add any fill or stroke styles we wish to the elements within the `<clipPath>`. On the object to be clipped we add a clip-path style property whose value references the `<clipPath>` element. Note that the property is hyphenated and not capitalized; the element is capitalized and not hyphenated. In Example 9-1, the object being clipped is a small version of the cat picture from Chapter 1, producing Figure 9-1.

Example 9-1. Clipping to a rectangular path

```
<defs>
<clipPath id="rectClip">
    <rect id="rect1" x="15" y="15"
        width="40" height="45"
        style="stroke: gray; fill: none;"/>
</clipPath>
</defs>

<!-- clip to rectangle -->
<use xlink:href="minicat.svg#cat" style="clip-path: url(#rectClip);"/>

<!--
    for reference, show entire picture with clipping area outlined -->
<g transform="translate(100,0)">
    <use xlink:href="#rect1"/>    <!-- show clip rectangle -->
    <use xlink:href="minicat.svg#cat"/>
</g>
```

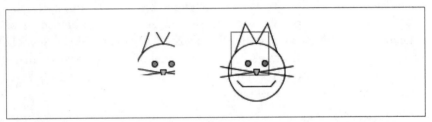

Figure 9-1. Simple rectangular clipping

As the name `<clipPath>` implies, you can clip to any arbitrary path.
Indeed, the `<clipPath>` element can contain any number of basic shapes,
`<path>` elements, or `<text>` elements. Example 9-2 shows a group of
shapes clipped to a curved path and the same group of shapes clipped by
text.

Example 9-2. Complex clip paths

```
<defs>
<clipPath id="curveClip">
    <path id="curve1"
        d="M5 55 C 25 5, 45 -25, 75 55, 85 85, 20 105, 40 55 Z"
        style="stroke: black; fill: none;"/>
</clipPath>

<clipPath id="textClip">
    <text id="text1" x="20" y="20" transform="rotate(60)"
        style="font-size: 48pt; stroke: black; fill: none;">
    CLIP
    </text>
</clipPath>
```

Example 9-2. Complex clip paths (continued)

```
<g id="shapes">
<rect x="0" y="50" width="90" height="60" style="fill: #999;"/>
<circle cx="25" cy="25" r="25" style="fill: #666;"/>
<polygon points="30 0 80 0 80 100" style="fill: #ccc;"/>
</g>
</defs>

<!-- draw with curved clip-path -->
<use xlink:href="#shapes" style="clip-path: url(#curveClip);" />

<g transform="translate(100,0)">
    <use xlink:href="#shapes"/>
    <use xlink:href="#curve1"/>   <!-- show clip path -->
</g>

<!-- draw with text as clip-path -->
<g transform="translate(0,150)">
    <use xlink:href="#shapes" style="clip-path: url(#textClip);"/>
</g>

<g transform="translate(100,150)">
    <use xlink:href="#shapes"/>
    <use xlink:href="#text1"/>
</g>
```

To help you see the areas better, the preceding SVG draws the clipping path above the entire figure; you see this in the right half of Figure 9-2.

The coordinates for the preceding clip paths have been specified in user coordinates. If you wish to express coordinates in terms of the object bounding box, then set clipPathUnits to objectBoundingBox (the default is userSpaceOnUse). Example 9-3 uses a clip path that will produce a circular (or oval) window on any object that it's applied to.

Example 9-3. clipPathUnits using objectBoundingBox

```
<defs>
<clipPath id="circularPath" clipPathUnits="objectBoundingBox">
    <circle cx="0.5" cy="0.5" r="0.5"/>
</clipPath>

<g id="shapes">
<rect x="0" y="50" width="100" height="50" style="fill: #999;"/>
<circle cx="25" cy="25" r="25" style="fill: #666;"/>
<polygon points="30 0 80 0 80 100" style="fill: #ccc;"/>
</g>

<g id="words">
<text  x="0"  y="19" style="font-size: 12;">
<tspan x="0"  y="19">If you have form'd a circle</tspan>
```

Example 9-3. clipPathUnits using objectBoundingBox (continued)

```
<tspan x="12" y="33">to go into,</tspan>
<tspan x="0"  y="47">Go into it yourself</tspan>
<tspan x="12" y="61">and see how you would do.</tspan>
<tspan x="50" y="80">&#xad;William Blake</tspan>
</text>
</g>
</defs>

<use xlink:href="#shapes" style="clip-path: url(#circularPath);" />
<use xlink:href="#words" transform="translate(110,0)"
    style="clip-path: url(#circularPath);"/>
```

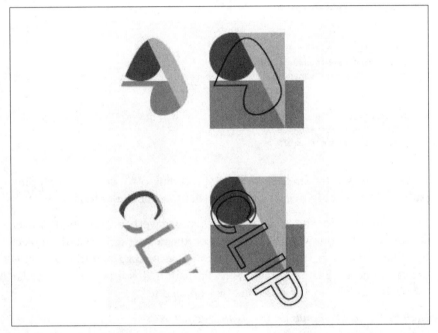

Figure 9-2. Complex path clipping

In Figure 9-3, the geometric figures happen to have a square bounding box, so the clipping appears circular. The text is bounded by a rectangular area, so the clipping area appears to be an oval.

Specify a clipping rectangle for <marker> and <symbol> tags with the clip style property. Its value is four whitespace-separated numbers specifying the rectangle's top, right, bottom, and left bounds. This sets the clip rectangle to match the marker or symbol's viewBox, rather than its viewport.

. nave form'd a cn ..
to go into,
Go into it yourself
and see how you would dr
–William Rlal–

Figure 9-3. Use of a circular/oval clipping path

Masking

A mask in SVG is the exact opposite of the mask you wear to a costume party. With a costume party mask, the parts that are opaque hide your face; the parts that are translucent let people see your face dimly, and the holes (which are transparent) let people see your face clearly. An SVG mask, on the other hand, transfers its transparency to the object that it masks. Where the mask is opaque, the pixels of the masked object are opaque. Where the mask is translucent, so is the object, and the transparent parts of the mask make the corresponding parts of the masked object invisible.

You use the <mask> element to create a mask. You may specify the mask's dimensions with the x, y, width, and height attributes. These dimensions are in terms of the masked objectBoundingBox. If you want the dimensions to be in terms of user space coordinates, set maskUnits to userSpaceOnUse.

Between the beginning <mask> and ending </mask> tags are any basic shapes, text, or paths that you wish to use as the mask. The coordinates on these elements are expressed in user coordinate space by default. If you wish to use the object bounding box for the contents of the mask, set maskContentUnits to objectBoundingBox. (The default is userSpaceOnUse.)

The question then becomes: how does SVG determine the transparency, or alpha value of the mask? We know that each pixel is described by four values: its red, green, and blue color value, and its opacity. While at first glance it would seem logical to use only the opacity value, SVG decides to use all the information available to it rather than throwing away three-fourths of a pixel's information. SVG uses this formula:

```
( 0.2125 * red value +
0.7154 * green value +
0.0721 * blue value ) *
 opacity value
```

where all of the values are floating point numbers in the range zero to one. You may be surprised that the proportions aren't equal, but if you look at fully saturated red, green, and blue, the green appears to be the brightest, red darker, and blue the darkest. (You can see this in Figure 9-4 [see additional color insert].) The darker the color, the smaller the resulting alpha value will be, and the less opaque the masked object will be.

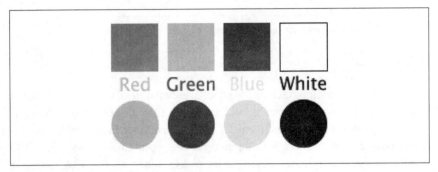

Figure 9-4. Effect of color values on transparency

Example 9-4 creates black text and a black circle masked by a totally opaque red, green, blue, and white square. The text and circle are grouped together, and the group uses a `mask` style property to reference the appropriate mask.

Example 9-4. Masking with opaque colors

```
<defs>
<mask id="redmask" x="0" y="0" width="1" height="1"
    maskContentUnits="objectBoundingBox">
    <rect x="0" y="0" width="1" height="1" style="fill: #f00;"/>
</mask>

<mask id="greenmask" x="0" y="0" width="1" height="1"
    maskContentUnits="objectBoundingBox">
    <rect x="0" y="0" width="1" height="1" style="fill: #0f0;"/>
</mask>

<mask id="bluemask" x="0" y="0" width="1" height="1"
    maskContentUnits="objectBoundingBox">
    <rect x="0" y="0" width="1" height="1" style="fill: #00f;"/>
</mask>

<mask id="whitemask" x="0" y="0" width="1" height="1"
    maskContentUnits="objectBoundingBox">
    <rect x="0" y="0" width="1" height="1" style="fill: #fff;"/>
</mask>
</defs>
```

Example 9-4. Masking with opaque colors (continued)

```
<!-- display the colors to show relative brightness (luminance) -->
<rect x="10" y="10" width="50" height="50" style="fill: #f00;"/>
<rect x="70" y="10" width="50" height="50" style="fill: #0f0;"/>
<rect x="130" y="10" width="50" height="50" style="fill: #00f;"/>
<rect x="190" y="10" width="50" height="50"
    style="fill: #fff; stroke: black;"/>

<g style="mask: url(#redmask);
    font-size: 14pt; text-anchor: middle;">
<circle cx="35" cy="115" r="25"  style="fill: black;"/>
<text x="35" y="80">Red</text>
</g>

<g style="mask: url(#greenmask);
    font-size: 14pt; text-anchor: middle;">
<circle cx="95" cy="115" r="25" style="fill: black;"/>
<text x="95" y="80">Green</text>
</g>

<g style="mask: url(#bluemask);
    font-size: 14pt; text-anchor: middle;">
<circle cx="155" cy="115" r="25" style="fill: black;"/>
<text x="155" y="80">Blue</text>
</g>

<g style="mask: url(#whitemask);
    font-size: 14pt; text-anchor: middle;">
<circle cx="215" cy="115" r="25" style="fill: black;"/>
<text x="215" y="80">White</text>
</g>
```

Figuring out the interaction between color, opacity, and final alpha value is not exactly intuitive. If you fill and/or stroke the mask contents in white, the "color factor" adds up to 1.0, and the opacity will then be the only factor that controls the mask's alpha value. Example 9-5 is written this way, and the result is in Figure 9-5.

Example 9-5. Mask alpha using opacity only

```
<defs>
<mask id="fullmask" x="0" y="0" width="1" height="1"
    maskContentUnits="objectBoundingBox">
    <rect x="0" y="0" width="1" height="1"
        style="fill-opacity: 1.0; fill: white;"/>
</mask>

<mask id="three-fourths" x="0" y="0" width="1" height="1"
```

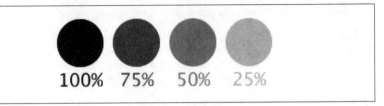

Figure 9-5. Alpha value equal to opacity

Example 9-5. Mask alpha using opacity only (continued)

```
    maskContentUnits="objectBoundingBox">
    <rect x="0" y="0" width="1" height="1"
        style="fill-opacity: 0.75; fill: white;"/>
</mask>

<mask id="one-half" x="0" y="0" width="1" height="1"
    maskContentUnits="objectBoundingBox">
    <rect x="0" y="0" width="1" height="1"
        style="fill-opacity: 0.5; fill: white;"/>
</mask>

<mask id="one-fourth" x="0" y="0" width="1" height="1"
    maskContentUnits="objectBoundingBox">
    <rect x="0" y="0" width="1" height="1"
        style="fill-opacity: 0.25; fill: white;"/>
</mask>
</defs>

<g style="font-size: 14pt; text-anchor:middle; fill:black;">
    <g style="mask: url(#fullmask);">
    <circle cx="35" cy="35" r="25"/>
    <text x="35" y="80">100%</text>
    </g>

    <g style="mask: url(#three-fourths);">
    <circle cx="95" cy="35" r="25"/>
    <text x="95" y="80">75%</text>
    </g>

    <g style="mask: url(#one-half);">
    <circle cx="155" cy="35" r="25"/>
    <text x="155" y="80">50%</text>
    </g>

    <g style="mask: url(#one-fourth);">
    <circle cx="215" cy="35" r="25"/>
    <text x="215" y="80">25%</text>
    </g>
</g>
```

Case Study—Masking a Graphic

Example 9-6 adds a JPG image to the image that was constructed in the section "Case Study—Adding Text to a Graphic." As you can see in Figure 9-6 (reduced to save space and in grayscale to avoid using color ink), the image obscures the curve inside the main ellipse, and the blue sky intrudes horribly on the pale red section.

Example 9-6. Unmasked image

```
<defs>
    <font-face font-family="bakbatn">
        <font-face-src>
            <font-face-uri xlink:href="kfont.svg#kfont-defn"/>
        </font-face-src>
    </font-face>
</defs>

<!-- draws ellipse and text -->
<use xlink:href="ksymbol.svg#ksymbol"/>

<image xlink:href="kwanghwamun.jpg" x="72" y="92"
    width="160" height="120"/>
```

Figure 9-6. Unmasked image

The solution is to fade out the edges of the picture, which is easily done by using a radial gradient as a mask. Here's the code to be added to the <defs> section of the document:

```
<radialGradient id="fade">
    <stop offset="0%" style="stop-color: white; stop-opacity: 1.0;"/>
    <stop offset="85%" style="stop-color: white; stop-opacity: 0.5;"/>
```

```
    <stop offset="100%" style="stop-color: white; stop-opacity: 0.0;"/>
</radialGradient>
<mask id="fademask">
    <rect x="72" y="92" width="160" height="120"
        style="fill: url(#fade);"/>
</mask>
```

Then add a mask reference to the <image> tag, resulting in Figure 9-7 (see additional color insert).

```
<image xlink:href="kwanghwamun.jpg" x="72" y="92"
    width="160" height="120"
    style="mask: url(#fademask);"/>
```

Figure 9-7. Masked image

Using less of the picture can substantially improve the graphic as a whole.

10

Filters

The preceding chapters have given you a basis for creating graphics that convey information with great precision and detail. If you're going on a spring picnic, you want a precise map. When you look in the newspaper for the graphics that describe the weather forecast, you want "just the facts."

If you're asked later to describe the day of the picnic, nobody wants a crisp recitation of meteorological statistics. Similarly, nobody wants to see a graphic of a spring flower composed of pure vectors; Figure 10-1 fails totally to convey any warmth or charm.

Figure 10-1. Flower composed of plain vectors

Graphics are often designed to evoke feelings or moods as much as they are meant to convey information. Artists who work with bitmap graphics have many tools at their disposal to add such effects; they can produce blurred shadows, selectively thicken or thin lines, add textures to part of the drawing, make an object appear to be embossed or beveled, etc.

How Filters Work

Although SVG is not a bitmap description language, it still lets you use some of these same tools. When an SVG viewer program processes a graphic object, it will render the object to some bitmapped output device; at some point the program will convert the object's description into the appropriate set of pixels that appear on the output device. Now let's say that you use the SVG `<filter>` element to specify a set of operations that display an object with a blurred shadow offset slightly to the side, and attach that filter to an object:

```
<filter id="drop-shadow">
  <!-- filter operations go here -->
</filter>

<g id="spring-flower"
   style="filter: url(#drop-shadow);"/>
  <!-- drawing of flower goes here -->
</g>
```

Because the flower uses a filter in its presentation style, SVG will not render the flower directly to the final graphic. Instead, SVG will render the flower's pixels into a temporary bitmap. The operations specified by the filter will be applied to that temporary area and their result will be rendered into the final graphic.

Creating a Drop Shadow

In Chapter 4, in the section "The image Element," we created a drop shadow by offsetting a gray ellipse underneath a colored ellipse. It worked, but it wasn't elegant. Let's investigate a way to create a better-looking drop shadow with a filter.

Establishing the Filter's Bounds

The `<filter>` element has attributes that describe the clipping region for a filter. You specify an x, y, width, and height in terms of the percentage of the filtered object's bounding box. (That is the default.) Any portion of the resulting output that's outside the bounds will not be displayed. If you are intending to apply a filter to many objects, you may want to omit these attributes altogether and take the default values of x equal to -10%, y equal to -10%, width equal to 120%, and height equal to 120%. This gives extra space for filters—such as the drop shadow that we're constructing—that produce output larger than their input.

These attributes are in terms of the filtered object's bounding box; specifically, `filterUnits` has a value of `objectBoundingBox` by default. If you wish to specify boundaries in user units, then set the attribute's value to `userSpaceOnUse`.

Using feGaussianBlur for a Drop Shadow

Between the beginning and ending `<filter>` tags are the filter primitives that perform the operations you desire. Each primitive has one or more inputs, and exactly one output. An input can be the original graphic, specified as `SourceGraphic`, the alpha (opaqueness) channel of the graphic, specified as `SourceAlpha`, or the output of a previous filtering primitive. You will probably use the alpha source more often, since it avoids the interactions of alpha and color, as described in Chapter 9, in the section "Masking."

Example 10-1 is our first attempt to produce a drop shadow on the flower, using the `<feGaussianBlur>` filter primitive. We specify `SourceAlpha` as its input (the `in` attribute), and the amount of blur with the `stdDeviation` attribute. The larger this number, the greater the blur. If you give two numbers separated by whitespace as the value for `stdDeviation`, the first number is taken as the blur in the *x*-direction and the second as the blur in the *y*-direction.

Example 10-1. First attempt to produce a drop shadow

```
<defs>

<filter id="drop-shadow">
    <feGaussianBlur in="SourceAlpha" stdDeviation="2"/>
</filter>

</defs>
<g id="flower" filter="url(#drop-shadow)">
    <!-- drawing here -->
</g>
```

Figure 10-2 shows the result, which is probably not what you thought it would be.

Don't be surprised; remember, the filter returns the output, which is a blurred alpha channel, *instead* of the original source graphic. We could get the effect we want by putting the flower within the `<defs>` section of the document and changing our SVG to read:

Figure 10-2. Result of first attempt at a drop shadow

```
<use xlink:href="#flower" filter="url(#drop-shadow)"
    transform="translate(4, 4)"/>
<use xlink:href="#flower"/>
```

However, that would require SVG to execute all the elements that make up the flower twice. Instead, we will add more filter primitives, so that all the work can be handled during rendering.

Storing, Chaining, and Merging Filter Results

Example 10-2 is the updated filter.

Example 10-2. Improved drop shadow filter

```
<filter id="drop-shadow">
    <feGaussianBlur in="SourceAlpha" stdDeviation="2" result="blur"/> ❶
    <feOffset in="blur" dx="4" dy="4" result="offsetBlur"/> ❷
    <feMerge> ❸
        <feMergeNode in="offsetBlur"/>
        <feMergeNode in="SourceGraphic"/>
    </feMerge>
</filter>
```

❶ The `result` attribute specifies that the result of this primitive can be referenced later by the name `blur`. This isn't like an XML `id`; the name you give is a local name that's only valid for the duration of the primitives contained in the current `<filter>`.

❷ The `<feOffset>` primitive takes its input, in this case the `blur` result from the Gaussian blur, offsets it by the specified `dx` and `dy` values, and stores the resulting bitmap under the name `offsetBlur`.

❸ The `<feMerge>` primitive encloses a list of `<feMergeNode>` elements, each of which specifies an input. The inputs are stacked one on top of another in the order that they appear. In this case, we want the `offsetBlur` below the original `sourceGraphic`.

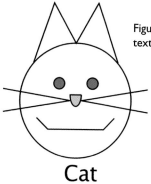

Figure 1-14. Stage seven—text and finished image

Cat

Figure 3-3. Demonstration of stroke color

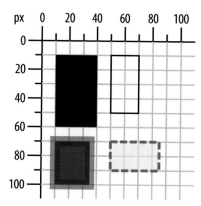

Figure 3-6. Demonstration of the rect element

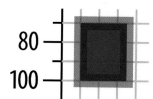

Figure 3-7. Close-up of transparent border

Figure 4-8. JPEG image included in an SVG file

Figure 6-5. Result of using elliptical arc

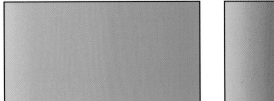

Figure 7-7. Simple two-color gradient

Figure 7-8. Three-stop gradient

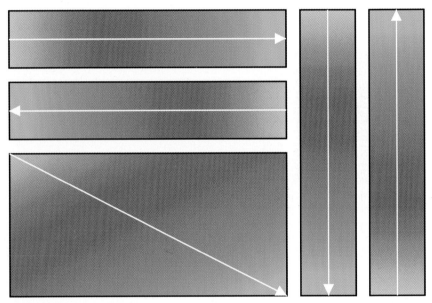

Figure 7-9. Defining vectors for a linear gradient

Figure 7-10. spreadMethod values pad, repeat, and reflect for a linear gradient

Figure 7-11. Radial gradient with three stops

Figure 7-12. Setting limits for a radial gradient

Figure 7-13. Setting focal point for a radial gradient

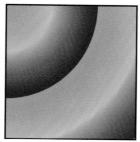

Figure 7-14. spreadMethod values pad, repeat, and reflect for a radial gradient

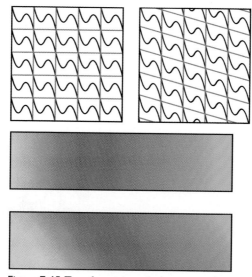

Figure 7-15. Transformation of a pattern and gradient

Figure 8-19. Text along path added to graphic

서울 – 대한민국

Seoul – Republic of Korea

Figure 9-4. Effect of color values on transparency

Figure 9-7. Masked image

서울 – 대한민국

Seoul – Republic of Korea

Figure 10-5. Drop shadow and glowing text

Spring Flower

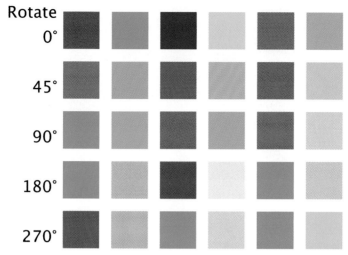

Figure 10-6. Result of hueRotate on fully saturated colors

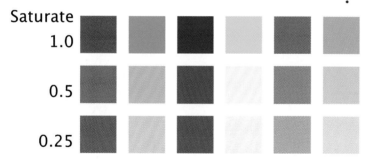

Figure 10-7. Result of saturate on primary colors

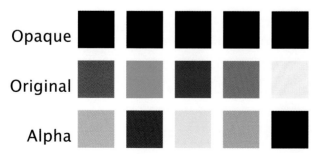

Figure 10-8. Result of luminanceToAlpha

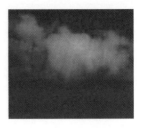

Figure 10-9. Result of
feImage

Figure 10-10. Result of linear
component transfer

Figure 10-12. Result of using
gamma correction

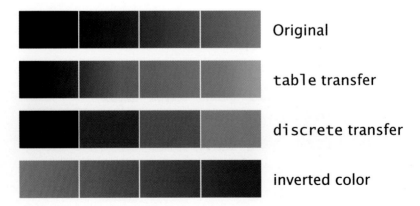

Original

table transfer

discrete transfer

inverted color

Figure 10-13. Result of using table and discrete transfers

linearRGB   sRGB

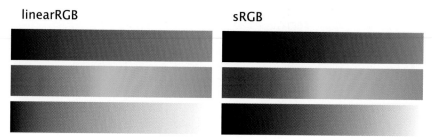

Figure 10-14. Comparsion of linearRGB and sRGB

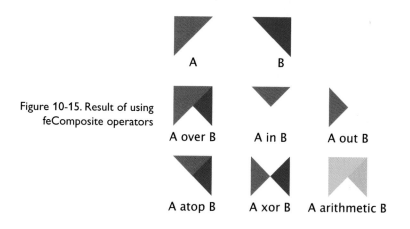

A   B

Figure 10-15. Result of using
feComposite operators

A over B   A in B   A out B

A atop B   A xor B   A arithmetic B

Opaque   50% Opaque

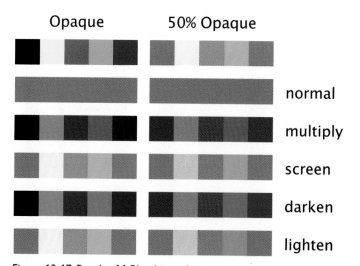

normal

multiply

screen

darken

lighten

Figure 10-17. Result of feBlend in and out

Figure 10-25. Result of using
feDisplacementMap

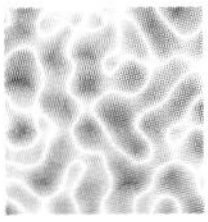

type="turbulence"   type="turbulence"   type="turbulence"
baseFrequency="0.1"   baseFrequency="0.1"   baseFrequency="0.05"
numOctaves="1"   numOctaves="5"   numOctaves="5"

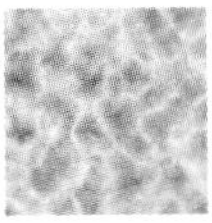

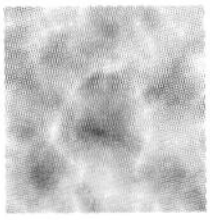

type="fractalNoise"   type="fractalNoise"   type="fractalNoise"
baseFrequency="0.1"   baseFrequency="0.1"   baseFrequency="0.05"
numOctaves="1"   numOctaves="5"   numOctaves="5"

Figure 10-27. Various values of feTurbulence attributes

Figure 11-12. Screenshot of
HTML and SVG interaction

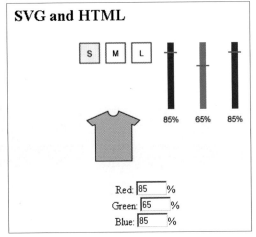

We now refer to this improved drop shadow filter sequence when drawing the flower, producing a surprisingly pleasant image in Figure 10-3.

```
<g id="flower" filter="url(#drop-shadow)">
    <!-- drawing here -->
</g>
```

Figure 10-3. Result of improved drop shadow

 When you first start working with filters, I strongly recommend that you do things in stages, testing filters one at a time. I created large numbers of stunningly ugly results during botched attempts to discover how a filter really works. You probably will, too. We'll just keep it as our little secret.

Similarly, when you first learn about filters, you will be tempted to apply as many of them as possible to a drawing, just to see what will happen. Since your purpose is experimentation, go ahead. Once you finish experimenting and begin production work, the purpose of the filter changes. Filters should support and enhance your message, not overwhelm it. Judicious use of one or two filters is a buoy; a flotilla of filters almost always sinks the message.

Creating a Glowing Shadow

The drop shadow works well on the flower, but looks totally unimpressive when applied to text, as we see in Figure 10-4.

Instead, we'd like a glowing turquoise area to surround the text, and we can do this with the `<feColorMatrix>` primitive to change black to a different color.

Figure 10-4. Drop shadow applied to text

The feColorMatrix Element

The `<feColorMatrix>` element allows you to change color values in a very generalized way. The sequence of primitives used to create a glowing turquoise shadow is shown in Example 10-3.

Example 10-3. Glow filter

```
<filter id="glow">
   <feColorMatrix type="matrix" ❶
      values=
          "0 0 0 0   0
           0 0 0 0.9 0
           0 0 0 0.9 0
           0 0 0 1   0"/>
   <feGaussianBlur stdDeviation="2.5" ❷
      result="coloredBlur"/> ❸
   <feMerge> ❹
      <feMergeNode in="coloredBlur"/>
      <feMergeNode in="SourceGraphic"/>
   </feMerge>
</filter>
```

❶ The `<feColorMatrix>` is a very versatile primitive, allowing you to modify any of the color or alpha values of a pixel. When the `type` attribute equals `matrix`, you must set the `value` to a series of twenty numbers describing the transformation.

To set up a transformation that adds color to the alpha values, set up your matrix values as follows:

```
values=
    "0 0 0 red 0
     0 0 0 green 0
     0 0 0 blue 0
     0 0 0 1 0"
```

where the red, green, and blue values are decimal numbers which usually range from zero to 1. In this example, we've set the red to zero, and the green and blue values to 0.9, which will produce a bright cyan color.

You'll note that we didn't specify an `in` attribute for the input to this primitive; the default is to use the `SourceGraphic`. We also didn't put a `result` attribute into this primitive. This means that the color matrix operation's output is available only as the implicit input to the next filter primitive. If you use this shortcut, then the next filter primitive must *not* have an `in` attribute.

❷ Now that we have a cyan-colored source, we use Gaussian blur to spread it out.

❸ The resulting cyan-colored blur is stored for future reference as `coloredBlur`.

❹ As in the previous example, we use `<feMerge>` to output the glow underneath the object in question.

With these two filters, we can create the new, improved Figure 10-5 (see additional color insert) with SVG like this:

```
<g id="flower" style="filter: url(#drop-shadow);">
    <!-- draw the flower -->
</g>
<text x="120" y="50"
    style="filter: url(#glow); fill: #003333; font-size:18;>
Spring <tspan x="120" y="70">Flower</tspan>
</text>
```

Figure 10-5. Drop shadow and glowing text

More About the feColorMatrix Element

We started with the most general kind of color matrix, where you get to specify any values you wish. There are three other values for the `type` attribute. Each of these "built-in" color matrices accomplishes a particular visual task and has its own way of specifying `values`.

hueRotate

The values is a single number that tells how many degrees the color values should be rotated. The mathematics used to accomplish this are very similar to those used in the rotate transformation as described in the section "The rotate Transformation" in Chapter 5. The relation between rotation and resulting color is not at all obvious, as shown in Figure 10-6 (see additional color insert).

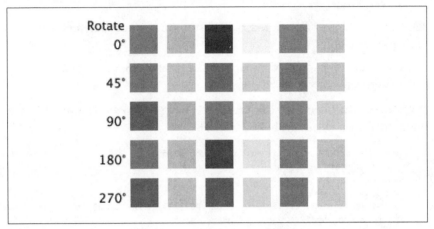

Figure 10-6. Result of hueRotate on fully saturated colors

saturate

The values attribute specifies a single number in the range zero to one. The smaller the number, the more "washed out" the colors will be, as you see in Figure 10-7 (see additional color insert).

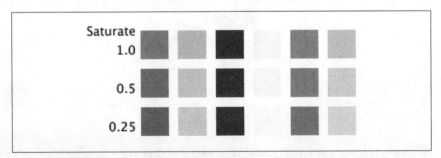

Figure 10-7. Result of saturate on primary colors

luminanceToAlpha

This filter creates an alpha channel based upon a color's luminance. The luminance is the inherent "brightness" of a color, as described in the section "Masking" in Chapter 9. In Figure 10-8 (see additional color insert), the luminance of the colored squares is used as an alpha channel for solid black squares. The lighter a color, the less the transparency it confers upon the filtered object. The `values` attribute is ignored for this type.

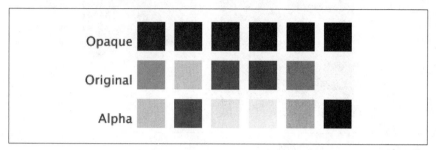

Figure 10-8. Result of luminanceToAlpha

The feImage Filter

Up to this point, we've used only the original graphic or its alpha channel as input to a filter. SVG's `<feImage>` element lets you use any JPG, PNG, or SVG file; or an SVG element with an `id` attribute as input to a filter. In Example 10-4, we import a picture of the sky with a cloud in it to use as a background in the picture of the flower.

Example 10-4. Using the feImage element

```
<defs>
<filter id="sky-shadow" filterUnits="objectBoundingBox">
    <feImage xlink:href="sky.jpg" result="sky"/>
    <feGaussianBlur in="SourceAlpha" stdDeviation="2" result="blur"/>
    <feOffset in="blur" dx="4" dy="4" result="offsetBlur"/>
    <feMerge>
        <feMergeNode in="sky"/>
        <feMergeNode in="offsetBlur"/>
        <feMergeNode in="SourceGraphic"/>
    </feMerge>
</filter>
</defs>

<g id="flower" style="filter: url(#sky-shadow)">
    <!-- flower graphic goes here -->
</g>

<!-- show original image -->
<image xlink:href="sky.jpg" x="170" y="10"
    width="122" height="104"/>
```

Since we're referencing a JPG image, it stretches to fill the bounding box of the filtered object. Figure 10-9 (see additional color insert) shows the result, with the original picture of the sky shown at right at its true size.

Figure 10-9. Result of feImage

The feComponentTransfer Filter

The problem with the background is that it is too dark. Using saturate isn't the answer; it raises or lowers all the color levels. What we need to do is increase the level of green and red more than the blue level, and the <feComponentTransfer> element lets us do just that.

You adjust the levels of red, green, blue, and alpha by placing a <feFuncR>, <feFuncG>, <feFuncB>, and <feFuncA> element inside the <feComponentTransfer>. Each of these sub-elements may independently specify a type attribute that tells how that particular channel is to be modified.

To simulate the effect of a brightness control, you specify the linear function, which places the current color value c into the formula: *slope* * c + *intercept*. The *intercept* provides a "base value" for the result; the *slope* is a simple scaling factor. Example 10-5 uses a filter that adds a brightened sky to the flower with the drop shadow. Note that the red and green channels are adjusted differently than the blue channel. This dramatically brightens the sky in Figure 10-10 (see additional color insert).

Example 10-5. Changing brightness with feComponentTransfer

```
<filter id="brightness-shadow" filterUnits="objectBoundingBox">
    <feImage xlink:href="sky.jpg" result="sky"/>
    <feComponentTransfer in="sky" result="sky">
        <feFuncB type="linear" slope="3" intercept="0"/>
        <feFuncR type="linear" slope="1.5" intercept="0.2"/>
        <feFuncG type="linear" slope="1.5" intercept="0.2"/>
    </feComponentTransfer>
    <feGaussianBlur in="SourceAlpha" stdDeviation="2" result="blur"/>
    <feOffset in="blur" dx="4" dy="4" result="offsetBlur"/>
```

Example 10-5. Changing brightness with feComponentTransfer (continued)

```
    <feMerge>
        <feMergeNode in="sky"/>
        <feMergeNode in="offsetBlur"/>
        <feMergeNode in="SourceGraphic"/>
    </feMerge>
</filter>
```

Figure 10-10. Result of linear component transfer

A simple linear adjustment will add and multiply the same amount to every color value within a channel. This is not the case with the gamma function, which places the current color value c into the formula: amplitude * $c^{exponent}$ + offset. The offset provides a "base value" for the result; the amplitude is a simple scaling factor, and exponent makes the result a curved line rather than a straight line. Since the color value is always between zero and one, the larger your exponent, the *smaller* the modified value will be. Figure 10-11 shows the curves generated with exponent values of 0.6 (the solid line) and 0.3 (the dashed line). Looking at the dashed line, you can see that a low original color value such as 0.1 will be boosted to 0.5, a 400% increase. An original value of 0.5, on the other hand, will increase only 80% to 0.9.

When you specify a gamma filter, you set the amplitude, exponent, and offset attributes to correspond to the values in the preceding formula. Example 10-6 uses gamma correction to adjust the sky. In this particular case, the differences between Figure 10-12 (see additional color insert) and Figure 10-10 are minor, but there are some images which can be improved much more by one method than by the other.

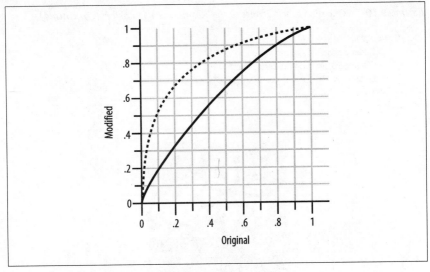

Figure 10-11. Gamma curve functions

Example 10-6. Gamma adjustment with feComponentTransfer

```
<feImage xlink:href="sky.jpg" result="sky"/>
<feComponentTransfer in="sky" result="sky">
    <feFuncB type="gamma"
        amplitude="1" exponent="0.2" offset="0"/>
    <feFuncR type="gamma"
        amplitude="1" exponent="0.707" offset="0"/>
    <feFuncG type="gamma"
        amplitude="1" exponent="0.707" offset="0"/>
</feComponentTransfer>
```

The astute reader (that's you) may have observed that both linear and gamma functions can produce color values greater than 1.0. The SVG specification says that this is not an error; after each filter primitive, the SVG processor will clamp the values to a valid range. Thus, any value greater than 1.0 is reduced to 1.0 and any value less than zero is set to zero.

`<feComponentTransfer>` has other options for the `type` attribute. Please note that you may mix and match any of these; you can gamma correct the red values while brightening the green values with a linear function.

Figure 10-12. Result of using gamma correction

`identity`

A "do-nothing" function. This lets you explicitly state that a color channel should remain unaffected. (This is the default if you don't provide an `<feFuncX>` element for a particular channel.)

`table`

Lets you divide the color values into a series of equal intervals, each of which will be proportionately scaled. Consider the following remapping, which doubles the value of the lowest quarter of the color range, squeezes the next quarter into a range of one tenth, keeps the third quarter in exact proportion, then squeezes the last quarter of the values into the remaining 15% of the color range:

Original value range	Modified value range
0.00—0.25	0.00—0.50
0.25—0.50	0.50—0.60
0.50—0.75	0.60—0.85
0.75—1.00	0.85—0.100

You would specify this mapping for the green channel by listing the endpoints of the remapped range in the `tableValues` attribute.

```
<feFuncG type="table"
    tableValues ="0.0, 0.5, 0.6, 0.85, 1.0"/>
```

If you are dividing the input spectrum into n different sections, you must provide $n+1$ items in `tableValues`, separated by whitespace or commas.

`discrete`

Lets you divide the color values into a series of equal intervals, each of which will be mapped to a single discrete color value. Consider the following remapping, which maps the value of the lowest quarter of the color range to 0.125, sets the next quarter to 0.375, the third quarter to 0.625, and remaining quarter to 0.875. (That is, each quarter of the range is mapped to its center point.)

Original value range	Modified value
0.00—0.25	0.125
0.25—0.50	0.375
0.50—0.75	0.625
0.75—1.00	0.875

You would specify this mapping for the green channel by listing the discrete values, separated by commas or whitespace, in the `tableValues` attribute.

```
<feFuncG type="discrete"
    tableValues ="0.125 0.375 0.625 0.875"/>
```

Dividing the input channel into *n* sections requires *n* entries in the `tableValues` attribute. **Exception**: If you want to remap all the input values to a single output value, you must place that entry into `tableValues` twice; thus, to set any input value of the blue channel to 0.5, you would say: `<feFuncB type="discrete" tableValues="0.5 0.5"/>`.

If you want to invert the range of color values for a channel (that is, change increasing values from a minimum to maximum into decreasing values from the maximum to the minimum), use this:

```
<feFuncX type="table"
    tableValues="maximum minimum"/>
```

Figure 10-13 (see additional color insert) shows the results of using discrete and table transfers as well as inversion via a table transfer.

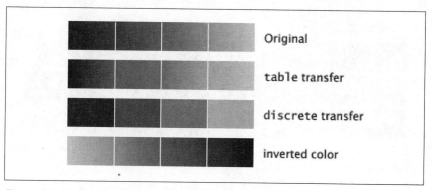

Original

table transfer

discrete transfer

inverted color

Figure 10-13. Result of using table and discrete transfers

Ordinarily, the values for red, green, or blue run in a straight line from zero to one, with zero being none of the color and one being 100% of the color. This is called a linear color space. However, when SVG calculates the color values between gradient stops (as described in Chapter 7, in the section "Gradients"), it uses a special way of representing color such that the values do not follow a straight line from zero to one. This representation is called the standard RGB or *sRGB* color space, and its use can make gradients much more natural-looking. Figure 10-14 (see additional color insert) shows a comparison. The first gradient goes from black to green, the second from red to green, and the third from black to white.

By default, filter arithmetic calculates any interpolated ("in-between") values in the linear RGB space, so if you apply a filter to an object that has been filled with a gradient, you will get results that aren't at all what you expect. In order to get the correct result, you must tell the filter to do its calculations in sRGB space by adding a `color-interpolation-filters="sRGB"` attribute to your `<filter>` element. Alternatively, you may leave the filter alone and apply `color-interpolation="linearRGB"` to the `<gradient>` element, so that it uses the same color space as the default for filters.

The feComposite Filter

So far we have combined the results of filters by using `<feMerge>` to layer the intermediate results one over another. We will now investigate the much more general `<feComposite>` element. This element takes two inputs, specified with the `in` and `in2` attributes, and an `operator` that tells

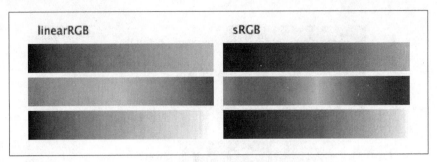

Figure 10-14. Comparsion of linearRGB and sRGB

how the two are to be combined. In the following explanation, we'll pre-sume that you've specified in="A" and in2="B".

<feComposite operator="**over**" in="A" in2="B"/>
> Produces the result of layering A over B, exactly as <feMergeNode> does. In fact, <feMergeNode> is really just a convenient shortcut for a <feComposite> element that specifies an over operation.

<feComposite operator="**in**" in="A" in2="B"/>
> The result is the part of A that is within the boundaries of B. Don't confuse the name of this attribute value with the in attribute.

<feComposite operator="**out**" in="A" in2="B"/>
> The result is the part of A that is outside the boundaries of B.

<feComposite operator="**atop**" in="A" in2="B"/>
> The result is the part of A that is inside B, as well as the part of B out-side A. To quote the article in which these operators were first defined: "...*paper* atop *table* includes *paper* where it is on top of *table*, and *table* otherwise; area beyond the edge of the table is out of the picture."[*]

<feComposite operator="**xor**" in="A" in2="B"/>
> The result is the part of A that is outside B together with the part of B that is outside A.

<feComposite in="A" in2="B" operator="**arithmetic**" .../>
> The ultimate in flexibility. You provide four coefficients, k1, k2, k3, and k4. The result for each pixel is calculated as:

    k1 * A * B + k2 * A + k3 * B + k4

---

[*] "Compositing Digital Images," T. Porter, T. Duff, SIGGRAPH '84 Conference Proceedings, Association for Computing Machinery, Volume 18, Number 3, July 1984.

The arithmetic operator is useful for doing a "dissolve" effect. If you want to have a resulting image that is *a*% of image A and *b*% of image B, set k1 and k4 to zero, k2 to *a*/100, and k3 to *b*/100. So, to make a blend with 30% of A and 70% of B, you'd use this:

```
<feComposite in="A" in2="B" result="combined"
    k1="0" k2="0.30" k3="0.70" k4="0"/>
```

Figure 10-15 (see additional color insert) shows the combinations that we've described; the arithmetic blend is 50% of A and 50% of B.

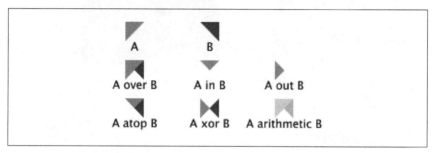

Figure 10-15. Result of using feComposite operators

Example 10-7 uses the in and out operators to do "cut-outs." The drop shadow has been eliminated from this example to produce a more visually pleasing result in Figure 10-16.

Example 10-7. Use of feComposite in and out

```
<defs>
<filter id="sky-in" filterUnits="objectBoundingBox">
    <feImage xlink:href="sky.jpg" result="sky"/>
    <feComposite in="sky" in2="SourceGraphic"
        operator="in"/>
</filter>

<filter id="sky-out" filterUnits="objectBoundingBox">
    <feImage xlink:href="sky.jpg" result="sky"/>
    <feComposite in="sky" in2="SourceGraphic"
        operator="out"/>
</filter>

<g id="flower">
    <!-- flower graphic goes here -->
</g>
</defs>
```

Example 10-7. Use of feComposite in and out (continued)

```
<use xlink:href="#flower" transform="translate(10,10)"
    style="filter: url(#sky-in);"/>

<use xlink:href="#flower" transform="translate(170,10)"
    style="filter: url(#sky-out);"/>
```

Figure 10-16. Result of feComposite in and out

The feBlend Filter

But wait, there's more! Yes, filters provide yet another way to combine
images. The <feBlend> element requires two inputs, specified with the in
and in2 attributes, and a mode that tells how the inputs are to be blended.
The possible values are: normal, multiply, screen, lighten, and darken.
Given opaque inputs <feBlend in="A" in2="B" mode="*m*"/>, the following
table shows the color of the resulting pixel for each mode:

Mode	Effect
normal	B only; this is the same as the over operator in <feMerge>.
multiply	As the name suggests, the resulting color value is the product of A's color value and B's color value. This tends to dramatically weaken light colors.
screen	Adds the color values together, then subtracts their product. This tends to strengthen light colors more than dark colors.
darken	Takes the minimum of A and B. This is the darker color, hence the name.
lighten	Takes the maximum of A and B. This is the lighter color, hence the name.

Note that the appropriate calculation is done independently for each of
the red, green, and blue values. So, if you were to darken a pure red

square with RGB values of (100%, 0%, 0%) and a gray square with RGB values of (50%, 50%, 50%), the resulting color would be (50%, 0%, 0%). If the inputs are not opaque, then all the modes except for screen factor in the transparencies when making the calculations.

Finally, once the color value is calculated, the opacity of the result is determined by the formula 1 - (1 - *opacity of A*) * (1 - *opacity of B*). Using this formula, two opaque items will still be opaque; two items that are 50% opaque will combine to one that is 75% opaque.

Figure 10-17 (see additional color insert) shows the result of blending an opaque solid gray (50%, 50%, 50%) bar with opaque and 50% opaque color squares that have RGB values of black (#000), yellow (#ff0), red (#f00), medium-bright green (#0c0), and dark blue (#009).

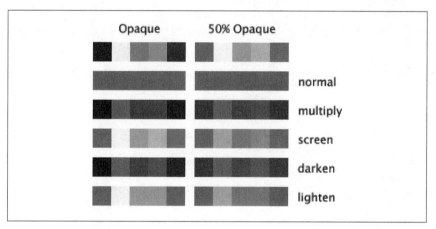

Figure 10-17. Result of feBlend in and out

The feFlood and feTile Filters

The `<feFlood>` and `<feTile>` elements are "utility filters." Much like `<feOffset>`, they allow you to carry out certain common operations within a series of filter primitives rather than having to create extra SVG elements in your main graphic.

`<feFlood>` provides a solid colored area for use in compositing or merging. You provide the `flood-fill-color` and `flood-fill-opacity`, and the filter does the rest.

`<feTile>` takes its input and tiles it horizontally and vertically to fill the area that is specified in the filter. The size of the tile itself is specified by the `<feImage>` element used as the input to `<feTile>`.

Example 10-8 uses <feComposite> to cut out the flooded and tiled area to the shape of a flower. The image used as a tile is shown for reference at the upper right of Figure 10-18.

Example 10-8. Example of feFlood and feTile

```
<defs>
<filter id="flood-filter" x="0" y="0" width="100%" height="100%">
    <feFlood flood-color="#993300" flood-opacity="0.8" result="tint"/>
    <feComposite in="tint" in2="SourceGraphic"
        operator="in"/>
</filter>

<filter id="tile-filter" x="0" y="0" width="100%" height="100%">
    <feImage xlink:href="cloth.jpg" width="32" height="32"
        result="cloth"/>
    <feTile in="cloth" result="cloth"/>
    <feComposite in="cloth" in2="SourceGraphic"
        operator="in"/>
</filter>

<g id="flower">
    <!-- flower graphic goes here -->
</g>

</defs>
<use xlink:href="#flower" transform="translate(0, 0)"
    style="filter: url(#flood-filter);"/>
<use xlink:href="#flower" transform="translate(110,0)"
    style="filter: url(#tile-filter);"/>
<image xlink:href="cloth.jpg" x="220" y="10"
    width="32" height="32"/>
```

Figure 10-18. Result of feFlood and feTile elements

Lighting Effects

If you draw a bright green circle with SVG, it looks like a refugee from a traffic signal, glowing by its own light and otherwise lying flat on the screen. If you look at a circle cut out of green construction paper, it looks more "real" because it is lit from an outside source and has some texture. A circle cut from green plastic not only is lit from outside, it also has reflected highlights. We call light from an outside source diffuse lighting, and the highlights that reflect off a surface specular lighting, from the Latin *speculum*, meaning *mirror*.

In order to achieve these effects, you must specify:

- The type of lighting you want (`<feDiffuseLighting>` or `<feSpecularLighting>`)

- The object you want to light

- The color of light you are using

- The type of light source you want (`<fePointLight>`, `<feDistantLight>`, or `<feSpotLight>`) and its location

You specify the location of a light source in three dimensions; this means you will need a *z*-value in addition to *x*- and *y*-values. The relationship of the *x*-, *y*-, and *z*-axes is shown in Figure 10-19; the positive *z* axis is "coming out of the screen" and pointing at you.

Both these lighting effects use the alpha channel of the object they are illuminating as a bump map; higher alpha values are presumed to be "raised" above the surface of the object.

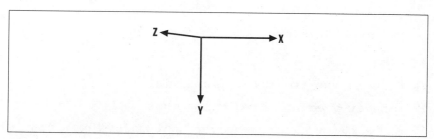

Figure 10-19. Relationship of x-, y,- and z-axes

Diffuse Lighting

The best way to show how the <feDiffuseLighting> element works is to
jump right into Example 10-9. We will shine a pale yellow light on a green
circle, textured with the curve pattern that we used in Example 7-1.

Example 10-9. Diffuse lighting with a point light source

```
<path id="curve" d="M 0 0 Q 5 20 10 10 T 20 20" ❶
    style="stroke: black; fill: none;"/>

<circle id="green-light" cx="50" cy="50" r="50" ❷
    style="fill: #060;"/>

<filter id="diff-light" color-interpolation-filters="sRGB" ❸
    x="0" y="0" width="100%" height="100%">

    <feImage xlink:href="#curve" result="tile" ❹
        width="20" height="20"/>

    <feTile in="tile" result="tile"/>

    <feColorMatrix type="luminanceToAlpha" in="tile" ❺
        result="alphaTile"/>

    <feDiffuseLighting in="alphaTile" ❻
        lighting-color="#ffffcc"
        surfaceScale="1" ❼
        diffuseConstant="0.5" ❽
        result="diffuseOutput"> ❾
        <fePointLight x="0" y="50" z="50"/> ❿
    </feDiffuseLighting> ⓫

    <feComposite in="diffuseOutput" in2="SourceGraphic" ⓬
        operator="in" result="diffuseOutput"/>

    <feBlend in="diffuseOutput" in2="SourceGraphic" ⓭
        mode="screen"/>
</filter>
```

❶ Define the curve that will be used as the tile.

❷ Define the object that we want to illuminate.

❸ Set the color interpolation method and the boundaries for the filter.

❹ Tile the area of the filter with the curve image. This will become our
    bump map...

❺ ...so convert it to a pure alpha map, named alphaTile.

❻ This tiled area is the input to the <feDiffuseLighting> element, which
    we will illuminate with a pale yellow light,as specified by the light-
    ing-color attribute.

❼ The surfaceScale attribute tells the height of the surface for an alpha value of 1. (Specifically, it's the factor by which the alpha value is multiplied.)

❽ diffuseConstant is a multiplicative factor that is used in determining the final RGB values of a pixel. It must have a value greater than or equal to zero; its default value is one. The brighter your lighting-color, the smaller this number should be. Unless you like having your picture washed out.

❾ The result of this filter will be named diffuseOutput.

❿ In this example, we are using a point light source, which means a source that radiates light in all directions. We will position it at the left center of the area we wish to illuminate, and set it 50 units in front of the screen. The farther you set it away from the object, the more evenly the object is illuminated. In this example, we've moved the light up close and personal to get the greatest possible effect.

⓫ The end of the <feDiffuseLighting> element.

 The input to this filter was an alpha channel; the output is a *totally opaque* RGB bitmap; its alpha channel is equal to 1.0 at every point.

⓬ We use <feComposite>'s in operator to clip the filter's output to the boundaries of the source graphic (the circle).

⓭ Finally, we use <feBlend> in screen mode, which tends to lighten the input, to create the final image.

Once this is all defined, the following statement activates the filter on the desired object to produce Figure 10-20:

```
<use xlink:href="#green-light" style="filter: url(#diff-light);"/>
```

Specular Lighting

Specular lighting, on the other hand, gives highlights rather than illumination. Example 10-10 shows how this works.

Example 10-10. Specular lighting with a distant light

```
<path id="curve" d="M 0 0 Q 5 20 10 10 T 20 20" ❶
   style="stroke: black; fill: none;"/>
<circle id="green-light" cx="50" cy="50" r="50"
```

Figure 10-20. Result of applying diffuse lighting filter

Example 10-10. Specular lighting with a distant light (continued)

```
    style="fill: #060;"/>

<filter id="spec-light" color-interpolation-filters="sRGB" ❷
    x="0" y="0" width="100%" height="100%">

    <feImage xlink:href="#curve" result="tile" ❸
        width="20" height="20"/>

    <feTile in="tile" result="tile"/>

    <feColorMatrix type="luminanceToAlpha" in="tile"
        result="alphaTile"/>

    <feSpecularLighting in="alphaTile" ❹
        lighting-color="#ffffcc"
            surfaceScale="1" ❺
            specularConstant="1" ❻
            specularExponent="4" ❼
            result="specularOutput"> ❽
            <feDistantLight elevation="25" azimuth="0"/> ❾
    </feSpecularLighting> ❿

    <feComposite in="specularOutput" in2="SourceGraphic" ⓫
        operator="in" result="specularOutput"/>

    <feComposite in="specularOutput" in2="SourceGraphic" ⓬
        operator="arithmetic" k1="0" k2="1" k3="1" k4="0"/>
</filter>
```

❶ As in the previous example, the first six lines define the curve and circle.

❷ The only difference between this and the previous example is the filter name.

❸ As in the previous example, this section tiles the curve into an alpha
   channel.

❹ Starts the definition of the `<feSpecularLighting>` filter and specifies the `lighting-color` to be a pale yellow light.

❺ The `surfaceScale` attribute tells the height of the surface for an alpha value of 1. (Specifically, it's the factor by which the alpha value is multiplied.)

❻ `specularConstant` is a multiplicative factor that is used in determining the final RGB values of a pixel. It must have a value greater than or equal to zero; its default value is one. The brighter your `lighting-color`, the smaller this number should be.

❼ `specularExponent` is another factor that is used in determining the final RGB values of a pixel. This attribute must have a value from 1 to 128; the default value is 1. The larger this number, the more "shiny" the result.

❽ The result of this filter will be named `specularOutput`.

❾ In this example, we are using a distant light source, which means that is *z*-value is effectively infinity. The `elevation` tells how far up or down the light is above the horizon, and the `azimuth` specifies the angle of the light in the plane of the screen—whether it's to the left, right, top, or bottom of the object being illuminated.

❿ The end of the `<feSpecularLighting>` element.

The input to this filter was an alpha channel; the output contains both alpha **and** color information (unlike `<feDif-fuseLighting>`, which always produces an opaque result).

⓫ We use `<feComposite>`'s in operator to clip the filter's output to the boundaries of the source graphic (the circle).

⓬ Finally, we use `<feComposite>` with the `arithmetic` operator to do a straight addition of the lighting and the source graphic.

Once this is all defined, the following statement activates the filter on the desired object, producing the highlighting relief effect in Figure 10-21.

```
<use xlink:href="#green-light" style="filter: url(#spec-light);"/>
```

Figure 10-21. Result of applying specular lighting filter

 An excellent tutorial on lighting effects in three dimensions is available at *http://www.webreference.com/3d/lesson12/.* We're working in only two dimensions, but much of the information is applicable.

A third type of light source, `<feSpotLight>`, is specified with these attributes: x, y, and z, the location of the spotlight (default value is zero); pointsAtX, pointsAtY, and pointsAtZ, the place that the spotlight is pointing at (default value is zero); specularExponent, a value that controls the focus for the light source (default value is one); and limitingConeAngle, which restricts the region where the light is projected. This is the angle between the spot light axis and the cone. Thus, if you want a 30 degree spread for the entire cone, specify the angle as 15. (The default value is to allow unlimited spread.)

Accessing the Background

In addition to the SourceGraphic and SourceAlpha filter inputs, a filtered object may access the part of the image that has already been rendered onto the canvas when you invoke a filter. These parts are called BackgroundImage (*not* BackgroundGraphic) and BackgroundAlpha. In order to access these inputs, the filtered object must be within a container element that has set the enable-background attribute to the value new. Example 10-11 performs a Gaussian blur on the background alpha channel.

Example 10-11. Accessing the background

```
<defs>
<filter id="blur-background">
    <feGaussianBlur in="BackgroundAlpha" ❶
        stdDeviation="2" result="blur"/>
    <feOffset in="blur" dx="4" dy="4" result="offsetBlur"/>
    <feMerge>
```

Example 10-11. Accessing the background (continued)

```
            <feMergeNode in="offsetBlur"/>
            <feMergeNode in="SourceGraphic"/>
        </feMerge>
    </filter>
    </defs>

    <g enable-background="new"> ❷
        <circle cx="30" cy="30" r="30" style="fill: #fff;"/> ❸
        <rect x="0" y="0" width="60" height="60"
            style="filter: url(#blur-background); ❹
            fill: none; stroke: blue;" />
    </g>
```

❶ This is similar to the blur filter used for drop shadows, except that the input is now the BackgroundAlpha rather than the SourceAlpha.

❷ Since <g> is a container element, it is a perfect candidate for placing the enable-background. All the children of this element will have access to the background image and alpha.

❸ We render a white circle onto the canvas; this makes it "invisible" against a white background.

❹ We now draw a rectangle and use the filter. The background alpha that it picks up will be circular, so Figure 10-22 shows a square with a circular shadow. (Strange, but true!)

Figure 10-22. Result of accessing background alpha

The feMorphology Element

The <feMorphology> element lets you "thin" or "thicken" a graphic. You specify an operator with a value of erode to thin or dilate to thicken a graphic. The radius attribute tells us how much the lines are to be thickened or thinned. It's ordinarily applied to alpha channels; in Example 10-12 we erode and dilate a simple line drawing. As you see in Figure 10-23, erosion can wreak havoc on a drawing that has thin lines to begin with.

Example 10-12. Thickening and thinning with feMorphology

```
<defs>
<g id="cat" stroke-width="2">
    <!-- drawing of a cat -->
</g>

<filter id="erode1">
    <feMorphology operator="erode" radius="1"/>
</filter>

<filter id="dilate2">
    <feMorphology operator="dilate" radius="2"/>
</filter>
</defs>

<use xlink:href="#cat"/>
<text x="75" y="170" style="text-anchor: middle;">Normal</text>

<use xlink:href="#cat" transform="translate(150,0)"
    style="filter: url(#erode1);"/>
<text x="225" y="170" style="text-anchor: middle;">Erode 1</text>

<use xlink:href="#cat" transform="translate(300,0)"
    style="filter: url(#dilate2);"/>
<text x="375" y="170" style="text-anchor: middle;">Dilate 2</text>
```

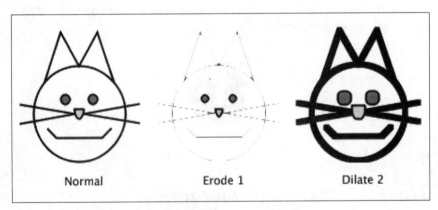

Figure 10-23. Result of using feMorphology

The feConvolveMatrix Element

The `<feConvolveMatrix>` element lets you calculate a pixel's new value in terms of the values of its neighboring pixels. This filter lets you do effects such as blurring, sharpening, embossing, and beveling. It works by combining a pixel with its neighboring pixels to produce a resulting pixel value. Imagine a pixel P and its eight neighboring pixels (the usual case that is used with this filter):

```
A   B   C
D   P   E
F   G   H
```

You then specify a list of nine numbers in the kernelMatrix attribute. These numbers tell how much to multiply each pixel by. These products will be added up. The sum could well come out to be greater than one (if all the factors are positive, for example), so, to even the intensity, the result is divided by the total of the factors. Let's say you specify these nine numbers:

```
<feConvolveMatrix kernelMatrix="
    0   1   2
    3   4   5
    6   7   8"/>
```

The new value of pixel P will then be:

```
P' = ((0*A) + (1*B) + (2*C) +
      (3*D) + (4*P) + (5*E) +
      (6*F) + (7*G) + (8*H)) / ( 0 + 1 + 2 + 3 + 4 + 5 + 6 + 7 + 8)
```

Example 10-13 achieves the embossing effect shown in Figure 10-24 by taking the upper left neighbor minus the lower right neighbor of each pixel.

Example 10-13. Embossing with feConvolveMatrix

```
<defs>
<filter id="emboss">
    <feConvolveMatrix
        kernelMatrix="
        1 0 0
        0 0 0
        0 0 -1"/>
</filter>

<g id="flower">
    <!-- flower graphic goes here -->
</g>
</defs>

<use xlink:href="#flower" style="filter: url(#emboss);"/>
```

Although the default matrix size is three columns by three rows, you can specify any size you want with the order attribute. If you specify order="4", then the matrix will require sixteen numbers (4 by 4) in the kernelMatrix attribute. A matrix with three columns and two rows would be specified by order="3 2" and would require six numbers. The larger your kernel matrix, the more computation is required to produce the result.

Figure 10-24. Result of using feConvolveMatrix

For a pixel in the middle of a graphic, the neighbors are easy to identify. What do you do with the pixels on the edges of the graphic? Who are their neighbors? This decision is made by the setting that you give the edgeMode attribute. If you set its value to be duplicate, then <feConvolve-Matrix> duplicates the edge values in the required direction to produce a neighbor. The value wrap wraps around to the opposite side to find a neighbor. For example, the neighbor above a pixel at the top is the pixel at the bottom, and the neighbor to the left of a pixel at the left edge is the corresponding pixel at the right edge. The value of none will provide a transparent black pixel (red, green, blue, and alpha values of zero) for any missing neighbors.

The default behavior of <feConvolveMatrix> is to apply the calculations to all the channels, including alpha. If you want to apply calculations only to the red, green, and blue values, specify preserveAlpha as true (the default value is false).

You may also add a fixed offset to the result of each calculation by specifying a value for the bias attribute, although this particular feature does not work in the current 1.0 release of Batik. Some sample convolve effects (which were not designed specifically for SVG) are available at *http://www.nebulus.org/tutorials/2d/pictpub/udf/*.

The feDisplacementMap Element

This fascinating filter uses the color values of its second input to decide how far to move the pixels in the first input. You specify which color channel should be used to affect the *x*-coordinate of a pixel with the xChannelSelector attribute; the yChannelSelector attribute specifies the color channel used to affect the *y*-coordinate. The legal values for these selectors are "R", "G", "B", and "A" (for the alpha channel). You must specify how far to displace pixels; the scale attribute gives the appropriate scaling factor. If you don't specify this attribute, the filter won't do anything.

Example 10-14 creates a gradient rectangle as the second input. The displacement factor will be set to ten, the red channel will be used as an *x* offset, and the green channel will be used as a *y* offset. Figure 10-25 (see additional color insert) shows the result of applying this displacement to the flower.

Example 10-14. Using a gradient as a displacement map

```
<defs>
<linearGradient id="gradient">
    <stop offset="0" style="stop-color: #ff0000;" />
    <stop offset="0.5" style="stop-color: #00ff00;"/>
    <stop offset="1" style="stop-color: #000000;"/>
</linearGradient>

<rect id="rectangle" x="0" y="0" width="100" height="200"
    style="fill: url(#gradient);"/>

<filter id="displace">
    <feImage xlink:href="#rectangle" result="grad"/>

    <feDisplacementMap
        scale="10"
        xChannelSelector="R"
        yChannelSelector="G"
        in="SourceGraphic" in2="grad"/>
</filter>


<g id="flower">
    <!-- flower graphic goes here -->
</g>
</defs>

<use xlink:href="#flower" style="filter: url(#displace);"/>
```

It's possible to use the same graphic for both inputs. This means that a graphic's displacement is controlled by its own coloration. This effect, as written in Example 10-15 and displayed in Figure 10-26, can be quite eccentric.

Example 10-15. Using a Graphic as Its Own Displacement Map

```
<defs>
<filter id="self-displace">
    <feDisplacementMap
        scale="10"
```

Figure 10-25. Result of using feDisplacementMap

Example 10-15. Using a Graphic as Its Own Displacement Map (continued)

```
      xChannelSelector="R"
      yChannelSelector="G"
      in="SourceGraphic" in2="SourceGraphic"/>
</filter>

<g id="flower">
   <!-- flower graphic goes here -->
</g>
</defs>

<use xlink:href="#flower" style="filter: url(#self-displace);"/>
```

Figure 10-26. Same graphic used as both inputs to feDisplacementMap

The feTurbulence Element

The `<feTurbulence>` elements lets you produce artificial textures for effects like marble, clouds, etc. by using equations developed by Ken Perlin. An excellent summary is available at *http://freespace.virgin.net/hugo.elias/ models/m_perlin.htm*. You specify these attributes:

type

One of `turbulence` or `fractalNoise`. Fractal noise is smoother in appearance.

baseFrequency

The larger the number you give as the value for this attribute, the more quickly colors change in the result. This number must be greater than zero and should be less than one. You may also give two numbers for this attribute; the first will be the frequency in the *x* direction and the second will be the frequency in the *y* direction.

numOctaves

This is the number of noise functions that should be added together when generating the final result. The larger this number, the more fine-grained the texture. The default value is one.

seed

The starting value for the random number generator that this filter uses. The default value is zero; change it to get some variety in the result.

Figure 10-27 (see additional color insert) is a screenshot of an SVG file that shows various values of the first three of these attributes.

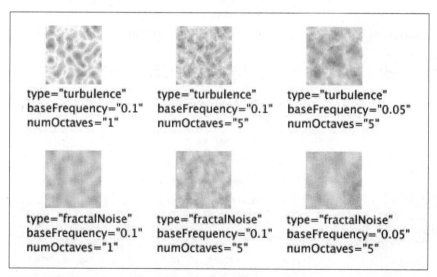

Figure 10-27. Various values of feTurbulence attributes

Filter Reference Summary

The `<filter>` element contains a series of filter primitives, each of which takes one or more inputs and provides a single result for use with other filters. The result of the last filter in the series is rendered into the final graphic. You specify the dimensions of the canvas to which the filter applies with the x, y, width, and height attributes.

Table 10-1 presents a filter reference summary. Each of the filter primitive elements has an in attribute that gives the source for the primitive, and may also specify an x, y, width, and height. Default attributes are in bold-face.

Table 10-1. Filter reference summary

Element	Attributes
`<feBlend>`	`in2="`*second source*`"`
	`mode="`**`normal`**`" | "multiply" | "screen" | "darken" | "lighten"`
`<feColorMatrix>`	`type="matrix" | "saturate" | "hueRotate" | "luminanceToAlpha"`
	`values="`*matrix values*`" | "`*saturation value (0-1)*`" | "`*rotate degrees*`"`
`<feComponentTransfer>`	container for `<feFuncR>`, `<feFuncG>`, `<feFuncB>`, and `<feFuncA>` elements.
`<feFuncX>`	`type="identity" | "table" | "discrete" | "linear" | "gamma"`
	`tableValues="`*intervals for table, steps for discrete*`"`
	`slope="`*linear slope*`"`
	`intercept="`*linear intercept*`"`
	`amplitude="`*gamma amplitude*`"`
	`exponent="`*gamma exponent*`"`
	`offset="`*gamma offset*`"`
`<feComposite>`	`in2="`*second source*`"`
	`operator="over" | "in" | "out" | "atop" | "xor" | "arithmetic"`

Table 10-1. Filter reference summary (continued)

Element	Attributes
`<feComposite>` *(continued)*	The following attributes are used with `arithmetic`:
	`k1="`*factor for in1*in2*`"`
	`k2="`*factor for in1*`"`
	`k3="`*factor for in2*`"`
	`k4="`*additive offset*`"`
`<feConvolveMatrix>`	`order="`*columns rows*`"` (default 3 by 3)
	`kernel="`*values*`"`
	`bias="`*offset value*`"`
`<feDiffuseLighting>`	Container for a light source element.
	`surfaceScale="`*height*`"` (default 1)
	`diffuseConstant="`*factor*`"` (must be non-negative; default 1)
`<feDisplacementMap>`	`scale="`*displacement factor*`"` (default 0)
	`xChannelSelector="R"` | `"G"` | `"B"` | `"A"`
	`yChannelSelector="R"` | `"G"` | `"B"` | `"A"`
	`in2="`*second input*`"`
`<feFlood>`	`flood-fill-color="`*color specification*`"`
	`flood-fill-opacity="`*value (0-1)*`"`
`<feGaussianBlur>`	`stdDeviation="`*blur spread*`"` (larger is blurrier; default 0)
`<feImage>`	`xlink:href="`*image source*`"`
`<feMerge>`	container for `<feMergeNode>` elements
`<feMergeNode>`	`in="`*intermediate result*
`<feMorphology>`	`operator="erode"` | `"dilate"`
	`radius="`*x-radius y-radius*`"`
	`radius="`*radius*`"`
`<feOffset>`	`dx="`*x offset*`"` (default 0)
	`dy="`*y offset*`"` (default 0)
`<feSpecularLighting>`	Container for a light source element.
	`surfaceScale="`*height*`"` (default 1)
	`specularConstant="`*factor*`"` (must be non-negative; default 1)
	`specularExponent="`*exponent*`"` (range 1-128; default 1)
`<feTile>`	tiles the *in* layer

Table 10-1. Filter reference summary (continued)

Element	Attributes
<feTurbulence>	type="turbulence" | "fractalNoise"
	baseFrequency="*x-frequency y-frequency*"
	baseFrequency="*frequency*"
	numOctaves="*integer*"
	seed="*number*"
<feDistantLight>	azimuth="*degrees*" (default 0)
	elevation="*degrees*" (default 0)
<fePointLight>	x="*coordinate*" (default 0)
	y="*coordinate*" (default 0)
	z="*coordinate*" (default 0)
<feSpotLight>	x="*coordinate*" (default 0)
	y="*coordinate*" (default 0)
	z="*coordinate*" (default 0)
	pointsAtX="*coordinate*" (default 0)
	pointsAtY="*coordinate*" (default 0)
	pointsAtZ="*coordinate*" (default 0)
	specularConstant="*focus control*" (default 1)
	limitingConeAngle="*degrees*"

11

Animating and
Scripting SVG

Up to this point we have produced static images; once constructed, they never change. In this chapter, we will examine two methods of making graphic images move. The first method, animation, is movement that is controlled by you, the author. The second method, scripting, lets the person viewing the graphic interact with and modify the image.

In Chapter 10 we suggested that filters should be used as a means to enhance a graphic's message, not as an end in themselves. This suggestion is even more crucial with animation. Drunk with the power of animation, you will be tempted to turn your every graphic into an all-dancing, all-singing, Broadway spectacular. As long as your goal is experimentation, this is fine. If your goal is to convey a message, however, nothing is worse than gratuitous use or overuse of animation. Let me state this clearly: nobody except the company CEO is interested in repeated viewing of a spinning, flashing, color-changing, strobe-lit version of the company logo.

In this chapter, our message *is* the animation, so most of our examples will be remarkably free of any content. We will, of course, avoid gratuitous and overwrought animation as much as possible.

Animation Basics

The animation features of SVG are based on the World Wide Web Consortium's Synchronized Multimedia Integration Language Level 2 (SMIL2) specification *http://www.w3.org/TR/smil20/*. In this system, you specify the starting and ending values of the attribute, color, motion, or transformation that you wish to animate; the time at which the animation should begin; and the duration of the animation. Example 11-1 shows this in action.

Example 11-1. The incredible shrinking rectangle

```
<rect x="10" y="10" width="200" height="20" stroke="black" fill="none"> ❶
    <animate ❷
        attributeName="width" ❸
        attributeType="XML" ❹
        from="200" to="20" ❺
        begin="0s" dur="5s" ❻
        fill="freeze" /> ❼
</rect> ❽
```

❶ A <rect> element *without* the ending />. The animation will be contained within the element.

❷ Begin specification of animation

❸ Specify the attribute whose value should change over time.

❹ Width is an XML attribute in the <rect> element. The other common value of attributeType is CSS, indicating that the property we want to change is a CSS property. If you leave this off, the default value of auto is used; it searches through CSS properties first and then XML attributes.

❺ The starting and ending values for the attribute. In this example, the starting value is 200 and the ending value is 20.*

❻ The beginning and duration times for the animation. In this example, we measure time in seconds, specified by the s after the number. For more details, see the section "How Time Is Measured."

❼ After the five-second duration, keep the attribute at its end value. If you remove this line, the attribute will return to its original value of 200 after the five-second animation has finished. This is the SMIL fill attribute, which tells the animation engine how to fill up the remaining time. Don't confuse it with SVG's fill attribute, which tells SVG how to paint an object.

❽ We have to close the <rect> element, since it is now a container element.

Figure 11-1 and Figure 11-2 show the beginning and ending stages of the animation. They can't do justice to the actual effect, so we strongly

---

* There is also a by attribute, which you may use instead of to; it is an offset that is added to the starting from value; the result is the ending value.

recommend that you download the Adobe SVG Viewer plugin and try the example. Type it into a file, enclosed in the appropriate `<?xml?>` and `<svg>` tags, and open it within your browser.

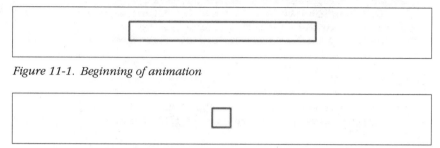

Figure 11-1. Beginning of animation

Figure 11-2. Ending of animation

Let's move on to a more ambitious example. In Example 11-2 we'll start with a 20-by-20 green square that will grow to 250-by-200 over the space of 8 seconds. For the first three seconds, the opacity of the green will increase, then decrease for the next three seconds. Note that `fill-opacity` is referred to with `attributeType="CSS"` since it was set in a style.

Example 11-2. Multiple animations on a single object

```
<rect x="10" y="10" width="20" height="20"
    style="stroke: black; fill: green; style: fill-opacity: 0.25;">
<animate attributeName="width" attributeType="XML"
    from="20" to="250" begin="0s" dur="8s" fill="freeze"/>
<animate attributeName="height" attributeType="XML"
    from="20" to="200" begin="0s" dur="8s" fill="freeze"/>
<animate attributeName="fill-opacity" attributeType="CSS"
    from="0.25" to="1" begin="0s" dur="3s" fill="freeze"/>
<animate attributeName="fill-opacity" attributeType="CSS"
    from="1" to="0.25" begin="3s" dur="3s" fill="freeze"/>
</rect>
```

Our last simple example, Example 11-3, animates a square and a circle. The square will expand from 20-by-20 to 120-by-120 over the space of eight seconds. Two seconds after the beginning of the animation, the circle's radius will start expanding from 20 to 50 over the space of four seconds. Figure 11-3 shows a combined screenshot of the animation at four times: zero seconds, when the animation begins; two seconds, when the circle starts to grow; six seconds, when the circle finishes growing; and eight seconds, when the animation is finished.

Example 11-3. Simple animation of multiple objects

```
<rect x="10" y="10" width="20" height="20"
    style="stroke: black; fill: #cfc;">
    <animate attributeName="width" attributeType="XML"
        begin="0s" dur="8s" from="20" to="120" fill="freeze"/>
    <animate attributeName="height" attributeType="XML"
        begin="0s" dur="8s" from="20" to="120" fill="freeze"/>
</rect>

<circle cx="70" cy="70" r="20"
    style="fill: #ccf; stroke: black;">
    <animate attributeName="r" attributeType="XML"
        begin="2s" dur="4s" from="20" to="50" fill="freeze"/>
</circle>
```

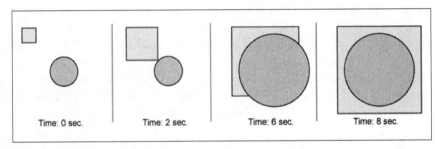

Time: 0 sec.   Time: 2 sec.   Time: 6 sec.   Time: 8 sec.

Figure 11-3. Stages of multi-object animation

How Time Is Measured

SVG's animation clock starts ticking when the SVG has finished loading, and it stops ticking when the user leaves the page. You may specify a beginning or duration for a particular animation segment as a numeric value in one of these ways:

- A full clock value in hours, minutes, and seconds (1:20:23).

- A partial clock value in minutes and seconds (2:15).

- A time value followed by a "metric," which is one of h (hours), min (minutes), s (seconds), or ms (milliseconds), for example dur="3.5s" begin="1min". If no metric is specified, the default is seconds. You may not put any whitespace between the value and the metric.

You may also tie an animation's beginning time to the beginning or end of another animation. Example 11-4 shows two circles; the second one will start expanding as soon as the first one has stopped shrinking. Figure 11-4 shows the important stages of the animation.

Example 11-4. Synchronization of animations

```
<circle cx="60" cy="60" r="30" style="fill: #f9f; stroke: gray;">
    <animate id="c1" attributeName="r" attributeType="XML"
        begin="0s" dur="4s" from="30" to="10" fill="freeze"/>
</circle>

<circle cx="120" cy="60" r="10" style="fill: #9f9; stroke: gray;">
    <animate attributeName="r" attributeType="XML"
        begin="c1.end" dur="4s" from="10" to="30" fill="freeze"/>
</circle>
```

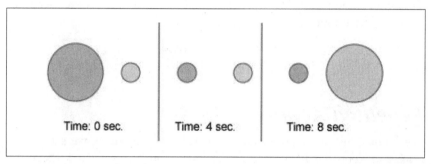

Figure 11-4. Stages of synchronized animations

It is also possible to add an offset to this synchronization. To make an animation start two seconds after another animation, you would use a construction of the form `begin="otherAnim.end+2s"`. (You may add whitespace around the plus sign.) The offset must be positive; to make an animation's start point `begin="otherAnim.end-2s"` would require the computer to look into the future, and there is no such thing as Psychic Vector Graphics. In Example 11-5, the second circle begins to grow one and a fourth seconds after the first circle begins shrinking.

Example 11-5. Synchronization of animations with offsets

```
<circle cx="60" cy="60" r="30" style="fill: #f9f; stroke: gray;">
    <animate id="c1" attributeName="r" attributeType="XML"
        begin="0s" dur="4s" from="30" to="10" fill="freeze"/>
</circle>

<circle cx="120" cy="60" r="10" style="fill: #9f9; stroke: gray;">
    <animate attributeName="r" attributeType="XML"
        begin="c1.begin+1.25s" dur="4s" from="10" to="30" fill="freeze"/>
</circle>
```

Now that we know about synchronizing animations, we can introduce the end attribute, which sets an end time for an animation. This is *not* a substitute for the dur attribute! The following animation will start six seconds after the page loads, and will last for twelve seconds or until an animation named otherAnim ends; whichever comes first.

```
<animate attributeName="width" attributeType="XML"
    begin="6s" dur="12s" end="otherAnim.end"
    from="10" to="100" fill="freeze"/>
```

You can, of course, set the value of end to a number; this is useful for halting an animation partway through so that you can see if everything is in the right place. This is how we were able to create Figure 11-3. The following animation starts at six seconds, and should last for twelve seconds, but is halted at nine seconds.

```
<animate attributeName="width" attributeType="XML"
    begin="6s" dur="12s" end="9s"
    from="10" to="100" fill="freeze"/>
```

Repeated Action

The animations we've produced so far occur exactly once; we set fill to freeze to keep the final stage of the animation. If we want to have the object return to its pre-animation state, we omit the attribute. (This is equivalent to setting fill to the default value of remove.)

Two other attributes allow you to repeat an animation. The first of them, repeatCount, is set to an integer value telling how many times you want a particular animation to repeat. The second, repeatDur, is set to a time telling how long the repetition should last. If you want an animation to repeat until the user leaves the page, set either repeatCount or repeatDur to the value indefinite. The animation in Example 11-6 shows two circles. The upper circle moves from left to right in two repetitions of five seconds each. The second circle moves from right to left for a total of eight seconds.

Example 11-6. Example of repeated animation

```
<circle cx="60" cy="60" r="30" style="fill: none; stroke: red;">
    <animate attributeName="cx" attributeType="XML"
        begin="0s" dur="5s" repeatCount="2"
        from="60" to="260" fill="freeze"/>
</circle>

<circle cx="260" cy="130" r="30" style="fill: #ccf; stroke: black;">
    <animate attributeName="cx" attributeType="XML"
        begin="0s" dur="5s" repeatDur="8s"
        from="260" to="60" fill="freeze"/>
</circle>
```

Just as it was possible to synchronize an animation with the beginning or ending of another animation, we can tie the start of one animation to the start of a specific repetition of another animation. You give the first animation an id, then set the begin of the second animation to id.repeat(count), where count is a number beginning at zero for the first repetition. In Example 11-7, we have an upper circle moving from left to right three times, requiring five seconds for each repetition. The lower square will go right to left only once, and will not begin until halfway through the second repetition. (We use an offset to achieve this effect.)

Example 11-7. Synchronizing an animation with a repetition

```
<circle cx="60" cy="60" r="30"
    style="fill: none; stroke: red;">
    <animate id="circle-anim" attributeName="cx" attributeType="XML"
        begin="0s" dur="5s" repeatCount="3"
        from="60" to="260" fill="freeze"/>
</circle>

<rect x="230" y="100" width="60" height="60"
    style="fill: #ccf; stroke: black;">
    <animate attributeName="x" attributeType="XML"
        begin="circle-anim.repeat(1) + 2.5s" dur="5s"
        from="230" to="30" fill="freeze"/>
</rect>
```

The set Element

All of these animations have modified numeric values over time. You may want to set a non-numeric attribute or property though. For example, you might want an initially invisible text item to become visible at a certain time; there's no real need for both a from and to. Thus, we have the convenient shorthand of the <set> element, which needs only a to attribute and the proper timing information. Example 11-8 shrinks a circle down to zero, then reveals text one-half second after the circle is gone.

Example 11-8. Example of set element

```
<circle cx="60" cy="60" r="30" style="fill: #ff9; stroke: gray;">
    <animate id="c1" attributeName="r" attributeType="XML"
        begin="0s" dur="4s" from="30" to="0" fill="freeze"/>
</circle>

<text text-anchor="middle" x="60" y="60" style="visibility: hidden;">
    <set attributeName="visibility" attributeType="CSS"
        to="visible" begin="4.5s" dur="1s" fill="freeze"/>
    All gone!
</text>
```

The animateColor Element

The `<animate>` element doesn't work with colors, since a color is not represented as a simple numeric value. Instead, the special `<animateColor>` element fills that purpose. Its `from` and `to` attributes are color values, as described in Chapter 3, in the section "stroke Color." In Example 11-9 we animate the fill and stroke colors of a circle, changing the fill from light yellow to red and the gray outline to blue. Both animations start two seconds after the page loads; this gives you time to see the original colors.

Example 11-9. Example of animateColor

```
<circle cx="60" cy="60" r="30"
        style="fill: #ff9; stroke: gray; stroke-width: 10;">
    <animateColor attributeName="fill"
        begin="2s" dur="4s" from="#ff9" to="red" fill="freeze"/>
    <animateColor attributeName="stroke"
        begin="2s" dur="4s" from="gray" to="blue" fill="freeze"/>
</circle>
```

 If you have several animations for a particular object, one animation can refer to the previous one with the keyword prev. We could rewrite the preceding example as Example 11-10. Tying two related animations together with prev lets you change them both by editing just the first one.

Example 11-10. Use of the prev keyword in animation

```
<circle cx="60" cy="60" r="30"
        style="fill: #ff9; stroke: gray; stroke-width: 10;">
    <animateColor attributeName="fill"
        begin="2s" dur="4s" from="#ff9" to="red" fill="freeze"/>
    <animateColor attributeName="stroke"
        begin="prev.begin" dur="4s" from="gray" to="blue" fill="freeze"/>
</circle>
```

The animateTransform Element

Just as `<animate>` doesn't work with colors, it doesn't work with rotate, translate, scale, or skew transformations either, since they're all "wrapped up" inside the `transform` attribute. The `<animateTransform>` element comes to the rescue. You set its `attributeName` to `transform`. The `type` attribute's value then specifies the transformation whose values should change (one of `translate`, `scale`, `rotate`, `skewX`, or `skewY`). The `from` and `to` values are specified as appropriate for the transform that you're animating.

Example 11-11 stretches a rectangle from normal scale to a scale of four times in the horizontal direction and two times in the vertical direction. Note that we've centered the rectangle around the origin so it doesn't move as it scales; we place it inside a <g> so it can be translated to a more convenient location. Figure 11-5 shows the beginning and end of the animation.

Example 11-11. Example of animateTransform

```
<g transform="translate(120,60)">
<rect x="-10" y="-10" width="20" height="20"
    style="fill: #ff9; stroke: black;">
    <animateTransform attributeType="XML"
        attributeName="transform" type="scale"
        from="1" to="4 2"
        begin="0s" dur="4s" fill="freeze"/>
    Stretch
</rect>
</g>
```

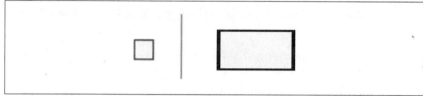

Figure 11-5. animateTransform—before and after

If you intend to animate more than one transformation, you must use the additive attribute. The default value of additive is replace, which replaces the specified transformation in the object being animated. This won't work in a series of animations, since the second animation would override the first one. By setting additive to sum, SVG will accumulate the transformations. Example 11-12 stretches and rotates the rectangle; the before and after pictures are in Figure 11-6.

Example 11-12. Example of multiple animateTransform elements

```
<rect x="-10" y="-10" width="20" height="20"
    style="fill: #ff9; stroke: black;">
    <animateTransform attributeName="transform" attributeType="XML"
        type="scale" from="1" to="4 2"
        additive="sum" begin="0s" dur="4s" fill="freeze"/>
    <animateTransform attributeName="transform" attributeType="XML"
        type="rotate" from="0" to="45"
        additive="sum" begin="0s" dur="4s" fill="freeze"/>
</rect>
```

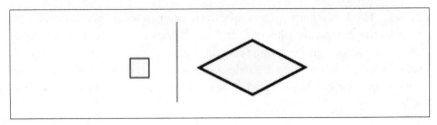

Figure 11-6. Multiple animateTransforms—before and after

The animateMotion Element

By using `translate` with the `<animateTransform>` element, you can cause an object to animate along a straight-line path. The `<animateMotion>` element lets you do this as well; additionally, it allows you to animate an object along an arbitrary path.

If you insist on using `<animateMotion>` for straight-line motion, you simply set the `from` and `to` attributes, assigning them each a pair of (*x*, *y*) coordinates. Example 11-13 moves a grouped circle and rectangle from (0,0) to (60,30).

Example 11-13. Animation along a linear path

```
<g>
    <rect x="0" y="0" width="30" height="30" style="fill: #ccc;"/>
    <circle cx="30" cy="30" r="15" style="fill: #cfc; stroke: green;"/>
    <animateMotion from="0,0" to="60,30" dur="4s" fill="freeze"/>
</g>
```

If you want a more complex path to follow, use the `path` attribute instead; its value is in the same format as the `d` attribute in the `<path>` element. Example 11-14, adapted from the SVG specification, animates a triangle along a cubic Bézier curve path.

Example 11-14. Animation along a complex path

```
<!-- show the path along which the triangle will move -->
<path d="M50,125 C 100,25 150,225, 200, 125"
        style="fill: none; stroke: blue;"/>

<!-- Triangle to be moved along the motion path.
    It is defined with an upright orientation with the base of
    the triangle centered horizontally just above the origin. -->
<path d="M-10,-3 L10,-3 L0,-25z" style="fill: yellow; stroke: red;">
    <animateMotion
        path="M50,125 C 100,25 150,225, 200, 125"
        dur="6s" fill="freeze"/>
</path>
```

As you can see in Figure 11-7, the triangle stays upright throughout its entire path.

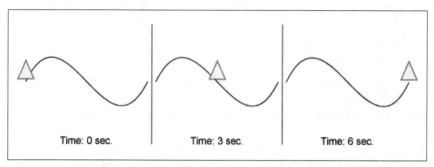

Figure 11-7. animateMotion along a complex path

If you would prefer that the object tilt so its x-axis is always parallel to the slope of the path, just add the rotate attribute with a value of auto to the <animateMotion> element. Example 11-15 shows the SVG and Figure 11-8 shows screenshots taken at various stages of the animation.

Example 11-15. Animation along a complex path with auto-rotation

```
<!-- show the path along which the triangle will move -->
<path d="M50,125 C 100,25 150,225, 200, 125"
      style="fill: none; stroke: blue;"/>

<!-- Triangle to be moved along the motion path.
   It is defined with an upright orientation with the base of
   the triangle centered horizontally just above the origin. -->
<path d="M-10,-3 L10,-3 L0,-25z" style="fill: yellow; stroke: red;" >
   <animateMotion
      path="M50,125 C 100,25 150,225, 200, 125"
      rotate="auto"
      dur="6s" fill="freeze"/>
</path>
```

Put simply, when you leave off the rotate attribute, you get the default value of zero, and the object acts like a hot-air balloon floating along the path. If you set rotate to auto, the object acts like a car on a roller coaster, tilting up and down as the path does.

You can also set rotate to a numeric value, which will set the rotation of the object throughout the animation. Thus, if you wanted an object rotated 45 degrees no matter what direction the path took, you'd use rotate="45".

In Example 11-15, we drew the path in blue so that it was visible, and then duplicated the path in the <animateMotion> element. You can avoid

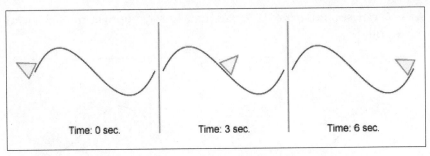

Figure 11-8. animateMotion along a complex path with auto-rotation

this duplication by adding an <mpath> element within the <animateMotion> element. The <mpath> will contain an xlink:href attribute that references the path you want to use. This also comes in handy when you have one path you wish to use to animate multiple objects. Here's the preceding example, rewritten as Example 11-16, using <mpath>.

Example 11-16. Motion along a complex path using mpath

```
<path id="cubicCurve" d="M50,125 C 100,25 150,225, 200, 125"
      style="fill: none; stroke: blue;"/>

<path d="M-10,-3 L10,-3 L0,-25z" style="fill: yellow; stroke: red;" >
    <animateMotion dur="6s" rotate="auto" fill="freeze">
        <mpath xlink:href="#cubicCurve"/>
    </animateMotion>
</path>
```

Using Links in SVG

To this point, you, the author of the SVG document, have made all the decisions about a graphic. You decide what a static image should look like, and if there are any animations, you decide when they start and stop. In this section, we will see how to hand some of that control over to the person who is viewing your document.

The easiest sort of interactivity to provide is linking, accomplished with the <a> element. By enclosing a graphic in this element, it becomes active; when clicked, you go to the URL specified in the xlink:href attribute. You can link to another SVG file or, depending upon your environment, a web page. In Example 11-17, clicking the word "Cat" will link to an SVG drawing of a cat; clicking the red, green, and blue shapes will link to the World Wide Web Consortium's SVG page. All the items within the second link are individually linked to the same destination, not the entire bounding box. When you test this example and move the cursor between the shapes, you will see that those areas are not linked.

Example 11-17. Links in SVG

```
<a xlink:href="cat.svg">
    <text x="100" y="30" style="font-size: 12pt;">Cat</text>
</a>

<a xlink:href="http://www.w3.org/SVG/">
    <circle cx="50" cy="70" r="20" style="fill: red;"/>
    <rect x="75" y="50" width="40" height="40" style="fill: green;"/>
    <path d="M120 90, 140 50, 160 90 Z" style="fill: blue;"/>
</a>
```

It's worth noting that xlink:href has a namespace prefix; though this attribute is duplicated in the SVG specification, it belongs to the XLink specification. The SVG DTD handles the namespace declaration.

Scripting SVG

The next step up from linking—and it's a big step—is scripting. You can write a program in ECMA Script (the European Computer Manufacturer's Association standard version of what is commonly called JavaScript) to interact with an SVG graphic. Interaction occurs when graphic objects respond to events.

Objects can respond to mouse events associated with clicking the mouse button: click, mousedown, and mouseup;[*] events associated with moving the mouse: mouseover (the mouse pointer is within the object), mouseout (the mouse pointer leaves the object), and mousemove; events associated with an object's status: load (the object has been fully parsed and is ready to render); and the non-standardized events associated with pressing keys: keydown and keyup.

 The names listed here are the names of the events. We'll be using attributes to specify the functions which should handle the events. These event handler attributes begin with the word on. Thus, onclick is an attribute whose value specifies a function that handles a click event.

To allow an object to respond to an event, you add an oneventName attribute to the element in question. The value of the attribute will be an ECMA Script statement, usually a function call. This function usually takes

---

[*] A click event is defined as a mousedown followed by a mouseup; all three are different events, and cannot be used synonymously.

the reserved word evt as one of its parameters. evt has properties and methods that describe the event that has occurred. The three methods you will use most often are getTarget(), which returns a reference to the graphic object that is responding to this event, and getClientX() and getClientY(), which return the *x*- and *y*- coordinates of the mouse when the event occurred. A value of (0,0) indicates the upper left corner of the SVG viewport. These functions return the position in the viewer window regardless of any zoom or pan that the user may have done.

Changing Attributes of a Single Object

The simplest type of event handling is where an event occurring on object *X* modifies some attribute of that object. Let's look at Example 11-18, which makes a circle respond to the mouseover event by making the circle's radius larger. The circle will respond to the mouseout event by making the radius smaller.

Example 11-18. Basic scripting—changing a single object

```
<script type="text/ecmascript"> ❶
<![CDATA[ ❷
function enlarge_circle(evt) ❸
{
    var circle = evt.getTarget(); ❹

    circle.setAttribute("r", 50); ❺
}

function shrink_circle(evt) ❻
{
    var circle = evt.getTarget();

    circle.setAttribute("r", 25);
}
// ]]> ❼
</script>

<circle cx="150" cy="100" r="25" fill="red" ❽
    onmouseover="enlarge_circle(evt)" ❾
    onmouseout="shrink_circle(evt)"/>

<text x="150" y="175" style="text-anchor: middle;">
    Mouse over the circle to change its size.
</text>
```

❶ The beginning <script> tag indicates that you are preparing to leave the world of SVG/XML and enter the ECMA Script environment. The type attribute tells which scripting language you are using.

❷ In XML, the less than sign introduces a tag, and the ampersand symbol is used for escaping characters (see Appendix A in the section "Entity References"). Since ECMA Script isn't XML, we want to turn off this special behavior. The <![CDATA[tells XML to stop treating the less than and ampersand symbols as special; they become ordinary content, which is the way ECMA Script likes it. This completes our exit from the SVG/XML world and immerses us in the ECMA Script environment.

❸ The first function, enlarge_circle, takes one parameter; the event that triggered the call.

❹ We use the evt.getTarget to return a reference to the graphic object that triggered the event, and store it in variable circle

❺ To change an attribute of a graphic object, call the object's **setAttribute** function with two parameters: the name of the attribute you wish to change, and its new value. setAttribute is a void function; it returns no value. There is a corresponding getAttribute function which takes as its parameter the name of the attribute; it returns a string representation of the attribute's current value. These functions are part of the DOM, or Document Object Model. The DOM is a standard API for accessing, modifying, and rearranging the elements in an XML document.

❻ This function, patterned exactly like the previous one, will set the r attribute of the event's target to 25.

❼ The]]> ends the <![CDATA[on the second line of the script. It returns the less than and ampersand to their special XML status, just in time for </script> on the next line, which leaves ECMA Script and returns you to the SVG/XML world. The leading slashes on line 16 introduce an ECMA Script comment, ensuring that the remainder of the line is not interpreted as part of the script. (This is not necessary with version 2.0 Adobe plugin, but other XML applications may require the slashes.)

❽ Since we will be setting an attribute to change the color, we specify the fill color with a presentation attribute. We can't use style, because its setting overrides the value of a presentation attribute.

❾ Here is our bridge between the SVG world and the ECMA Script world. The onmouseover event handler will call enlarge_circle, and the onmouseout event handler will call shrink_circle. In this context, evt is provided by the SVG viewer environment.

Changing Attributes of Multiple Objects

Sometimes you will want an event that occurs on object A to affect attributes of both object A and some other object B. Example 11-19 shows possibly the world's crudest example of SVGcommerce. Figure 11-9 shows a T-shirt whose size changes as the user clicks each labeled button. The currently selected size button is highlighted in light yellow.

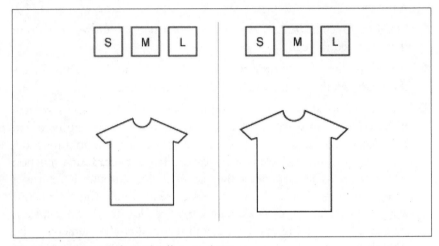

Figure 11-9. Screenshots of different selections

Example 11-19. Changing multiple objects in a script

```
<svg width="400" height="250"  viewBox="0 0 400 250"
    onload="init(evt)"> ❶

<script type="text/ecmascript">
<![CDATA[

var scaleChoice = 1; ❷
var scaleFactor = new Array( 1.25, 1.5, 1.75 );

function init( evt )
{
    transformShirt();
}

function setScale( n )
{
    obj = svgDocument.getElementById( "scale" + scaleChoice ); ❸
    obj.setAttribute( "fill", "white" );
    scaleChoice = n;
    obj = svgDocument.getElementById( "scale" + scaleChoice );
    obj.setAttribute( "fill", "#ffc" );
    transformShirt();
```

Example 11-19. Changing multiple objects in a script (continued)

```
}

function transformShirt( )
{
    var obj = svgDocument.getElementById( "shirt" ); ❹
    obj.setAttribute( "transform",
        "scale(" + scaleFactor[scaleChoice] + ")"
    );
    obj.setAttribute( "stroke-width",
        1 / scaleFactor[scaleChoice] );
}

// ]]>
</script>

<defs>
    <path id="shirt" ❺
        d="M -6 -30, -32 -19, -25.5 -13, -22 -14, -22 30, 23 30,
            23 -14, 26.5 -13, 33 -19, 7 -30
            A 6.5 6 0 0 1 -6 -30"
        fill="white" stroke="black"/> ❻
</defs>

<use xlink:href="#shirt" x="150" y="150"/>

<g onclick="setScale(0)"> ❼
<rect id="scale0" x="100" y="10" width="30" height="30"
    fill="white" stroke="black"/>
<text x="115" y="30" text-anchor="middle">S</text>
</g>

<g onclick="setScale(1)">
<rect id="scale1" x="140" y="10" width="30" height="30"
    fill="#ffc" stroke="black"/> ❽
<text x="155" y="30" text-anchor="middle">M</text>
</g>

<g onclick="setScale(2)">
<rect id="scale2" x="180" y="10" width="30" height="30"
    fill="white" stroke="black"/>
<text x="195" y="30" text-anchor="middle">L</text>
</g>

</svg>
```

❶ As soon as the document finishes loading, the load event occurs, and the onload handler will call the init function, passing it the event information. Most scripts will use this event handler to make sure that all their variables are set up properly.

❷ This script works by keeping track of which button (S, M, or L) has been chosen, and indexing into the corresponding entry in the scale-Factor array. The default is index number one, medium.

❸ svgDocument is a reference to the entire SVG document, and we'll be using its properties and methods to access the parts of the document that we need. This entire script hinges on the use of the document's getElementById function. getElementById takes a string as its parameter, and returns the object which has that string as its id. The setScale function finds the currently chosen button and turns its fill color to white. It then updates the current choice, and changes that button's fill color to light yellow. Finally, it updates the image of the shirt.

❹ In addition, the transformShirt function calls on the document's getElementById to access the graphic object with id of shirt, and changes its transform attribute to the proper scale. It also sets the stroke-width to the reciprocal of the scaling factor so the stroke width of the shirt's border always equals one.

❺ Here's the shirt; it's centered around (0,0) so it will appear to expand around its center.

❻ Since we're changing the attributes in the script, we have to use pre-sentation attributes here instead of styles. (If we used styles, they would override any attribute settings.)

❼ Each of the buttons will call the setScale function when clicked; the parameter gives the index for the scaling factor, and each button's <rect> element is named with the corresponding number at the end.

❽ The default button has a background set to light yellow when the document first loads.

Dragging Objects

Let us expand this example by adding "sliders" that can be dragged to set the color of the shirt, as shown in Figure 11-10.

We'll need a few more global variables in the script. The first of these, slideChoice, tells which slider (0, 1, or 2) is currently being dragged; its initial value is -1, meaning that no slider is active. We'll also use an array called rgb to hold the percent of red, green, and blue; the initial values are all 100, since the shirt is initially white.

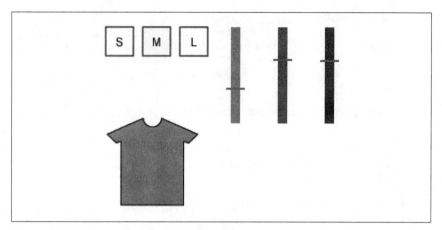

Figure 11-10. Screenshot of color sliders

```
var slideChoice = -1;
var rgb = new Array( 100, 100, 100);
```

We now draw the sliders themselves. The color bar and the slide indicator are drawn on a white background, and they are grouped together. The id attribute goes on the indicator <line> element, since its *y*-coordinate will be changing. The event handlers will be attached to the enclosing <g> element. The group will then capture the mouse events that happen on any of its child elements. (This is why we drew the white background; the mouse will still track even if you drag outside the colored bar.)

```
<g onmousedown="startColorDrag(0)"
    onmouseup="endColorDrag()"
    onmousemove="doColorDrag(evt,0)"
    transform="translate( 230, 10 )">
    <rect x="-10" y="-5" width="40" height="110" style="fill: white;"/>
    <rect x="5" y="0" width="10" height="100" style="fill: red;"/>
    <line id="slide0" x1="0" y1="0" x2="20" y2="0"
        style="stroke: gray; stroke-width: 2;"/>
</g>

<g onmousedown="startColorDrag(1)"
    onmouseup="endColorDrag()"
    onmousemove="doColorDrag(evt,1)"
    transform="translate( 280, 10 )">
    <rect x="-10" y="-5" width="40" height="110" style="fill: white;"/>
    <rect x="5" y="0" width="10" height="100" style="fill: green;"/>
    <line id="slide1" x1="0" y1="0" x2="20" y2="0"
        style="stroke: gray; stroke-width: 2;"/>
</g>

<g onmousedown="startColorDrag(2)"
    onmouseup="endColorDrag()"
    onmousemove="doColorDrag(evt,2)"
```

```
                transform="translate( 330, 10 )">
                <rect x="-10" y="-5" width="40" height="110" style="fill: white;"/>
                <rect x="5" y="0" width="10" height="100" style="fill: blue;"/>
                <line id="slide2" x1="0" y1="0" x2="20" y2="0"
                    style="stroke: gray; stroke-width: 2;"/>
        </g>
```

The corresponding functions are as follows:

```
/*
 * Stop dragging the current slider (if any)
 * and set the current slider to the one specified.
 * (0 = red, 1 = green, 2 = blue)
 */
function startColorDrag( which )
{
    endColorDrag( );
    slideChoice = which;
}


/*
 * Set slider choice to -1, indicating that no
 * slider is begin dragged.
 */
function endColorDrag( )
{
    slideChoice = -1;
}


/*
 * Move the specified slider in response to the
 * mousemove event.
 */
function doColorDrag( evt, which )
{
    /*
     * If no slider is active, or the event is on a
     * slider other than the active one, do nothing
     */
    if (slideChoice < 0 || slideChoice != which)
    {
        return;
    }

    /*
     * Get the slider indicator line object, and the
     * mouse position (relative to the top of the color bar)
     */
    var obj = evt.getTarget();
    var pos = evt.getClientY() - 10;

    /* Clamp values to range 0..100 */
    if (pos < 0) { pos = 0; }
    if (pos > 100) { pos = 100; }
```

```
/* Move the slider line to the new mouse position */
obj = svgDocument.getElementById( "slide" + slideChoice );
obj.setAttribute("y1", pos );
obj.setAttribute("y2", pos );

/* Calculate the new color value for this slider */
rgb[slideChoice] = 100-pos;

/*
 * Put together all the color values and
 * change the shirt's color accordingly.
 */
var colorStr = "rgb(" + rgb[0] + "%," +
    rgb[1] + "%," + rgb[2] + "%)";
obj = svgDocument.getElementById( "shirt" );
obj.setAttribute("fill", colorStr );
}
```

There's only one minor point to take care of—the document will respond to an onmouseup only if it occurs within the slider area. So, if you click the mouse on the red color bar, drag the mouse down to the shirt, then release the mouse button, the document will be unaware of it. When you then move the mouse over the red slider again, it will still follow the mouse. To solve this problem, we insert a transparent rectangle that completely covers the viewport, and have it respond to a mouseup event by calling stopColorDrag. It will be the first, and therefore bottom-most object in the graphic. To make the rectangle as unobtrusive as possible, it will be set to style="fill: none;". "But wait," you interject. "A transparent area cannot respond to an event!" No, ordinarily it can't, but we can set the pointer-events attribute to visible, meaning that an object can respond to events as long as it is visible, no matter what its opacity.*

```
<rect x="0" y="0" width="400" height="300" style="fill: none;"
    onmouseup="endColorDrag()"
    pointer-events="visible"/>
```

Modifying Text

Although the sliders do give us the interactivity we want, it's hard to judge the percentages by eye. We'd much prefer to show the percentages of red, green, and blue below each slider, as depicted in Figure 11-11.

---

* Other values for pointer-events let you respond to an object's events in the filled areas only (fill), outline areas only (stroke), or the fill and outline together (painted), whether visible or not. Corresponding attribute values of visibleFill, visibleStroke, and visible-Painted take the object's visibility into account as well.

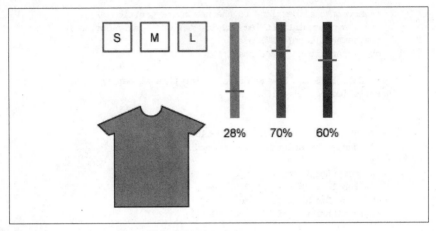

Figure 11-11. Screenshot of labeled color sliders

Here's the SVG for the text underneath the red slider; the ones under the blue and green slider have ids of pct1 and pct2. This element will go into a separate group from the color bar and slider line so that it does not also become clickable.

```
<text id="pct0" x="10" y="120"
    style="font-size: 9pt; text-anchor: middle;">100%</text>
```

The number we want to change as we drag the mouse is not an attribute; it's the child of the <text> element, so we can't use setAttribute to modify the text. Instead, we have to create a new text node and insert it into the document tree in place of the old one. Here's the code that we add at the end of the doColorDrag function. The first line retrieves the <text> element. (The obj variable has already been declared, so we don't need to say var again.) The second line asks the document to create a new text node whose content is the percentage of the currently chosen slider. This text node needs to be placed in its proper location within the document tree. That's what the third line does; it replaces the first child of the text element with the newly created node.

```
obj = svgDocument.getElementById( "pct" + slideChoice );
var newText = svgDocument.createTextNode( rgb[slideChoice] + "%" );
obj.replaceChild( newText, obj.getFirstChild() );
```

You can do much more than simply modify the text in a document. You can remove elements, change their order, or even create new elements with attributes and add them to the document under script control. A list of the functions that manipulate the Document Object Model are listed in Appendix E of the World Wide Web Consortium's Document Object Model (DOM) Level 1 Specification at *http://www.w3.org/TR/1998/REC-DOM-Level-1-19981001*. A detailed explanation of what the functions do can be found in the *DOM Reference* chapter of *XML in a Nutshell*, by Elliotte Rusty Harold and W. Scott Means. Although the examples in that book use Java rather than ECMA Script, the explanations apply to both.

Interacting with an HTML Page

It is possible to embed an SVG graphic in a web page using the `<embed>` element. The relevant attributes are the `src` for the graphic (a URL), the `width` and `height` of the graphic, and the `type` attribute, which will be `image/svg+xml`. Once embedded, you can add code to the SVG script and the HTML page's script so they can communicate with one another.

Our goal in this example is to embed the preceding SVG example into a web page. This web page will have a form that lets users type in the red, green, and blue percentages. The values they enter will be reflected in the sliders. If they adjust the sliders, the values in the form fields will be updated accordingly.

Here is the HTML document, with references to the (as yet unwritten) `updateSVG` function. This function will take the input field number and the value currently within the input field.

```
<html>
<head>
<title>SVG and HTML</title>
</head>

<body bgcolor="white">
<h2>SVG and HTML</h2>
```

```
<div align="center">
<embed src="shirt_interact.svg"
    width="400" height="250"
    type="image/svg+xml" />

<form name="rgbForm">
    Red: <input id="fld0" type="text" size="5" value="100"
              onchange="updateSVG(0, this.value)" />% <br />
    Green: <input id="fld1" type="text" size="5" value="100"
              onchange="updateSVG(1, this.value)" />% <br />
    Blue: <input id="fld2" type="text" size="5" value="100"
              onchange="updateSVG(2, this.value)" />%
</form>
</div>
</body>
</html>
```

Here is the script that goes into the head of the HTML document. Function updateSVG checks to see that the input value is an integer (it will discard any decimal part), and, if so, calls setShirtColor. setShirtColor is actually a reference to a function that exists in the SVG document, and it will be the SVG document's responsibility to connect the function to this HTML reference.

Function updateHTMLField will be called from the SVG document's script. It will receive a form field number and a percent value, which it will display in the appropriate form field.

```
<script language="Javascript">
<!--
function updateSVG( which, amount )
{
    amount = parseInt( amount );
    if (!isNaN(amount))
    {
        window.setShirtColor( which, amount );
    }
}

function updateHTMLField( which, percent )
{
    document.rgbForm[ "fld" + which ].value = percent;
}
// -->
</script>
```

Let us now turn our attention to the SVG document. The parent of the document is the browser window in which it is embedded. We use the reserved word parent in the init function to connect the SVG document's svgSetShirtColor function to the HTML page's setShirtColor reference.

```
function init( evt )
{
    parent.setShirtColor = svgSetShirtColor;
    svgDocument = evt.getTarget().getOwnerDocument();
    transformShirt();
}
```

Since there are now effectively two ways to set the color values, we'll make things more modular by rewriting doColorDrag to call the new svgSetShirtColor function:

```
function doColorDrag( evt, which )
{
    /*
     * If no slider is active, or the event is on a
     * slider other than the active one, do nothing
     */
    if (slideChoice < 0 || slideChoice != which)
    {
        return;
    }

    /*
     * Get the slider indicator line object, and the
     * mouse position (relative to the top of the color bar)
     */
    var obj = evt.getTarget();
    var pos = evt.getClientY() - 10;

    /*
     * Since pos=0 is at the 100% point on the scale,
     * take 100-pos and send that to svgSetShirtColor
     * along with the slider number.
     */
    svgSetShirtColor( which, 100 - pos );
}
```

Function svgSetShirtColor will do what the remainder of doColorDrag used to do, with two major differences. It uses the slider number that it is given as the first parameter, not the global sliderChoice variable. The second parameter is now a percentage; in the original version it was the *y*-position of the mouse. These are the sorts of changes you have to make when you decide to modularize simple code that was written for an ad-hoc example.

```
function svgSetShirtColor( which, percent )
{
    var obj;
    var colorStr;
    var newText;

    /* Clamp values to range 0..100 */
```

```
    if (percent < 0) { percent = 0; }
    if (percent > 100) { percent = 100; }

    /* Move the slider line to the new mouse position */
    obj = svgDocument.getElementById( "slide" + which );
    obj.setAttribute("y1", 100-percent );
    obj.setAttribute("y2", 100-percent );
    rgb[which] = percent;

    /*
     * Put together all the color values and
     * change the shirt's color accordingly.
     */
    colorStr = "rgb(" + rgb[0] + "%," +
        rgb[1] + "%," + rgb[2] + "%)";
    obj = svgDocument.getElementById( "shirt" );
    obj.setAttribute("fill", colorStr );

    /*
     * Change text to match slider position
     */
    obj = svgDocument.getElementById( "pct" + which );
    newText = svgDocument.createTextNode( rgb[which] + "%" );
    obj.replaceChild( newText, obj.getFirstChild());
}
```

This code accomplishes the HTML to SVG communication. Our last step is to communicate from SVG back to HTML if the user decides to choose colors with the slider. Rather than continuously update the HTML fields, we have made the design decision to update the HTML when dragging stops. We add the boldface code to function **endColorDrag**. The result is shown in Figure 11-12 (see additional color insert; the screenshot has been edited to eliminate unnecessary whitespace).

```
function endColorDrag( )
{
    /*
     * If a slider was being moved, send the slider number
     * and its value back to the updateHTMLField function
     * in the parent web browser window.
     */
    if (slideChoice >= 0)
    {
        parent.updateHTMLField( slideChoice, rgb[slideChoice] );
    }

    /* In any case, nobody's being dragged now */
    slideChoice = -1;
}
```

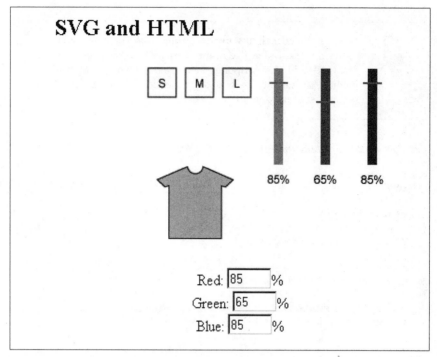

Figure 11-12. Screenshot of HTML and SVG interaction

Scripting and Animation Together

Scripting and animation can work together. You can start an animation in response to an event, and you can use the beginning, end, or repetition of an animation to invoke a function. Example 11-20 shows a trapezoid and a button. When you click the button, a message saying "Animation in progress" appears, and the trapezoid rotates 360 degrees. When it finishes rotating, the message disappears. Relevant screenshots are shown in Figure 11-13.

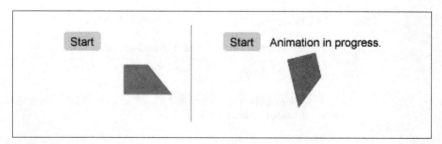

Figure 11-13. Screenshot of two stages of scripting with animation

The numbered callouts in the example are in conceptual order, not text order. I've found it easier to design the SVG first and add the scripting later. One advantage of this method is that I can see if the base drawing looks good before I start making it react to events.

Example 11-20. Scripting and Animation Together

```
<script type="text/ecmascript">
<![CDATA[

function init( evt )
{
    /* initialization code goes here */
}

function setMessage( visStatus )  ❶
{
    var message = svgDocument.getElementById( "message" );
    message.setAttribute( "visibility", visStatus );
}

// ]]>
</script>

<g id="button">  ❷
    <rect x="10" y="10" width="40" height="20" rx="4" ry="4"
        style="fill: #ddd;"/>
    <text x="30" y="25" style="text-anchor: middle;">Start</text>
</g>

<text id="message" x="60" y="25" visibility="hidden">  ❸
    Animation in progress.
</text>

<g transform="translate(100, 60)">
    <path d="M-25 -15, 0 -15, 25 15, -25 15 Z"
        style="stroke: gray; fill: #699;">

        <animateTransform id="trapezoid" attributeName="transform"
            type="rotate" from="0" to="360"
            begin="button.click"  ❹
            dur="6s"
            onbegin="setMessage('visible')"  ❺
            onend="setMessage('hidden')"/>
    </path>
</g>
```

❶ Here's the function, which takes the visibility status that was passed to it, and sets the message's visibility property accordingly.

❷ The start button is a simple rounded rectangle with text. The entire group gets the id.

❸ The message, initially hidden. Again, we use a presentation attribute here rather than a style, since we'll be modifying the attribute.

❹ Instead of giving the begin time for the animation in terms of seconds, we begin whenever a click event is detected on the button object. Since we're waiting for the event, we use click rather than the event handler attribute onclick.

❺ The next two lines *are* event handlers, so they begin with the prefix on. When the animation begins (onbegin), we call setMessage with the argument 'visible'; when it ends (onend) we call the same function with the argument 'hidden'.*

Animation via Scripting

Because SMIL2 animation is integrated with SVG, your animations become part of the document structure. Since it's all XML, animated SVG documents remain easy for humans to read and for XML tools to process. The addition of scripting, as we showed in the preceding section, makes it possible to add some user interaction with an animation.

While animation can handle most of the things you'll want to move, there are some things the animation elements can't do easily. For example, it's hard to change a <path> dynamically. We're not talking about making an object move along a path (<animateMotion>); we want the path itself to change over time. The path isn't a transformation, so <animateTransform> won't work; in addition, it's not a simple numeric value, so we can't use <animate>. We'll have to use scripting instead.

Example 11-21 uses scripting alone to repeatedly change the d attribute of the path over time. The key to doing animation via scripting is the set-Interval function. setInterval sets an "alarm clock" to go off repeatedly at regular intervals. When the alarm goes off, the scripting engine performs the ECMA Script statements you want. The simplest form is:

---

* The event handler onrepeat is invoked each time an animation repeats after the first iteration.

```
timer_variable =
    setInterval( "ECMA Script function",
        interval time in milliseconds);
```

This function returns a reference to the timer that it set. You should save that reference in a global variable so that other functions can access it. You call setInterval once, and, the *ECMA Script function* you've specified will be called every *interval* milliseconds. The repetition will continue until you call clearInterval(*timer_variable*).

Example 11-21 shows a cubic Bézier curve. When the user clicks the start button, we'll move the control points every tenth of a second for five seconds (fifty movements in all). The control points will move towards each other in the *x* direction starting at five pixels per interval. They will move away from each other in the *y* direction at three-fourths of a pixel per interval. Note especially the boldfaced line and its commentary!

Example 11-21. Animating a path with scripting

```
<svg width="300" height="200" viewBox="0 0 300 200"
    onload="init(evt)">
<script type="text/ecmascript">
<![CDATA[

/* Starting coordinates for both control points */
var cp1 = new Array( 100, 50 );
var cp2 = new Array( 200, 200 );

var moveLimit = 50;      // total number of moves to make
var currentMove = 0;     // current number of moves

var deltaX;              // X movement amount
var deltaY;              // Y movement amount

var delay = 100;         // one-tenth second

var timer;               // store the alarm clock

function init( evt )
{
    /* do any global initialization here */
}

/*
 * Initialize movement; set control points back to their
 * starting positions, set the current number of moves
 * to zero, and set an interval timer to move the
 * control points every "delay" milliseconds.
 */
function setupMove()
{
```

Example 11-21. Animating a path with scripting (continued)

```
    var i;

    currentMove = 0;
    deltaX = 5;          /* start X at five pixels per interval */
    deltaY = 0.75;       /* start Y at 3/4 pixels per interval */
    setGraphicInfo();
    timer = setInterval( "moveControlPoints()", delay );
}

function setGraphicInfo()
{
    var obj;
    var pathString;

    /*
     * Construct a path that describes a cubic
     * Bezier curve using the current coordinates
     * for the control points.
     */
    pathString = "M 50 120 C " +
        (cp1[0] + currentMove * deltaX) + " " +
        (cp1[1] - currentMove * deltaY) + ", " +
        (cp2[0] - currentMove * deltaX)  + " " +
        (cp2[1] + currentMove * deltaY) + ", " +
        "250, 120";

    obj = svgDocument.getElementById( "cubic" );
    obj.setAttribute( "d", pathString );
}

function moveControlPoints()
{
    currentMove++;        // we've done one more move
    setGraphicInfo();     // adjust the control points and path

    /*
     * If we have finished moving, clear the timer, which
     * will stop the repeated wake-up calls.
     */
    if (currentMove >= moveLimit)
    {
        clearInterval( timer );
    }
}

function stopMovement()
{
    clearInterval( timer );
}

/*
 * setInterval expects its first argument to be found in
```

Example 11-21. Animating a path with scripting (continued)

```
* the main window. We oblige it by creating a reference
* to this script's moveControlPoints function as a
* window property
*/
window.moveControlPoints = moveControlPoints;

// ]]>
</script>

<g id="button" onclick="setupMove();">
    <rect x="10" y="10" width="40" height="20" rx="4" ry="4"
        style="fill: #ddd;"/>
    <text x="30" y="25" style="text-anchor: middle;">Start</text>
</g>

<g id="button" onclick="stopMovement()">
    <rect x="70" y="10" width="40" height="20" rx="4" ry="4"
        style="fill: #ddd;"/>
    <text x="90" y="25" style="text-anchor: middle;">Stop</text>
</g>

<path id="cubic" style="stroke: blue; fill: none;"
    d="M 50 120 C 100 50, 200 200, 250 120" />

</svg>
```

Figure 11-14 shows the path in its initial and final states.

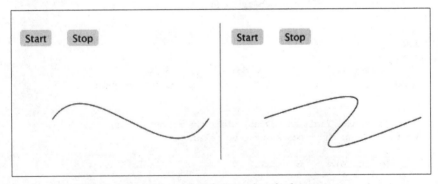

Figure 11-14. Beginning and ending of scripted path change

In this example, the moveControlPoints function didn't need any parameters. Let's say the function needed two parameters, pathColor and path-
StrokeWidth To ensure that moveControlPoints got those parameters
every time it was called, we would add them at the end of our call to set
up the interval timer:

```
timer = setInterval("moveControlPoints()", delay,
    pathColor, pathStrokeWidth );
```

setInterval* is the *only* safe way to script repeated actions with a delay interval. Using setInterval is like leaving a message with a desk clerk at a hotel to give you a wake-up call every hour; between calls you are free to sleep or do other things. In scripting terms, this kind of code leaves the computer free to do other tasks between actions:

```
function startGoodAction()
{
    timer = setInterval( "doGoodAction()", delay );
}

function doGoodAction()
{
    obj.setAttribute( "x", value );
    value = value + increment;
    repetitions = repetitions + 1;
    if ( repetitions == limit )
    {
        clearInterval( timer );
    }
}
```

Beginning programmers will often do something like this:

```
function doBadAction()
{
    obj.setAttribute( "x", value );
    value = value + increment;
    if ( repetitions != limit )
    {
        waitCount = 0;
        while (waitCount < waitLimit)
            waitCount++;
        doBadAction();
    }
}
```

---

* Or its variant, setTimeout, which sets the timer to go off exactly once. The generic model for calling this function is:

    timer_variable = setTimeout("*action_function(parameters)*", *delay*);

Use clearTimeout(*timer_variable*) to cancel a pending timer event.

This technique is akin to constantly looking at your watch and asking, "Is it time yet?" This gives you no time to sleep or do anything else. In an SVG script, it gives the computer little chance to attend to other tasks. Additionally, this uses a *recursive* style, which, if not carefully controlled, can consume your system resources faster than you can say "Error: stack overflow."

Though the preceding example was a simple one, this technique has great power. If you choose to use scripting to do animation, you will then have available all the interactivity features of scripting; you can make animation dependent on mouse position or complex conditions involving multiple variables. If you're doing simple animation, we recommend that you use SVG's animation elements.

12

Generating SVG

The previous chapters have described the major features of SVG. All the examples have been relatively modest and have been written in an ordinary text editor. For graphics of any great complexity, though, few people will write the SVG from scratch. Let's face it: almost nobody does this by hand. Instead, graphic designers and programmers will use some sort of graphic tool that outputs SVG, or they will take existing raw data and convert it to SVG. If you're dealing with a graphic program's output that is already in SVG format, you can sit back and relax; all the heavy lifting has been done for you. If you ever take a look at the SVG that it generated, it may be hard to read. Some programs, for example, may not use groups (the <g> element) efficiently or they may not optimize paths. When you use these programs, you are trading off the ease of generating SVG for the absolute control you have when you write the entire file by hand.

If you're dealing with data that's already in XML format, you may just need to extract the pertinent data and plug it into an SVG framework. In such a case, you can use tools that implement Extensible Stylesheet Language Transformations (XSLT). If the data is in XML but needs a fair amount of processing, you may need to write a program in Java or some other language to do the conversion. Luckily, you can take advantage of freely available XML parsers to do the busy work for you.

Finally, if you are dealing with data that isn't in XML format, you have some work ahead of you. If you have raw data in either ASCII or binary form you may need to write custom code to do the conversion.

In this chapter, we'll start with a custom Perl program to convert geographical mapping data that's not in an XML format to an SVG file. Then

we will use Java to convert a representation of a matrix in Mathematical
Markup Language (MathML) format to SVG. The last example will use
XSLT to convert an XML-formatted aeronautical weather report to SVG.

Using Perl to Convert Custom Data to SVG

If anyone lives a life that revolves around graphics display, it's a map-
maker. Cartographers are finding XML markup in general and SVG in particular to be excellent vehicles for putting data into a portable format. At
present, though, much of the data that is currently available is in custom
or proprietary formats. One of these is the proprietary format developed
by Earth Science Resources, Inc. for use by their ARC/INFO Geographic
Information System. Data created in this system can be exported in an
ASCII "ungenerate" form. Such a file contains a series of polygon descriptions, followed by a line with the word END on it. Each polygon starts with
a line that consists of an integer polygon identification number and the x-
and y-coordinates of the polygon's centroid. This line is followed by the
x- and y-coordinates of the polygon's vertices, one vertex per line. A line
with the word END on it marks the end of the polygon. Here is a sample
file:

```
      1        -0.122432044171565E+03        0.378635608621089E+02
   -0.122418712172884E+03        0.378527169597E+02
   -0.122434402770255E+03        0.378524342437443E+02
   -0.122443301934511E+03        0.378554484803880E+02
   -0.122446316168374E+03        0.378610463416856E+02
   -0.122438565286068E+03        0.378683666259093E+02
   -0.122418712172884E+03        0.378527169591107E+02
END
      2        -122.36                  37.82
   -122.378               37.826
   -122.377               37.831
   -122.370               37.832
   -122.378               378.826
END
END
```

Converting such a file to SVG is a simple task. The only twist is that ARC/
INFO stores data in Cartesian coordinates, so we will have to flip the y-
coordinates upside-down. The program we'll write in Perl will run from
the command line as follows:

```
perl mapSVG.pl input-file width decimals
```

Where the `width` is the width of the resulting SVG graphic in pixels, and `decimals` is an optional parameter giving the number of digits you wish to keep after the decimal point in coordinate values.

The program will start with a utility subroutine that grabs one token at a time from the input file:

```perl
#!/usr/bin/perl

#
#   @line_buffer is a global
#
@line_buffer = ( );

#
#   Input file PFILE is opened in main
#   part of program.
#
sub get_token
{
    my ($data);
    if ((scalar @line_buffer) == 0) # out of data?
    {
        $data = <PFILE>;              # grab a line
        $data =~ s/^\s+//;            # get rid of leading...
        $data =~ s/\s+$//;            # ...and trailing whitespace
        @line_buffer = split /\s+/, $data;  # place tokens into a buffer
    }
    $data = shift @line_buffer;       # take one token out and return it
    return $data;
}
```

Here is the remainder of the program:

```perl
if (scalar @ARGV < 2) ❶
{
    print "Usage: $0 polygon_file width (decimals)\n";
    print "polygon_file - file in ARC/INFO ungenerate format\n";
    print "width - desired width of output SVG\n";
    print "decimals - optional # of decimal places to keep\n";
    print "Output SVG goes to standard output.\n";
    exit 0;
}

open PFILE, $ARGV[0] or die("Cannot open polygon file $ARGV[1]");

$width = $ARGV[1];
if ($width <= 0)
{
    die("Width must be greater than zero.");
}

$n_decimals =  ((scalar @ARGV) == 3) ? $ARGV[2] : 0;
```

```
#
#   Set maxima and minima ❷
#
$min_x = 1.0e100;
$min_y = 1.0e100;
$max_x = -1.0e100;
$max_y = -1.0e100;

undef @polygon_list;

#
#   a file consists of a series of polygon numbers followed
#   by pairs of x-y coordinates. Each polygon is finished
#   by an END token, and the file is marked by an END token
#   instead of a polygon number
#
while (1)    ❸
{
    $polygon_number = get_token();
    last if ($polygon_number =~ /END/);

    undef   @polygon;   # the storage area for this particular polygon

    while (1)
    {
        $x = get_token();
        last if ($x =~ /END/);
        $y = get_token();
        push @polygon, $x, $y;

        #
        # keep track of maximum and minimum coordinates
        #
        if ($x < $min_x) {$min_x = $x;}
        if ($x > $max_x) {$max_x = $x;}
        if ($y < $min_y) {$min_y = $y;}
        if ($y > $max_y) {$max_y = $y;}
    }

    push @polygon_list, [ @polygon ];  ❹

}

close PFILE;

print STDERR "max x=$max_x  min x=$min_x width=", $max_x-$min_x, "\n";
print STDERR "max y=$max_y  min y=$min_y height=", $max_y-$min_y, "\n";

#
#   Figure out the scaling factor to make the width equal to
#   the one specified on the command line, then find the
#   corresponding height.
#
$scale = $width / ($max_x - $min_x );
```

```
$height = ($max_y - $min_y) * $scale;

#
#    Round it up so viewport and viewBox are integral
#
$height = int ($height + 0.5);

#
#    Insert extra pixels for padding
#
$pad_width = $width + 30;
$pad_height = $height + 30;

#
#    Begin constructing the SVG file
#
print <<"SVG_HEADER";        ❺
<!DOCTYPE svg PUBLIC "-//W3C//DTD SVG 1.0//EN"
    "http://www.w3.org/TR/2001/REC-SVG-20010904/DTD/svg10.dtd">

<svg width="$pad_width" height="$pad_height"
    viewBox="0 0 $pad_width $pad_height">
<title>Map constructed from $ARGV[0]</title>
<g transform="translate(15,15)" style="fill: none; stroke: black;">
SVG_HEADER

$poly_num = 1;
foreach $poly (@polygon_list)
{
    $n = 0;
    print qq%<polyline id="poly$poly_num" points="\n\t%;

    #
    #    get rid of first coordinate
    #
    shift @$poly;        ❻
    shift @$poly;

    foreach $coord (@$poly)
    {
        if ($n % 2 == 0)      # x-coordinate
        {
            $coord = ($coord - $min_x) * $scale;
        }
        else                  # flip y-coordinate
        {
            $coord = ($max_y - $coord) * $scale; ❼
        }
        if ($n_decimals != 0)
        {
            $coord = int($coord * (10**$n_decimals))/(10**$n_decimals);
        }

        print $coord, " ";
```

```
    #
    #    to avoid excessively long text lines, place only
    #    eight coordinates on a line
    #
    $n = ($n+1) % 8;
    print "\n\t" if ($n == 0);
  }
  print qq%" />\n%;    # close off the <path> element
  $poly_num++;
}


#
#  Close off open tags to end the file.
#
print "</g>\n</svg>\n";
```

❶ Obligatory argument retrieval and error checking.

❷ Set up variables. The initial maxima and minima are huge enough to handle the coordinates of a map of anything smaller than a minor galaxy. The variable @polygon_list will be a list of the polygons, each of which will itself be represented as a list.

❸ The outer loop reads polygon ID numbers, and the inner loop stores the coordinates in the @polygon list.

❹ The square brackets are very important. They create an anonymous list to contain the coordinates in @polygon, and that list is pushed onto @polygon_list. Without the brackets, it would simply append all the coordinates, ungrouped, to the end of @polygon_list.

❺ This line prints, verbatim, all the text up to (but not including) a line that begins with the literal SVG_HEADER. Because SVG_HEADER is enclosed in double quotes, we can use variable interpolation in the verbatim text.

❻ The $poly loop variable, set in the outer foreach, is an entire list, which is why it must be preceded by an @ to be accessed properly.

❼ We had to keep track of the maximum and minimum *x*-coordinate to calculate the width scaling factor properly; we kept track of the maximum *y*-coordinate so we could change from Cartesian coordinates to SVG style coordinates.

Running this program with the data for the state of Michigan with an output width of 250 pixels and a decimal accuracy of three digits produces Figure 12-1. Michigan was chosen because it requires several polygons to draw, and its outline is more visually interesting than that of, say, Colorado. The data came from the U.S. Census Bureau Cartographic Boundary Files Web Site at *http://www.census.gov/geo/www/cob/*.

Figure 12-1. Conversion from ARC/INFO ungenerate to SVG

Using Java to Convert XML to SVG

While preparing to write Appendix D, I had to decide how to produce the matrix equations. At that time, I didn't have a definitive answer from the production staff at O'Reilly on the format in which to submit the data. I decided on an ad-hoc subset of MathML,* an XML application for describing the presentation and content of mathematical information. This choice gave me the maximum flexibility; I would not be tied down to a proprietary equation editor, conversion to the TEX typesetting language (a common format among publishers) could be done with a trivial XSLT file, and using MathML would give me an example for this chapter.

This example is atypical in that the majority of its output will be <text> elements. It is further atypical in that it is not a general tool, nor is it intended to be. It is, however, typical in that it shows how to parse an input XML document, construct a new XML document in memory and output through a serializer.

The subset of MathML in this example is as follows; all the elements are container elements:

MathML element	Contains
<math>	root element of a MathML document
<mrow>	a formula
<mtable>	a matrix (table)

---

* You can find out about the complete MathML specification at *http://www.w3.org/Math/*.

MathML element	Contains
<mtr>	a matrix row
<mtd>	a data cell within a row
<mn>	a numeric value
<mi>	an identifier (variable)
<mo>	a mathematical operator
<msub>	subscripted content

The general outline of the program is as follows:

- Parse the input document to create a Document Object Model in memory.

- Find the matrix with the maximum number of rows; this will determine the height of the output SVG document.

- Go through the formula and output matrices and operators as specified. These become elements in an SVG Document that is also built in memory.

- If the operator is a parenthesis, make it as large as the largest matrix in the entire formula. This is an assumption that saves a lot of programming, and works well for most of the formulas that the appendix needs.

- Each matrix is output within an SVG group (<g>) element. Again, for ease of programming, the matrix is drawn with its upper left corner at (0,0) and will be moved to its proper place with a `translate` transformation. The square brackets that enclose the matrix's values will be drawn with a <path> element.

- Once the SVG document has been built, use the parser's `serialize` method to create an output file.

This program uses the Xerces XML parser from the Apache Software Foundation; you may download it and read its documentation at *http://xml.apache.org*. The program starts with a large number of imports from the standard Java libraries and the Xerces parser.

```
import java.awt.Dimension;
import java.awt.Font;
import java.awt.FontMetrics;
import java.awt.Graphics;
import java.awt.Image;
import java.awt.image.BufferedImage;

import java.io.OutputStreamWriter;
import java.io.PrintWriter;
import java.io.UnsupportedEncodingException;
```

```
import java.io.IOException;

import org.w3c.dom.Attr;
import org.w3c.dom.Document;
import org.w3c.dom.DocumentFragment;
import org.w3c.dom.DocumentType;
import org.w3c.dom.DOMImplementation;
import org.w3c.dom.Element;
import org.w3c.dom.NamedNodeMap;
import org.w3c.dom.Node;
import org.w3c.dom.NodeList;
import org.w3c.dom.Text;

import org.apache.xerces.parsers.DOMParser;
import org.apache.xml.serialize.XMLSerializer;
import org.apache.xml.serialize.OutputFormat;
```

The program itself starts with constants that establish the default line
height, font height for normal characters, font height for subscripted characters, extra height at the top and bottom of the image, and extra horizontal space between items:

```
public class MLtoSVG {

    //
    // Constants
    //

    private static final int LINE_HEIGHT = 24;
    private static final int FONT_HEIGHT = 14;
    private static final int SUBSCRIPT_HEIGHT = 12;
    private static final int EXTRA_HEIGHT = 10;
    private static final int X_SPACING = 2;
```

Although global variables are considered a mortal sin, I was too lazy to
pass parameters ad infinitum, so the input document, output document,
and root element of the output document became properties of the class:

```
    /** The "before" document */
    protected Document mlDocument;

    /** The "after" document */
    protected Document svgDocument;

    /** Permanent pointer to SVG document's root element */
    protected Element svgRoot;
```

The **main** function is entirely straightforward:

```
    public static void main(String argv[]) {

        // is there anything to do?
        if ( argv.length == 0 ) {
```

```
                System.err.println("usage: java MLtoSVG filename");
                System.exit(1);
        }

        // vars
        MLtoSVG converter = null;

        converter = new MLtoSVG();
        converter.readDocument( argv[0] );
        converter.processDocument( );
        converter.printDocument( );

    } // main(String[])
```

The **readDocument** method will set up a DOM parser and read the input
file. However, the standard parser does not come with any error handling.
Thus, there is the following implementation of the `org.xml.saxEr-`
`rorHandler` abstract class. Rather than reinvent the wheel, I stole the code
outright from a sample program that came with the Xerces parser, and
produced the **ParserErrorHandler** class.

```
/*
 * ParserErrorHandler code taken from DOMWriter.java sample code.
 * Copyright (c) 1999 The Apache Software Foundation.  All rights
 * reserved. For licensing details, see http://www.apache.org/
 */

import org.xml.sax.ErrorHandler;
import org.xml.sax.SAXException;
import org.xml.sax.SAXParseException;
import org.xml.sax.SAXNotRecognizedException;
import org.xml.sax.SAXNotSupportedException;

public class ParserErrorHandler
    implements ErrorHandler {

    //
    // ErrorHandler methods
    //

    /** Warning. */
    public void warning(SAXParseException ex) {
        System.err.println("[Warning] "+
                        getLocationString(ex)+": "+
                        ex.getMessage());
    }

    /** Error. */
    public void error(SAXParseException ex) {
        System.err.println("[Error] "+
                        getLocationString(ex)+": "+
                        ex.getMessage());
```

```
        }

        /** Fatal error. */
        public void fatalError(SAXParseException ex) throws SAXException {
            System.err.println("[Fatal Error] "+
                               getLocationString(ex)+": "+
                               ex.getMessage());
            throw ex;
        }

        //
        // Private methods
        //

        /** Returns a string of the location. */
        private String getLocationString(SAXParseException ex) {
            StringBuffer str = new StringBuffer();

            String systemId = ex.getSystemId();
            if (systemId != null) {
                int index = systemId.lastIndexOf('/');
                if (index != -1)
                    systemId = systemId.substring(index + 1);
                str.append(systemId);
            }
            str.append(':');
            str.append(ex.getLineNumber());
            str.append(':');
            str.append(ex.getColumnNumber());

            return str.toString();

        } // getLocationString(SAXParseException):String

    }
```

This program uses the Xerces parser explicitly; some programs will put the parser name in a string and then instantiate it dynamically:

```
String parserName = "org.apache.xerces.parsers.DOMParser";
DOMParser parser =
(DOMParser)Class.forName(parserName).newInstance();
```

I didn't see the need for this, so I constructed the parser directly, set the error handler, parsed the file whose name is the input to the **readDocument** function, and saved the document that is returned. Failure at any point is met with a stack trace.

```
        /** Read the input document and construct a document tree. */
        public void readDocument( String uri ) {
            ParserErrorHandler errHandler = new ParserErrorHandler();
            mlDocument = null;
            try {
```

```
            DOMParser parser = new org.apache.xerces.parsers.DOMParser();
            parser.setErrorHandler( errHandler );
            parser.parse( uri );
            mlDocument = parser.getDocument();
        } catch ( Exception e ) {
            e.printStackTrace(System.err);
        }
    } // readDocument(String)
```

Similarly, once the SVG document has been built, sending it to a file—in this case the standard output—is no great challenge. Most of this function performs error-checking.

```
    public void printDocument( ) {

        if (svgDocument == null)
        {
            return;
        }
        PrintWriter out = null;
        try{
            out =
            new PrintWriter(new OutputStreamWriter(System.out, "UTF8"));❶
        }
        catch (Exception e)
        {
            System.out.println("Error creating output stream");
            System.out.println(e.getMessage());
            System.exit(1);
        }
        OutputFormat oFormat = new OutputFormat( "xml", "UTF8", true );❷
        XMLSerializer serial = new XMLSerializer( out, oFormat );❸
        try
        {
            serial.serialize( svgDocument );
        }
        catch (java.io.IOException e)
        {
            System.out.println(e.getMessage());
        }
    }
```

❶ First, construct an output stream with your favorite encoding method.

❷ A serializer requires an output format. This constructor's three parameters are the output method (which is normally one of "xml", "html", or "text"); the character encoding, which should be "UTF8" to keep your international clients happy; and a Boolean that tells whether the output should be indented or not.

❸ The OutputFormat is used when creating the serializer.

This leaves the majority of the work to the processDocument function.

```
public void processDocument( )
{
    svgDocument = null;

    /* anything to do? */
    if (mlDocument == null)
    {
        return;
    }

    /* Create the output document */
    DOMImplementation dImplement = mlDocument.getImplementation();  ❶
    DocumentType dType = dImplement.createDocumentType(  ❷
        "svg",
        "-//W3C//DTD SVG 1.0//EN",
        "http://www.w3.org/TR/2001/REC-SVG-20010904/DTD/svg10.dtd"
    );
    svgDocument = dImplement.createDocument( null, "svg", dType);
    svgRoot = (Element) svgDocument.getDocumentElement();

    Element      mrowElement;    // store <mrow> element for ease
                                 //   of access
    NodeList     matrices;       // list of all <mtable> elements
    NodeList     rows;           // list of all <mtr> elements
    NodeList     nodes;          // immediate children of <mrow>
    int          i;              // ubiquitous counter

    /* current x  position while creating matrices */
    int currX = 0;

    /* maximum number of rows in any one matrix */
    int maxRows = 0;
    int totalHeight;

  ❸

    /* Find the first <mrow> node */
    nodes = mlDocument.getElementsByTagName("mrow");  ❹
    mrowElement = (Element) nodes.item(0);

    /* Find the maximum number of rows among all the matrices */
    matrices = mrowElement.getElementsByTagName("mtable");  ❺
    for (i = 0; i < matrices.getLength(); i++)
    {
        rows = ((Element) matrices.item(i)).getElementsByTagName("mtr");
        if (rows.getLength() > maxRows)
        {
            maxRows = rows.getLength();
        }
    }
```

```
                    /* Calculate total height */
                    totalHeight = maxRows * LINE_HEIGHT + EXTRA_HEIGHT;

                    /* Now create the SVG for the matrices and operators */
                    nodes = mrowElement.getChildNodes(); ⑥
                    for (i=0; i < nodes.getLength(); i++) ⑦
                    {
                        if (nodes.item(i).getNodeName().equals("mtable"))
                        {
                            currX += generateMatrix( nodes.item(i), currX, totalHeight );
                        }
                        else if (nodes.item(i).getNodeName().equals("mo"))
                        {
                            currX += generateOperator( nodes.item(i), currX, totalHeight );
                        }
                    }

                    currX += 2 * X_SPACING; // put some padding at the right

                    svgRoot.setAttribute("width", Integer.toString( currX )); ⑧
                    svgRoot.setAttribute("height", Integer.toString( totalHeight) );
                    svgRoot.setAttribute("viewBox",
                        "0 0 " + currX + " " + totalHeight);

                }
```

❶ The `processDocument` function starts by creating the SVG document. Since every parser implementation has its own way of storing the objects, you must ask the `DOMImplementation` class to give you the details.

❷ The implementation is asked to create a document. The `createDocumentType` function's parameters will be used when producing the `<!DOCTYPE>` in the output; you provide a root element name, and a public and system identifier for the DTD. The `createDocument` function's parameters are the namespace URI (in this case, none is needed), the name of the top-level document element, and the document type. The root element is retrieved for future reference by calling `getDocumentElement`.

❸ Now it's time to extract information from the MathML document. Among the methods you use to access information in the Document Object Model are the following:

NodeList getElementsByTag (DOMString *tagName*)

Calling *element*.`getElementsByTag("`*name*`")` returns a list of all the descendant nodes of the specified element that have the specified tag name. These are not just the child nodes; they are descendants at any depth, which is very advantageous in this program.

Node item (int *n*)
> Calling *nodeList*.item(*n*) retrieves node number *n* from the given node list.

NodeList getChildNodes ( )
> Calling *node*.getChildNodes( ) retrieves a list of all the immediate children of the given node.

short getNodeType ( )
> Calling *node*.getNodeType( ) returns an integer that tells which kind of node this is (element, text, CDATA, entity, etc.).

String getNodeName ( )
> Calling *node*.getNodeName( ) returns a string based on the node type. If the node is an element, the tag name is returned; if it's a text node, the string "#text" is returned.

Node getNextSibling ( )
> Calling *node*.getNextSibling( ) retrieves the given node's next sibling, or null if this is the last of the siblings. Sibling nodes are nodes that are all descendants of a common parent, listed in the order in which they appear in the document.

❹ The first <mrow> element encloses the entire matrix expression. The easiest way to find it is to grab all the tags and store the address of the first one. The code casts the results of the item call to **Element**. This is safe, since the node lists were constructed by calls that return only **Elements**.

❺ In order to center all the matrices vertically, we need to find the matrix with the largest number of rows. Presuming that there are no nested matrices, this is done by walking through each <mtable> element, extracting a list of all its <mtr> descendants, and checking that list's length. This maximum number of rows is used to calculate the *totalHeight* of the resulting graphic.

❻ We then call the getChildNodes function to retrieve a NodeList of all the immediate children of the <mrow> element.

❼ The program iterates through these children, generating a matrix when encountering an <mtable>, or an operator symbol when encountering an <mo> element. Everything else is ignored, which conveniently skips over the "hidden" text nodes that come from carriage returns between lines in the source file.

The generateMatrix and generateOperator create the output SVG. Once they are done, the *currX* variable will contain the total width of the graphic.

8 The `processDocument` function wraps up by using the `setAttribute` function to add the `width`, `height`, and `viewBox` attributes to the *svg-Root* variable.

`setAttribute` is just one of the functions used to populate the new document. Other functions include:

Element createElement (DOMString *elementName*)

Calling *document*.`createElement("`*name*`")` returns an element which belongs to the specified document, but is *not* part of the document hierarchy (it hasn't been placed in the "tree" yet).

Text createTextNode (String *data*)

Calling *document*.`createTextNode("`*value*`")` returns a text node whose content is the given value. Again, this node belongs to the specified document, but it is *not* part of the document hierarchy (it hasn't been placed in the "tree" yet).

void setAttribute (DOMString *data*, DOMString *value*)

Calling *element*.`setAttribute("`*attr*`", "`*value*`")` sets the particular attribute of the specified element to the given value. If the attribute already exists, any previous value it had is replaced with the new value.

Node appendChild (Node *newchild*)

Calling *parentNode*.`appendChild(`*newchild*`)` appends the given new child node to the child nodes of the parent node. It returns a reference to the new child node. This puts the node into the document hierarchy.

Node insertBefore (Node *newchild*, Node *refchild*)

Calling *parentNode*.`insertBefore(`*newChild*, *referenceChild*`)` inserts the new child node into the list of child nodes of the parent node just before the child node specified in the second parameter. The function returns a reference to the new child node. (The sample program doesn't use this function, but it's included here because it's generally useful.)

Let us now turn our attention to the `generateMatrix` function.

```
public int generateMatrix( Node mtableNode, int currX, int totalHeight )
{
    double      y;                    1
    int         x = 0;
    NodeList    rowList;      // list of all <mtr> elements
    NodeList    cellList;     // list of all <mtd> elements
    Element     newElement;   // a catch-all "new element"
    Element     gElement;     // a created <g> element
```

```
Element      startColumn;     // marks beginning of a column
Element      textElement;     // a created <text> element

int          nRows;           // number of rows in table
int          nCells;          // number of cells per row
int          i;               // ubiquitous loop counter
int          row, col;        // more counter variables
int          colWidth;        // maximum width of a column

Dimension    textInfo;        // holds text width and height
```

❷

```
rowList = ((Element) mtableNode).getElementsByTagName("mtr");
nRows = rowList.getLength();

/* Check to see that all rows have the same number of cells */
cellList = ((Element) rowList.item(0)).getElementsByTagName("mtd");
nCells = cellList.getLength();

for (i = 1; i < nRows; i++)
{
    cellList = ((Element) rowList.item(i)).getElementsByTagName("mtd");
    if (cellList.getLength() != nCells)
    {
        System.err.println("All rows must have " + nCells + " cells ");
        System.exit(1);
    }
}

y = (totalHeight - nRows * LINE_HEIGHT) / 2.0;    ❸

newElement = svgDocument.createElement("g");    ❹
newElement.setAttribute("transform",
    "translate(" + currX + ", " + y + ")" );
newElement.setAttribute("font-family", "sans-serif");
newElement.setAttribute("font-size",
    Integer.toString(FONT_HEIGHT));
gElement = (Element) svgRoot.appendChild( newElement );

newElement = svgDocument.createElement("path");    ❺
newElement.setAttribute("d",
    "M3 0h-3v" + (nRows*LINE_HEIGHT) +
        "h3");
newElement.setAttribute("fill", "none");
newElement.setAttribute("stroke", "black");

/* The next "nCells" siblings of this element ❻
   will be the first column of the matrix */
startColumn = (Element) gElement.appendChild( newElement );

/* Now get all the <mtd> cells in order */ ❼
cellList = ((Element) mtableNode).getElementsByTagName("mtd");

x = X_SPACING;
```

```
textElement = null;

for (col = 0; col < nCells; col++)
{
    Node      currNode;

    colWidth = 0;
    for (row = 0; row < nRows; row++)
    {
        currNode = cellList.item( row * nCells + col );
        newElement = svgDocument.createElement("text"); ❽
        textInfo = constructTextNode( newElement, currNode,
            FONT_HEIGHT );
        textElement = (Element) gElement.appendChild( newElement );
        textElement.setAttribute("y",
            Integer.toString( row * LINE_HEIGHT + textInfo.height ) );
        textElement.setAttribute("text-anchor", "middle");
        textElement.setAttribute("font-size",
            Integer.toString(FONT_HEIGHT));
        if (textInfo.width > colWidth)
        {
            colWidth = textInfo.width;
        }
    }

    /* go back and put in the "x" coordinates */ ❾
    startColumn = (Element) startColumn.getNextSibling();
    for (row = 0; row < nRows; row++)
    {
        startColumn.setAttribute("x",
            Double.toString( x + colWidth/2.0 ) );
        startColumn = (Element) startColumn.getNextSibling();
    }
    x += colWidth + X_SPACING;
    startColumn = textElement;

}

x += X_SPACING;
/* the closing bracket */ ❿
newElement = svgDocument.createElement("path");
newElement.setAttribute("d",
    "M" + (x-3) + " 0h3v" + (nRows*LINE_HEIGHT) +
    "h-3");
newElement.setAttribute("fill", "none");
newElement.setAttribute("stroke", "black");
startColumn = (Element) gElement.appendChild( newElement );

return x + 2*X_SPACING;
}
```

❶ We start off with a clump of declarations. I tend to use a lot of temporary variables so that I don't have to constantly call the DOM access functions.

❷ The function starts by extracting the number of rows in this matrix and seeing that all the rows have the same number of cells in them.

❸ After this sanity check, the function calculates where the top y coordinate of the matrix should be when the matrix is vertically centered.

❹ Once the top position of the matrix is known, the program creates a <g> element to enclose the matrix. The transform attribute positions it, and the font-family and font-size will apply to all the text in that matrix. We are using presentation attributes because it's easier to set them individually than to construct a string for the appropriate style attribute.

The resulting element is appended to the root element's children, and, for ease of future access, is stored in the variable *gElement*.

❺ The first thing inside the <g> is a <path> that draws the left bracket enclosing the matrix.

❻ Following the bracket, generateMatrix draws the matrix's cells column by column. Each cell will become a <text> element. As we insert each cell for a particular column into the output tree, we'll keep track of its text width. At the end of the column, we'll know the column's maximum width, and we will go back and update the x attributes of each of the <text> elements. This requires us to remember the starting point after which we began adding cells. That's why we had to save the position of the <path> element in *startColumn*.

❼ Here's the code that creates the cells for the entire matrix. Note that we grabbed all the <mtd> descendants of the <mtable> node. This bypasses any intervening elements, but that's OK since we don't have any nested tables.

❽ The actual task of building the cell contents is left to the construct-TextNode function; in this segment of the code we set the y, font-size, and text-anchor attributes of the cell.

❾ Here is the code that goes back to fill in the x attribute after each column is complete. The getNextSibling function proceeds through the text elements that were just added. Once this is done, we reset the *startColumn* variable to point to the very last *textElement* element we added, for its siblings will become the next column.

❿ Finally, the function creates another `<path>` element for the right bracket of the matrix, and the matrix has been generated. We return the total width of the matrix, plus a bit of extra padding.

Now let's look at the `constructTextNode` function. The way the program is set up, text may be subscripted within an `<msub>` element, which this function should handle. If the text is enclosed in `<mi>` or `<mn>` elements, `constructTextNode` ignores the tags and takes only the enclosed text. The parameters to `constructTextNode` are the destination node to which the text is to be added in the output tree, the parent source node that contains the original text, and the font size for the text.

```
public Dimension constructTextNode( Node destNode, Node parentNode,
    int size )
{
    NodeList    children = parentNode.getChildNodes();  ❶
    Node        currNode;
    int         i;
    Dimension   d = new Dimension(0, 0);
    Dimension   subDim;

    for (i=0; i < children.getLength(); i++ )
    {
        subDim = new Dimension(0,0);
        currNode = children.item(i);
        if (currNode.getNodeName().equals("#text"))     ❷
        {
            Text    textNode;
            String  value = currNode.getNodeValue();

            subDim = stringInfo( value, size );
            textNode = svgDocument.createTextNode( value );
            destNode.appendChild( textNode );
        }
        else if (currNode.getNodeName().equals("msub"))  ❸
        {
            Element newElement;
            newElement = svgDocument.createElement("tspan");
            newElement.setAttribute( "baseline-shift",
                "sub");
            newElement.setAttribute("font-size",
                Integer.toString(SUBSCRIPT_HEIGHT));
            newElement = (Element) destNode.appendChild( newElement );
            subDim = constructTextNode( newElement, currNode,
                SUBSCRIPT_HEIGHT );
        }
        else if (currNode.getNodeType() == Node.ELEMENT_NODE)  ❹
        {
            subDim = constructTextNode( destNode, currNode, size );
        }
```

```
            d.width += subDim.width;  ❺
            if (subDim.height > d.height)
            {
                d.height = subDim.height;
            }
        }
        return d;
    }

    public Dimension stringInfo( String str, int fontSize )  ❻
    {
        BufferedImage buffer = new BufferedImage(
            100, 100, BufferedImage.TYPE_INT_RGB);
        Graphics g = buffer.getGraphics();
        Font f = new Font("SansSerif", Font.PLAIN, fontSize);
        g.setFont( f );
        FontMetrics fm = g.getFontMetrics();

        return new Dimension( fm.stringWidth( str ), fm.getAscent() );
    }
```

❶ The function starts by getting all the immediate children of the source node and setting the total width and height of the text, stored in variable *d*, to zero.

❷ We look at each of the children of the current source node in turn. If the child is a text element, we create a text node for it, find its width and ascent height by calling **stringInfo**, and append it to the destination node's children.

❸ However, if the child is an <msub> element, we must create a <tspan> element in the output with a baseline-shift attribute for subscripting. We then recursively call **constructTextNode** to add all the enclosed text to this new <tspan> node.

❹ If it's not text and not subscripted, it's some other element node that we don't care to handle, so just do a recursive call to gather all its text and append it to the destination node.

❺ No matter what course of action we took, *subDim* now contains the width and height of the text that was appended. We add the width to the total and keep track of the maximum height.

❻ **constructTextNode** calls the **stringInfo** function to determine the width and ascent height of text. Because we don't know how an SVG viewer will render text, and thus can't determine its length exactly, we have to do the best we can. In this instance, we load the generic sans-serif font, set its size, get the font metrics, and use the results from that. Since the output will come from the Batik SVG viewer, which is also Java-based, it's reasonable to presume that the numbers will come out fairly close to the final results. `stringInfo` opens up an in-memory image in order to access a graphics environment.

The last function to consider is `generateOperator`, which contains no new DOM concepts. It checks to see if the first child of the <mo> element is a text node whose value is a left or right parenthesis. If so, the function produces an elliptical arc as tall as the largest matrix in the entire expression. Otherwise, it's some other mathematical operator, and is treated as plain text by calling the `constructTextNode` function.

```
public int generateOperator( Node moNode, int currX, int totalHeight )
{
    double      y;
    int         fontsize;
    Element     newElement, textElement;
    Dimension   textInfo;

    currX += X_SPACING;
    y = (totalHeight) / 2.0;

    fontsize = FONT_HEIGHT;
    if (moNode.getFirstChild().getNodeType() == Node.TEXT_NODE)
    {
        String str = moNode.getFirstChild().getNodeValue();
        if (str.equals( "(" ))
        {
            newElement = svgDocument.createElement("path");
            newElement.setAttribute( "d",
                "M" + (currX+12) + " 8 a12 " + y + " 0 0 0 " +
                    "0" + " " + (totalHeight-EXTRA_HEIGHT - 8) );
            newElement.setAttribute( "fill", "none");
            newElement.setAttribute( "stroke", "black" );
            svgRoot.appendChild( newElement );
            return 16 + X_SPACING;
        }
        else if (str.equals( ")" ))
        {
            newElement = svgDocument.createElement("path");
            newElement.setAttribute( "d",
                "M" + currX + " 8 a12 " + y + " 0 0 1 " +
                    "0" + " " + (totalHeight-EXTRA_HEIGHT - 8) );
            newElement.setAttribute( "fill", "none");
            newElement.setAttribute( "stroke", "black" );
            svgRoot.appendChild( newElement );
            return 10 + X_SPACING;
        }
    }

    newElement = svgDocument.createElement("text");
    textInfo = constructTextNode( newElement, moNode, fontsize );

    textElement = (Element) svgRoot.appendChild( newElement );
```

```
    if (fontsize != FONT_HEIGHT)
    {
        y = 0;
        textElement.setAttribute("stroke-width",
            Double.toString( (FONT_HEIGHT * 1.0 / fontsize )) );
    }
    textElement.setAttribute("transform",
        "translate(" + currX + ", " + (y+textInfo.height/2.0) + ")" );
    textElement.setAttribute("font-size",
        Integer.toString(fontsize));

    return textInfo.width + 2 * X_SPACING;
}
```

What do we get when we put this all together? The following MathML matrices:

```
<math>
<mrow>
<mo>(</mo>
<mtable>
<mtr>
    <mtd> <mi>x</mi><msub><mn>1</mn></msub> </mtd>
    <mtd> <mi>y</mi><msub><mn>1</mn></msub> </mtd>
    <mtd> <mi>1</mi> </mtd>
</mtr>
</mtable>
<mo>*</mo>
<mtable>
<mtr>
    <mtd> <mo>cos(</mo><mi>a</mi><mo>)</mo> </mtd>
    <mtd> <mo>-sin(</mo><mi>a</mi><mo>)</mo> </mtd>
    <mtd> <mn>0</mn> </mtd>
</mtr>

<mtr>
    <mtd> <mo>sin(</mo><mi>a</mi><mo>)</mo> </mtd>
    <mtd> <mo>cos(</mo><mi>a</mi><mo>)</mo> </mtd>
    <mtd> <mn>0</mn> </mtd>
</mtr>

<mtr>
    <mtd> <mn>0</mn> </mtd>
    <mtd> <mn>0</mn> </mtd>
    <mtd> <mn>1</mn> </mtd>
</mtr>
</mtable>
<mo>)</mo>
<mo>=</mo>
<mtable>
<mtr>
    <mtd> <mi>x</mi><msub><mn>2</mn></msub> </mtd>
    <mtd> <mi>y</mi><msub><mn>2</mn></msub> </mtd>
```

```
        <mtd> <mi>1</mi> </mtd>
    </mtr>
    </mtable>
    </mrow>
</math>
```

become this SVG:

```
<?xml version="1.0" encoding="UTF8"?>
<!DOCTYPE svg PUBLIC "-//W3C//DTD SVG 20001102//EN"
    "http://www.w3.org/TR/2000/CR-SVG-20001102/DTD/svg-20001102.dtd">
<svg height="82" viewBox="0 0 378 82" width="378">
    <path d="M14 8 a12 41.0 0 0 0 0 64" fill="none" stroke="black"/>
    <g font-family="sans-serif" font-size="14"
        transform="translate(18, 29.0)">
        <path d="M3 0h-3v24h3" fill="none" stroke="black"/>
        <text font-size="14" text-anchor="middle" x="15.5"
            y="15">x<tspan baseline-shift="sub" font-size="12">1</tspan>
        </text>
        <text font-size="14" text-anchor="middle" x="44.0"
            y="15">y<tspan baseline-shift="sub" font-size="12">1</tspan>
        </text>
        <text font-size="14" text-anchor="middle"
            x="68.5" y="15">1</text>
        <path d="M79 0h3v24h-3" fill="none" stroke="black"/>
    </g>
    <text font-size="14" transform="translate(106, 48.5)">*</text>
    <g font-family="sans-serif" font-size="14"
        transform="translate(115, 5.0)">
        <path d="M3 0h-3v72h3" fill="none" stroke="black"/>
        <text font-size="14" text-anchor="middle"
            x="28.5" y="15">cos(a)</text>
        <text font-size="14" text-anchor="middle"
            x="28.5" y="39">sin(a)</text>
        <text font-size="14" text-anchor="middle"
            x="28.5" y="63">0</text>
        <text font-size="14" text-anchor="middle"
            x="86.5" y="15">-sin(a)</text>
        <text font-size="14" text-anchor="middle"
            x="86.5" y="39">cos(a)</text>
        <text font-size="14" text-anchor="middle"
            x="86.5" y="63">0</text>
        <text font-size="14" text-anchor="middle"
            x="127.5" y="15">0</text>
        <text font-size="14" text-anchor="middle"
            x="127.5" y="39">0</text>
        <text font-size="14" text-anchor="middle"
            x="127.5" y="63">1</text>
        <path d="M138 0h3v72h-3" fill="none" stroke="black"/>
    </g>
    <path d="M262 8 a12 41.0 0 0 1 0 64" fill="none" stroke="black"/>
    <text font-size="14" transform="translate(274, 48.5)">>=</text>
    <g font-family="sans-serif" font-size="14"
        transform="translate(288, 29.0)">
```

```
<path d="M3 0h-3v24h3" fill="none" stroke="black"/>
<text font-size="14" text-anchor="middle" x="15.5"
    y="15">x<tspan baseline-shift="sub" font-size="12">2</tspan>
</text>
<text font-size="14" text-anchor="middle" x="44.0"
    y="15">y<tspan baseline-shift="sub" font-size="12">2</tspan>
</text>
<text font-size="14" text-anchor="middle"
    x="68.5" y="15">1</text>
<path d="M79 0h3v24h-3" fill="none" stroke="black"/>
    </g>
</svg>
```

which becomes Figure 12-2.

$$\left(\begin{bmatrix} x_1 & y_1 & 1 \end{bmatrix} * \begin{bmatrix} \cos(a) & -\sin(a) & 0 \\ \sin(a) & \cos(a) & 0 \\ 0 & 0 & 1 \end{bmatrix} \right) = \begin{bmatrix} x_2 & y_2 & 1 \end{bmatrix}$$

Figure 12-2. Sample converted from MathML to SVG

You can find out more about manipulating XML with Java in the aptly named book *Java & XML* by Brett McLaughlin, published by O'Reilly & Associates.

Using XSLT to Convert XML Data to SVG

Defining the Task

The final example in this chapter uses the Extensible Stylesheet Language Transformations (XSLT) to extract information from an XML file and insert it into an SVG file. The source data is in the Weather Observation Markup Format (OMF), defined at *http://zowie.metnet.navy.mil/~spawar/JMV-TNG/XML/OMF.html*. OMF is, for the most part, a wrapper for several different types of weather reports. The OMF elements add annotation, decoded information, and quantities calculated from the raw reports. Here is a sample report:

```
<Reports TStamp="997568716">
<SYN Title='AAXX' TStamp='997573600' LatLon='37.567, 126.967' BId='471080'
SName='RKSL, SEOUL' Elev='86'>
<SYID>47108</SYID>
<SYG T='22.5' TD='14.1' P='1004.1' P0='1014.1' Pd='0 0.1' Vis='22000'
```

```
Ceiling='INF' Wind='30-70, 1.5' WX='NOSIG' Prec=' ' Clouds='44070'>
32972 40703 10225 20141 30041 40141 50001 84070
</SYG></SYN>
</Reports>
```

Our objective is to extract the reporting station, the date and time, temperature, wind speed and direction, and visibility from the report. These data will be filled into the graphic template of Figure 12-3.

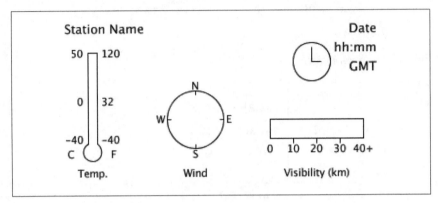

Figure 12-3. Graphic weather template

This example is atypical, in that all the information is contained in the attributes of the source XML rather than the content of the elements. Paradoxically, this makes our example typical, since real-world markup so often fails to follow the pristine examples found in textbooks or reference manuals. You'll eventually encounter such data, so it may as well be now. The OMF format attributes we're interested in are listed here, along with the plan for displaying them in the final graphic. The first two required attributes come from the <SYN> element, the rest are optional attributes from its child <SYG> element.

TStamp

> The timestamp in seconds since midnight, January 1, 1970 UTC. In the final graphic, the date and time will be represented in text, and the time will also be shown on an analog clock. The color of the clock face will be light yellow to indicate hours between 6 A.M. and 6 P.M., and light blue for evening and night hours.

SName

> The reporting station's call letters, possibly followed by a comma and the station's full name. The final graphic will represent this as text.

T

The air temperature in degrees Celsius. This will be displayed by coloring in the thermometer to the appropriate level. If the temperature is greater than zero, the coloring will be red; if less than or equal to zero, it will be blue.

Wind

A direction and speed, separated by a comma. The direction is measured in degrees; 0 indicates wind blowing from true north, and 270 indicates wind from the west. This will be represented by a line on the compass.

Wind direction may also be expressed as two numbers separated by a dash, indicating a range of directions. Thus, 0-40 indicates wind from the north to north-east. In this case, two dashed lines will be drawn on the compass.

The wind speed is expressed in meters per second. If two numbers are given, separated by a dash, the second number indicates the speed of gusts of wind. This information will be displayed in text form.

Vis

Surface visibility in meters, or the value INF for unlimited visibility. The final graphic will represent this by filling in a horizontal bar. Any visibility above 40 kilometers will be presumed to be unlimited.

How XSLT Works

To convert an OMF source file to its destination SVG format, we will create a list of specifications that tells which elements and attributes in OMF are of interest to us. These specifications will then detail what SVG elements to generate whenever we encounter an item of interest. If we were asking a human to do the transformation by hand, we could write out an English language description:

- Begin a new SVG document by typing this:

  ```
  <!DOCTYPE svg PUBLIC "-//W3C/DTD SVG 1.0//EN",
    "http://www.w3.org/TR/2001/REC-SVG-20010904/DTD/svg10.dtd">
  ```

- Go through the source document. As you find each element, look for instructions on how to process it.

- To process the <Reports> element, type the following into a text editor, then process any sub-elements as specified in comments.

```
<svg viewBox="0 0 350 200" height="200" width="350">
    <!-- process any SYN elements you find within this element -->
</svg>
```

- To process a <SYN> element, type this text and fill in the blanks:

```
<text font-size="10pt" x="10" y="20">
<!-- fill in the value of the SName attribute -->
</text>

<!-- process any SYG elements you find within this element -->
```

- To process a <SYG> element:

  1. Extract the value of the T attribute, and use that value when following the instructions for "how to draw a thermometer."

  2. Extract the value of the Wind attribute, and use that value as you follow the instructions for "how to draw a wind compass."

  3. (etc.)

- To draw a thermometer, calculate the height of the bar as 50 minus the value you got from the T attribute, and use that result where you see the italicized text as you type the following:

```
<path
    d = "M 25 height 25 90
    A 10 10 0 1 0 35 90
    L 35 height Z"
    style="stroke: none; fill: {$tint};"/>
<path
    d= "M 25 0 25 90 A 10 10 0 1 0 35 90 L 35 0 Z"
    style="stroke: black; fill: none;"/>
```

- To draw a wind compass (etc.).

Rather than writing our specifications in English and handing them to a human to perform, we will write the specifications in the XSLT markup format. We'll hand the XSLT file, along with the OMF file, to the Apache Software Foundation's Xalan processor, and it will process elements and fill in the blanks to produce an output SVG file. Here is a quick English-to-XSLT translation guide.

>

English	XSLT

Process an *element* element	`<xsl:template match="element">`
	`    <!-- output to produce -->`
	`</xsl:template>`

English	XSLT
Process any *items* within the current element	`<xsl:apply-templates select="items"/>`
Fill in the value of an *item*	`<xsl:value-of select="item"/>`

Use the value of an *item* as a variable named *var*	`<xsl:variable name="var">`
	   `<!-- instructions to produce item's value -->`
	`</xsl:variable>`

Developing an XSL Stylesheet

We'll add details as we proceed, but this gives us more than enough to start. The XSLT file begins like this:

```
<xsl:stylesheet version="1.0"
    xmlns:xsl="http://www.w3.org/1999/XSL/Transform">

<xsl:output method="xml" indent="yes" ❶
    doctype-public="-//W3C//DTD SVG 1.0//EN"
    doctype-system=
        "http://www.w3.org/TR/2001/REC-SVG-20010904/DTD/svg10.dtd"/>

<xsl:template match="Reports"> ❷
<svg width="350" height="200" viewBox="0 0 350 200">
    <defs>
        <path id="wind-line" d="M 40 40 h 25"
            style="stroke: black; fill: none;"/>
    </defs>
    <xsl:apply-templates select="SYN"/> ❸
</svg>
</xsl:template>
```

❶ The `<xsl:output>` specifies that the output will be an XML file and that we want it indented nicely. It also generates the appropriate `<!DOCTYPE ...>` instruction.

❷ `<xsl:template>` directs the XSLT processor to generate the specified output whenever it encounters a `<Reports>` element. This template will be called only once, since there's only one such element in the source document. It creates the outermost `<svg>` element and a `<defs>` element for later use.

❸ After outputting the `<svg>` and `<defs>`, `<xsl:apply-templates>` directs the processor to find any child `<SYN>` elements and generate whatever its `<xsl:template>` element specifies.

And how is the `<SYN>` element to be processed? Like this:

```
<xsl:template match="SYN">
    <!-- output the station name as a text element -->
    <text x="10" y="20" style="font-size: 10pt;">
        <xsl:value-of select="@SName"/>
    </text>

    <!-- process any child SYG elements -->
    <xsl:apply-templates select="SYG"/>
</xsl:template>
```

The `<xsl:value-of>` inserts the value of the selected item. The preceding @ indicates that we want the value of an attribute; in this case, the SName attribute. We also want the timestamp from this element, but it requires special handling, so we'll come back to it later.

The processor then finds all subordinate `<SYG>` elements and processes them as our XSLT document specifies.

In this example, we've only used element and attribute names as the values of a match or select. In reality, you can put any XPath expression as a value. XPath is a notation that lets you select parts of an XML document with extreme precision. For example, while processing an XHTML document, you could select only the odd `<td>` elements that are within `<tr>` elements that have been set align="right".

The majority of the work needs to be done when we encounter the `<SYG>` element, since it contains the temperature, wind, and visibility attributes. While it would be possible to output all the relevant SVG within one `<xsl:template>`, a modular approach is easier to read and maintain. XSLT lets you create templates that act somewhat like functions; they don't correspond to any element in the source document, but you may explicitly call them by name and pass parameters to them. We take advantage of this in the following template:

```
<xsl:template match="SYG">
    <!-- pass the temperature to the thermometer -->
    <xsl:call-template name="draw-thermometer">
        <xsl:with-param name="t" select="@T"/>
    </xsl:call-template>

    <!-- draw-wind needs wind speed and direction -->
    <xsl:call-template name="draw-wind">
```

```
        <xsl:with-param name="w" select="@Wind"/>
    </xsl:call-template>

    <!-- draw-visibility needs the value of the Vis attribute -->
    <xsl:call-template name="draw-visibility">
        <xsl:with-param name="v">
            <xsl:value-of select="@Vis"/>
        </xsl:with-param>
    </xsl:call-template>
</xsl:template>
```

If the value of a parameter is an attribute value, the easiest way to set it is with a select. Another way to set the value is to put the content between a beginning and ending tag, as is shown in the third call.

Now we can write the template for draw-thermometer. We need to use the passed-in parameter to determine the height to fill the thermometer, and whether the thermometer should be filled with red or blue.

```
<xsl:template name="draw-thermometer">
    <xsl:param name="t">0</xsl:param> ❶
    <xsl:variable name="height" select="50-$t"/> ❷
    <xsl:variable name="tint"> ❸
    <xsl:choose>
        <xsl:when test="$t &gt; 0">red</xsl:when>
        <xsl:otherwise>blue</xsl:otherwise>
    </xsl:choose>
    </xsl:variable>

<g id="thermometer" transform="translate(10, 40)">
    <path
        d = "M 25 {$height} 25 90 A 10 10 0 1 0 35 90 L 35 {$height} Z" ❹
        style="stroke: none; fill: {$tint};"/>

    <path d= "M 25 0 25 90 A 10 10 0 1 0 35 90 L 35 0 Z"
        style="stroke: black; fill: none;"/>

    <g id="thermometer-text"
        style="font-size: 8pt; font-family: sans-serif;">
        <text x="20" y="95" style="text-anchor: end;">-40</text>
        <text x="20" y="55" style="text-anchor: end;">0</text>
        <text x="20" y="5" style="text-anchor: end;">50</text>
        <text x="10" y="110" style="text-anchor: end;">C</text>
        <text x="40" y="95">-40</text>
        <text x="40" y="55">32</text>
        <text x="40" y="5">120</text>
        <text x="50" y="110">F</text>
        <text x="30" y="130" style="text-anchor: middle;">Temp.</text>

        <text x="30" y="145" style="text-anchor: middle;"> ❺
            <xsl:value-of select="$t"/> /
            <xsl:value-of select="round($t div 5 * 9 + 32)"/>
        </text>
```

```
    </g>
  </g>
</xsl:template>
```

❶ You can specify the default value for a parameter if none is passed in.

❷ XSLT lets you declare variables for use within a template. These are actually semi-variables; every time the template gets called, the variable will get set to an initial value, but for the duration of the template, it cannot be changed further. Note that XSLT can also do simple calculations such as the one shown in the select attribute, which figures out the height to which the thermometer should be filled. When referring to a variable or parameter in an expression, precede its name with a $.

❸ We must set the tint variable conditionally. This is done with the <xsl:choose> element, which contains one or more <xsl:when> elements. The first one whose test succeeds is the one whose output goes into the final document. The <xsl:otherwise> element is a catchall in case all the preceding tests fail.

In the test, we used the entity reference > for a greater than symbol to avoid problems with some XSLT processors; if you ever use a less than it *must* be written as <.

❹ When referring to parameters or variables in the values of attributes of the output document, you must enclose them within curly braces. This particular <path> draws the thermometer, filled to the proper height.

❺ The <text> elements preceding this one are all fixed; this one outputs the temperature in both degrees Celsius and degrees Fahrenheit. Note the use of div for division in the formula; this is because the forward slash is already used in XPath to separate levels of element nesting.

This would be a good time to test what we've done so far. Before we can test, we have to add four items to the stylesheet. The first two are empty templates to draw the wind compass and visibility bar; they'll be completed later. The third is an empty template to handle text nodes. XSLT processors are set up with default templates to ensure that they will visit all the elements and text in the source document. The default behavior is to send the text within elements directly to the destination document. In this transformation we want to throw away the text, so we construct an empty template for text nodes; they will not appear in the SVG file. Finally, we need the closing </xsl:stylesheet> tag.

```
<xsl:template name="draw-wind">
    <!-- watch this space -->
</xsl:template>

<xsl:template name="draw-visibility">
    <!-- to be determined -->
</xsl:template>

<xsl:template match="text()"/>
</xsl:stylesheet>
```

On a Unix system, we invoke the Xalan processor from the command line with the following shell script. Xalan is the XSLT processor and Xerces is the XML parser. The resulting graphic, Figure 12-4, shows the station name and the thermometer.

```
java -cp /usr/local/xmljar/xalan.jar:\
/usr/local/xmljar/xerces.jar\
org.apache.xalan.xslt.Process
    -IN weather.xml -XSL omf.xsl -OUT weather.svg
```

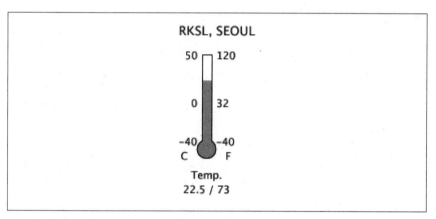

Figure 12-4. XSL-generated SVG file showing thermometer

You have seen that XSLT can do simple arithmetic; it can also do a reasonable amount of string manipulation. Here is the XSLT to handle the drawing of the wind compass. It uses the **substring-before** and **substring-after** functions to split the wind information into the parts that are needed for the drawing.

```
<xsl:template name="draw-wind">
    <xsl:param name="w" select="0"/>

    <xsl:variable name="dir" ❶
        select="substring-before($w, ',')"/>
    <xsl:variable name="speed"
        select="substring-after($w, ',')"/>
```

```
    <xsl:variable name="dir1"> ❷
        <xsl:choose>
        <xsl:when test="contains($dir, '-')">
            <xsl:value-of select="number(substring-before($dir,
                '-' ))-90"/>
        </xsl:when>
        <xsl:otherwise>
            <xsl:value-of select="number($dir) - 90"/>
        </xsl:otherwise>
        </xsl:choose>
    </xsl:variable>

    <xsl:variable name="dir2"> ❸
        <xsl:choose>
        <xsl:when test="contains($dir, '-')">
            <xsl:value-of select="number(substring-after($dir,
                '-' ))-90"/>
        </xsl:when>
        <xsl:otherwise>
            <xsl:value-of select="number($dir) - 90"/>
        </xsl:otherwise>
        </xsl:choose>
    </xsl:variable>

<g id="compass" font-size="8pt" font-family="sans-serif"
    transform="translate(110, 70)">
    <circle cx="40" cy="40" r="30" style="stroke: black; fill: none;"/>
    <path
        d= "M 40 10 L 40 14
            M 70 40 L 66 40
            M 40 70 L 40 66
            M 10 40 L 14 40"
        style="stroke: black; fill: none;"/>
    <use transform="rotate({$dir1},40,40)" xlink:href="#wind-line"> ❹
        <xsl:if test="$dir1 != $dir2">
            <xsl:attribute name="stroke-dasharray">3 3</xsl:attribute>
        </xsl:if>
    </use>
    <use transform="rotate({$dir2},40,40)" xlink:href="#wind-line">
        <xsl:if test="$dir1 != $dir2">
            <xsl:attribute name="stroke-dasharray">3 3</xsl:attribute>
        </xsl:if>
    </use>
    <text x="40" y="9" text-anchor="middle">N</text>
    <text x="73" y="44">E</text>
    <text x="40" y="80" text-anchor="middle">S</text>
    <text x="8" y="44" text-anchor="end">W</text>
    <text x="40" y="100" text-anchor="middle">Wind (m/sec)</text>
    <text x="40" y="115" text-anchor="middle">
        <xsl:value-of select="$speed"/> ❺
    </text>
</g>
</xsl:template>
```

❶ This splits the wind information into a direction and speed by grabbing the substring before and after the separating comma.

❷ If there is a hyphen in the direction, it must be split into two portions. This sets the first number, subtracting 90 degrees, since "north" is -90 degrees in SVG. If there's no hyphen, the first direction is simply offset by -90 degrees. The number function ensures string data is converted to numeric form after stripping leading and trailing whitespace.

❸ Similar code sets the second direction. You may wonder why we didn't use simpler code like this:

```
<xsl:choose>
<xsl:when test="contains($dir,'-')">
    <xsl:variable name="dir1"> ... </xsl:variable>
    <xsl:variable name="dir2"> ... </xsl:variable>
</xsl:when>
<xsl:otherwise>
    <xsl:variable name="dir1"> ... </xsl:variable>
    <xsl:variable name="dir2"> ... </xsl:variable>
</xsl:otherwise>
</xsl:choose>
```

Because a variable exists only within its enclosing block, this code won't work—the starting <xsl:when> or <xsl:otherwise> would create the variables, which would disppear immediately upon encountering the ending </xsl:when> or </xsl:otherwise>. This is why we have to repeat all the choice code within the variable declarations.

❹ After the boilerplate that creates the circle and the hash marks, we draw both wind direction lines. If a range of wind directions was specified in the source file, in which case variables $dir1 and $dir2 will be different, we want the direction lines to be dashed. We use an <xsl:if> element to test if the directions are unequal. If so, the <xsl:attribute> will add the named attribute, stroke-dasharray, to the current element, and the <xsl:attribute>'s content will become the value of that attribute. In this case, we'll add a stroke-dasharray to the currently open <use> element and give it a value of 3 3.

If the directions are the same, the <xsl:if> element does nothing, and we get the same solid line drawn twice.

❺ After the boilerplate text, we insert the wind speed.

Now we construct the XSLT commands to draw the visibility bar. We want to treat numbers greater than 40,000 as infinity, and we must also handle the special case of the word INF as a value for the visibility. This requires a three-way choice for an <xsl:choose> element to set the value of the width for the rectangle that will be drawn in green.

```
<xsl:template name="draw-visibility">
    <xsl:param name="v">0</xsl:param>
    <xsl:variable name="width"> ❶
        <xsl:choose>
        <xsl:when test="$v = 'INF'">100</xsl:when>
        <xsl:when test="$v &gt; 40000">100</xsl:when>
        <xsl:otherwise>
            <xsl:value-of select="$v * 100.0 div 40000.0"/>
        </xsl:otherwise>
        </xsl:choose>
    </xsl:variable>
<g id="visbar" transform="translate(220,110)"
    font-size="8pt" text-anchor="middle">


    <rect fill="green" stroke="none"
        x="0" y="0" width="{$width}" height="20"/>


    <rect x="0" y="0" width="100" height="20" stroke="black" fill="none"/>

    <path fill="none" stroke="black"
        d="M 25 20 L 25 25 M 50 20 L 50 25 M 75 20 L 75 25"/>

    <text x="0" y="35">0</text>
    <text x="25" y="35">10</text>
    <text x="50" y="35">20</text>
    <text x="75" y="35">30</text>
    <text x="100" y="35">40+</text>
    <text x="50" y="60">
        Visibility (km)
    </text>
    <text x="50" y="75">
        <xsl:value-of select="format-number($v div 1000.0,'0.###')"/> ❷
    </text>
</g>
</xsl:template>
```

❶ Setting the width of the area to be filled requires a three-way choice; the visibility could be the literal INF, a number greater than 40,000, or some other number. This <xsl:choose> scales the visibility to a maximum width of 100 for the fill.

❷ The visibility is in meters, but we want to show it in kilometers. To show it cleanly, we use the format-number function, which takes two parameters: the number to format and the formatting string. The formatting string used here says to print the integer part, even if it is zero, followed by at most three decimal places. Trailing zeroes will not be displayed.

Given these specifications, the weather report in Figure 12-5 is taking shape nicely, but it is still missing the date and time.

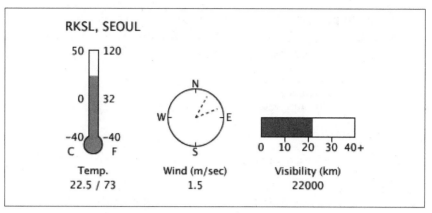

Figure 12-5. XSLT-generated SVG file without time data

Extending XSLT in Java

While XSLT contains some arithmetic operations and string functions, they are nowhere near powerful enough to handle timestamp conversion into the hour and minute of the day, much less a nicely formatted date string. Luckily, it is possible to write extensions to XSLT to handle such tasks. You may write extensions in Java, JavaScript, NetRexx, JPython (the Java version of Python), PerlScript, or any other language that supports the Bean Scripting Framework. For full details, see *http://xml.apache.org/ xalan-j/extensions.html*. Since Xalan is our tool of choice, and it is written in Java, we'll write this extension in Java.

To use an extension written in Java, you must add the text shown in bold-face to the root element of the XSLT stylesheet. The first line associates the java namespace with calls to Java extensions. The second line says that XSLT doesn't have to attach that namespace to any tags it generates.

```
<xsl:stylesheet version="1.0"
    xmlns:xsl="http://www.w3.org/1999/XSL/Transform"
    xmlns:java="http://xml.apache.org/xslt/java"
    exclude-result-prefixes="java">
```

We then write a class with static methods that take a timestamp as input and return the information we need. Since the hour and minute will only be used in a numeric context, we return them as Double. The following code is totally unsurprising; the only "gotcha" is that the OMF timestamp is measured in seconds since 1 January 1970, and Java's time and date methods are designed to work with time measured in *milliseconds* since 1 January 1970.

If you want to put your functions into a package, you may do so. You are not restricted to static methods, either. An extension may create an instance of a Java object and return it to be stored in an XSLT variable.

```
import java.util.Calendar;
import java.util.Date;
import java.text.DateFormat;

public class TimeStampUtils
{
    public static String getDate(String timeStampString)
    {
        DateFormat d = DateFormat.getDateInstance();
        long milliseconds = Long.parseLong( timeStampString ) * 1000;
        return
            d.format(new Date(milliseconds));
    }

    public static Double getHour(String timeStampString)
    {
        long milliseconds = Long.parseLong( timeStampString ) * 1000;
        Calendar c = Calendar.getInstance();
        c.setTime( new Date( milliseconds ) );
        return new Double( c.get( Calendar.HOUR_OF_DAY ) );
    }

    public static Double getMinute(String timeStampString)
    {
        long milliseconds = Long.parseLong( timeStampString ) * 1000;
        Calendar c = Calendar.getInstance();
        c.setTime( new Date( milliseconds ) );
        return new Double( c.get( Calendar.MINUTE ) );
    }
}
```

To call one of these methods from XSLT, you give the namespace—in this case java:—followed by the fully qualified name of the method you wish to call. To retrieve the date string associated with the timestamp, we add the code in boldface to the definition of the <SYN> template. We also retrieve the hour and minute, and pass them to a template that will display the time as text and also draw an analog clock face.

```
<xsl:template match="SYN">
    <xsl:variable name="tstamp" select="@TStamp"/>
    <text font-size="10pt" x="10" y="20">
        <xsl:value-of select="@SName"/>
    </text>
    <text font-size="10pt" x="345" y="20" text-anchor="end">
        <xsl:value-of select="java:TimeStampUtils.getDate( $tstamp )"/>
    </text>
```

```
<xsl:call-template name="draw-time-and-clock">
    <xsl:with-param name="hour"
        select="java:TimeStampUtils.getHour( $tstamp )"/>
    <xsl:with-param name="minute"
        select="java:TimeStampUtils.getMinute( $tstamp )"/>
</xsl:call-template>

    <xsl:apply-templates select="SVG"/>
</xsl:template>
```

Finally, here is the template for drawing the time and clock. The only new item here is the `<xsl:text>` element. Its contents, which must be pure text, are placed into the output document verbatim. We're using it here to avoid problems with whitespace. If the boldface line in the following listing had been simply the colon that separates the minutes and hours, the leading tab on that line and the next one would have made their way into the resultant SVG `<text>` element, which would have produced extra space around the colon in the final graphic.

```
<xsl:template name="draw-time-and-clock">
    <xsl:param name="hour">0</xsl:param>
    <xsl:param name="minute">0</xsl:param>

    <!-- clock face is light yellow from 6 AM to 6 PM, otherwise light
        blue -->
    <xsl:variable name="tint">
        <xsl:choose>
        <xsl:when test="$hour &gt; 6 and $hour &lt; 18">#ffffcc</xsl:when>
        <xsl:otherwise>#ccccff</xsl:otherwise>
        </xsl:choose>
    </xsl:variable>

    <!-- calculate angles for hour and minute hand of analog clock -->
    <xsl:variable name="hourAngle"
        select="(30 * ($hour mod 12 + $minute div 60)) - 90"/>
    <xsl:variable name="minuteAngle"
        select="($minute * 6) - 90"/>

<text x="345" y="40" style="font-size: 10pt; text-anchor: end;">
        <xsl:value-of select="$hour"/>
        <xsl:text>:</xsl:text>
        <xsl:value-of select="format-number($minute,'00')"/>
</text>
<text font-size="10pt" x="345" y="60" text-anchor="end">
GMT
</text>
<g id="clock" transform="translate(255, 30)">
    <circle cx="20" cy="20" r="20"
        style="fill: {$tint}; stroke: black;"/>
    <line transform="rotate({$minuteAngle}, 20, 20)"
        x1="20" y1="20" x2="38" y2="20" style="stroke: black;"/>
    <line transform="rotate({$hourAngle}, 20, 20)"
```

```
                   x1="20" y1="20" x2="33" y2="20" style="stroke: black;"/>
         </g>
         </xsl:template>
```

When you run this transformation, the classpath that you give to Xalan must include the directory where your class file lives. In this case, it's in the same directory as the OMF file and XSL file, so we changed the script to include . in the classpath:

```
java -cp /usr/local/xmljar/xalan.jar:\
/usr/local/xmljar/xerces.jar:\
.\
org.apache.xalan.xslt.Process\
  -IN weather.xml -XSL omf.xsl -OUT weather.svg
```

Putting this all together produces Figure 12-6.

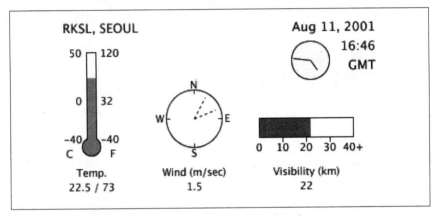

Figure 12-6. XSLT-generated SVG file showing complete data

There is room for improvement in this XSLT file. Few people are interested in the four-letter station code that precedes the station name; it should be eliminated. If the temperatures are outside the range of -40 to 50 degrees Celsius, as frequently happens in desert areas or in Antarctica, the thermometer will be filled improperly. If any of the attributes is missing from the original OMF file, bad things will happen. Numeric operations on the null string result in a value called "not a number," which displays as NaN in text, and will cause SVG errors if inserted into a path's description. Finally, if there is more than one <SYN> element in the document, the XSLT will generate multiple SVG descriptions of thermometers, compasses, and visibility bars one on top of the other.

These corrections and any improvements to the output are left for the astute reader, who has been sufficiently astute to purchase *XSLT* by Doug Tidwell, published by O'Reilly & Associates. Chapter 8 of that marvelous book also contains an example of using XSLT to generate SVG from an XML file that is far better-behaved than the one we've used here. If you're serious about XML, you would be well advised to have this book on your shelf.

13

Serving SVG Files

In most of the preceding chapters, we have presented a general view of SVG and have tried to be application-agnostic. The techniques you've seen can be applied to diagrams destined for print, for conversion of legacy data to a more transportable format, and, of course, for web graphics. In this chapter, we will consider the problem of accessing data in XML format, transforming it to SVG, and then sending it to a client on the Web.

Serving Web Files — The Task at Hand

We will present a list of airports on a web page, and let the users select one whose weather report they wish to see. The request will be sent to a Java servlet, which will retrieve the information in Weather Observation Markup Format (OMF) and send back a web page containing a graphic presentation of the data. Though SVG is the most compact representation—and this is a book about SVG, after all—some users may not have an SVG plugin for their browsers. Thus, we will offer them a choice of receiving the graphic in SVG or in one of two rasterized formats: PNG (Portable Network Graphics) or JPG. We offer JPG for users with older browsers that don't support PNG. The web page is shown in Figure 13-1.

This example uses a servlet without explaining the servlet mechanism in any great detail. You can find that information in *Java Servlet Programming* by Jason Hunter and William Crawford, published by O'Reilly & Associates.

Figure 13-1. Screenshot of web page

The resulting graphic will be a modified form of the graphic presented in Chapter 12, in the section "Using XSLT to Convert XML Data to SVG," showing the city name, time, temperature, wind speed and direction, and visibility. The most important modification is that the graphic will show the local time, rather than Greenwich Mean Time, which is the format for the original data. Figure 13-2 shows one such result.

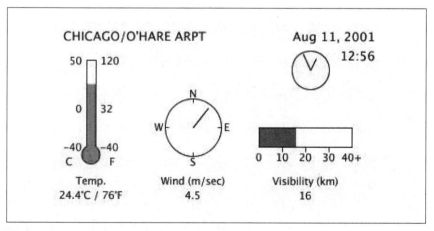

Figure 13-2. Screenshot of resulting graphic

Partitioning the Task

Our task can be broken down into three major subtasks: creating the web page, writing the servlet itself, and constructing the XSLT file that the servlet will use.

The Request Web Page

Example 13-1 is a listing of the HTML for the web page. The value of each select menu option consists of the four-letter station ID, city name, and time zone, separated by vertical bars. The time zone is chosen from the list provided by Java's java.util.TimeZone.getAvailableIDs() function. The action attribute points to the servlet running on localhost; you will change this depending on the server, server software, and servlet container you're using.

Example 13-1. HTML form for requesting OMF information

```
<html>
<head><title>OMF to SVG</title></head>

<body>
<h2>OMF Graphic Display</h2>
<form method="get"
 action="http://localhost:8080/omf_j/servlet/Weather">
<p>
See weather for:

<select name="call_id">
<option value="----|-----|---->Choose an airport</option>
<option value="SABE|Buenos Aires, Argentina|America/Buenos_Aires">
    Buenos Aires, Argentina
</option>
<option value="KORD|Chicago/O'Hare|America/Chicago">
    Chicago/O'Hare
</option>
<!-- etc. -->
</option>
<option value="KSJC|San Jose|America/Los_Angeles">
    San Jose, California
</option>
<option value="RKSS|Seoul/Kimp'o|Asia/Seoul">
    Seoul/Kimp'o
</option>
<option value="YSSY|Sydney, Australia|Australia/Sydney">
    Sydney, Australia
</option>
</select>
</p>
<p>
Format:
<input type="radio" name="imgtype" value="SVG"
    checked="checked" /> SVG
<input type="radio" name="imgtype" value="JPG" /> JPG
<input type="radio" name="imgtype" value="PNG" /> PNG
<input type="submit" value="Show Weather Graphic" />
</p>
</form>
```

Example 13-1. HTML form for requesting OMF information (continued)

```
</body>
</html>
```

The Weather Servlet

Let us now turn our attention to the Java servlet, Weather, that creates the web page on which the image will appear. This servlet merely creates HTML; it doesn't create the image itself. Instead, it will create an <embed> tag (or <img> tag) whose src attribute will be a reference to the Transform servlet that does the actual transformation. There are two reasons to do this: First, most applications create a web page with an image rather than returning an image alone. Second, returning only an image causes caching problems with some browsers; returning a web page doesn't. The source code for the servlet is listed in Example 13-2.

Example 13-2. Weather.java, a servlet for creating a web page

```
import java.io.*;
import java.text.*;
import java.util.*;

import java.net.URLEncoder; ❶
import javax.servlet.*;
import javax.servlet.http.*;

public class Weather extends HttpServlet {

    ResourceBundle rb = ❷
        ResourceBundle.getBundle("TransformFileStrings");

    public void doPost(HttpServletRequest request,
        HttpServletResponse response)
        throws ServletException, IOException
    {

        PrintWriter out = response.getWriter();

        try
        {
            response.setContentType("text/html"); ❸
            response.setHeader("Cache-Control",
                "no-cache, no-store, must-revalidate");
            response.setHeader("Cache-Control",
                "post-check=0, pre-check=0");
            String agent =
                request.getHeader("User-Agent").toLowerCase();

            // netscape chokes on Pragma no-cache so only
            // send it to explorer
```

Example 13-2. Weather.java, a servlet for creating a web page (continued)

```java
if (agent.indexOf("explorer") > -1){
  response.setHeader("Pragma", "no-cache");
}
response.setHeader("Expires",
    "Thu, 01 Dec 1994 16:00:00 GMT");

String params = request.getParameter( "call_id" ); ❹
String referer = request.getHeader( "Referer" );

/* if no airport chosen, return to caller */
if ( params.startsWith("----") && (referer != null) )
{
    response.setStatus( response.SC_MOVED_TEMPORARILY );
    response.setHeader( "Location", referer );
    return;
}

StringTokenizer info = new StringTokenizer( params, "|" ); ❺
info.nextToken();    /* we don't need the station ID */
String cityName = info.nextToken();

String imgType = request.getParameter( "imgtype" );

String transformURL = rb.getString( "transformURL" );

out.println("<html><head><title>" +
    cityName + "</title></head>");
out.println("<body>");

if (referer != null)    ❻
{
    out.println("<p><a href=\"" +
        request.getHeader("Referer") +
        "\">Back</a></p>");
}

/*
 * Construct parameters to pass to Transform servlet.
 * The servlet request.getParameter function decoded
 * the information, so we must re-encode it.
 */
params = "call_id=" + java.net.URLEncoder.encode(params) +
    "&imgtype=" + imgType;

if (imgType.equals("SVG"))    ❼
{
    out.println("<p><embed width=\"350\" height=\"200\" " +
        "type=\"image/svg+xml\" ");
    out.println(
        "src=\"" + transformURL +
        "?" + params +
        "\" /></p>");
```

Example 13-2. Weather.java, a servlet for creating a web page (continued)

```
            }
            else
            {
                out.println("<p><img width=\"350\" height=\"200\" ");
                out.println(
                    "src=\"" + transformURL +
                    "?" + params +
                    "\" /></p>");
            }
            out.println("</body></html>");
        }
        catch (Exception e)
        {
            out.println("<html><head><title>Error</title></head>");
            out.println("<body>");
            out.println("<p>Unable to extract information.</p>");
            out.println("</body></html>");
        }
    }

    public void doGet(HttpServletRequest request, ❽
                      HttpServletResponse response)
        throws IOException, ServletException
    {
        doPost( request, response );
    }
}
```

❶ Include all the connectivity and servlet routines.

❷ For ease of modification, all the file names and URL names for both servlets are stored in a resource file, which looks like this:

```
pathName=file:///home/httpd/html/omf_j/

#
#   for Weather servlet
#
transformURL=http://localhost:8080/omf_j/servlet/Transform

#
#   for Transform servlet
#
xslFileName=omf.xsl
svgErrFile=/home/httpd/html/omf_j/err.svg
imgErrFile=/home/httpd/html/omf_j/err.jpg
omfSource=http://url.of.omf.org/get-obs"
```

❸ The servlet sets the content type for a web page (text/html) and emits an inordinate amount of information to make sure the page doesn't get cached.

❹ Retrieve the weather station call letters (call_id) and the URL of the web page from which we were called (the referer). The referrer, whose keyword was misspelled when the API was created, will be null if the user typed the URL in the browser's location bar rather than calling the servlet from an actual web page.

❺ Split out the city name from the call_id parameter for use in the <title> element.

❻ If there was a referring page, create a link back to that page.

❼ Create the appropriate <object> or <img> tag. Note that the src attribute is a URL that will call the Transform servlet, passing on to it all the parameters that we received in this servlet.

❽ If this servlet is called from a GET request, handle it exactly the same as a POST request.

The Transform Servlet

When the Weather servlet is invoked, it will create a web page, one of whose tags will in turn invoke the Transform servlet. This servlet has to retrieve the XML, transform it to SVG, possibly convert it to JPG or PNG format, and send it to the client, as shown in Figure 13-3. We want a cross-platform, open source solution, so we will use Apache's Xalan processor for XSLT, and the Apache Batik project's transcoder.

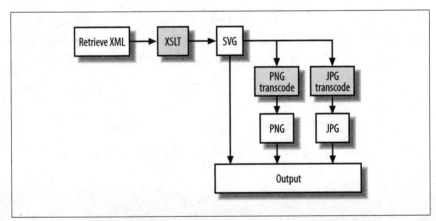

Figure 13-3. Information flow of Transform servlet

The servlet begins by importing a significant number of classes:

```
import java.io.*;
import java.text.*;
import java.util.*;

import java.net.URL;
import java.net.URLConnection;
import java.net.URLEncoder;
import java.net.URLDecoder;

import javax.servlet.*;
import javax.servlet.http.*;
import javax.xml.transform.*;
import javax.xml.transform.stream.StreamSource;
import javax.xml.transform.stream.StreamResult;

import org.apache.batik.transcoder.image.JPEGTranscoder;
import org.apache.batik.transcoder.image.PNGTranscoder;
import org.apache.batik.transcoder.TranscoderInput;
import org.apache.batik.transcoder.TranscoderOutput;

import org.xml.sax.helpers.XMLReaderFactory;

import org.apache.xalan.templates.OutputProperties;
```

The **init** function will read the XSL transformation file, compile it, and store the result in the class variable xslTemplate. This function is called only once, and the variable will persist throughout the servlet's lifetime. This means we don't have to re-parse the XSL file every time the servlet is called.

```
public class Transform extends HttpServlet {

    ResourceBundle rb =
        ResourceBundle.getBundle("TransformFileStrings");

    private Templates xslTemplate;

    public void init(ServletConfig config) throws ServletException
    {
        String path;
        String title;

        path = rb.getString("pathName");
        title = rb.getString( "xslFileName" );
        super.init(config);
        try
        {
            //for storing a compiled and resuseable style sheet
            TransformerFactory factory =
                TransformerFactory.newInstance();
```

```
        xslTemplate =
            factory.newTemplates(new StreamSource(path + title));
    }
    catch (Exception ex)
    {
        xslTemplate = null;
    }
}
```

This is followed by the main routine, doPost. Of particular interest is the
code in boldface, which passes the time zone string as a parameter to the
XSLT file.

```
public void doPost(HttpServletRequest request,
    HttpServletResponse response)
    throws ServletException, IOException
{
    StreamSource    xmlInput;
    StreamResult    svgOutput;
    StringWriter    svgWriter;
    String          svgString;
    String          stationID = "";
    String          cityName = "";
    String          timeZoneString ="";
    String          retrievedXML = "";

    /* If init failed, exit immediately */
    if (xslTemplate == null)
    {
        errorExit( request, response, "No template" );
        return;
    }

    try
    {
        /* Split out information from the parameter */
        String temp;
        temp = request.getParameter( "call_id" );
        StringTokenizer info = new StringTokenizer( temp, "|" );
        stationID = info.nextToken();
        cityName = info.nextToken();
        timeZoneString = info.nextToken();
    }
    catch (Exception e)
    {
        errorExit( request, response, "Can't split parameters" );
    }

    /*
     * The OMF source that we are using returns
     * an SVG document beginning with a <!DOCTYPE if there
     * is no error, or an HTML form document if it got
     * invalid input.
```

```
    */
retrievedXML = getOMFReports( request, cityName, stationID );
if (retrievedXML != null &&
 retrievedXML.startsWith("<!DOC"))
{
    try
    {
        xmlInput = new StreamSource(
            new StringReader( retrievedXML )
        );

        /*
         * Create an XSLT Transformer based on our template,
         * make it output UTF, and pass it the time zone
         */
        Transformer transformer = xslTemplate.newTransformer();
        transformer.setOutputProperty("encoding", "UTF-8");
        transformer.setParameter("timeZone", timeZoneString);

        /*
         * Transform the XML to SVG as one long
         * string.
         */
        svgWriter = new StringWriter( 2048 );
        svgOutput = new StreamResult( svgWriter );
        transformer.transform(
            xmlInput,
            svgOutput
        );

        svgString = svgWriter.toString();

        /*
         * Send back the appropriate output given the
         * image type that the user requested.
         */
        if ( request.getParameter("imgtype").equals("JPG") )
        {
            emitJPG( request, response, svgString );
        }
        else if (request.getParameter("imgtype").equals("PNG"))
        {
            emitPNG( request, response, svgString );
        }
        else
        {
            emitSVG( request, response, svgString );
        }
    }
    catch (Exception e)
    {
        errorExit( request, response, e.getMessage() );
    }
}
```

```
        else
        {
            errorExit( request, response, retrievedXML );
        }
    }

    /*
     * Treat get and post equivalently.
     */
    public void doGet(HttpServletRequest request,
                      HttpServletResponse response)
        throws IOException, ServletException
    {
        doPost( request, response );
    }
```

Here's the routine that accesses the OMF source. The particular source we're using will only accept POST requests; this code shows you how to do them. The OMF source we used while developing this chapter returns an XML file starting with a <!DOCTYPE ... > if the input data is valid; otherwise it returns an HTML page with an error message.

```
    private String getOMFReports( HttpServletRequest request,
        String cityName, String stationID )
    {
        URL url;
        URLConnection urlConn;

        DataOutputStream output;
        DataInputStream input;

        String  retrievedReport = null;

        try
        {
            /*
             * Open a URL connection to the OMF source URL
             */
            url = new URL( rb.getString("omfSource") );
            urlConn = url.openConnection();

            /*
             * We need to both send (output)
             * and receive (input) data
             * with this connection
             */
            urlConn.setDoOutput (true);
            urlConn.setDoInput (true);

            // Don't use any cached values
            urlConn.setUseCaches (false);

            // Specify the content type.
```

```
        urlConn.setRequestProperty("Content-Type",
            "application/x-www-form-urlencoded");

        /*
         * No user interaction such as authentication
         * dialogs is needed here.
         */
        urlConn.setAllowUserInteraction(false);

        /*
         * Write the POST data; this OMF source
         * is ordinarily called from an HTML form;
         * we are filling in the call_id field and
         * faking the "Retrieve" submit button
         */
        output = new DataOutputStream (urlConn.getOutputStream ());
        String content = "do-retrieve=Retrieve&call_id=" +
            URLEncoder.encode( stationID );
        output.writeBytes (content);
        output.flush ();
        output.close ();

        /*
         * Get response data, appending it to a
         * string buffer.
         */
        input = new DataInputStream(urlConn.getInputStream ());

        StringBuffer strBuf = new StringBuffer(2048);
        String str;
        while (null != ((str = input.readLine())))
        {
            strBuf.append(str);
            strBuf.append("\n");
        }

        /*
         * If the result begins with <!DOCTYPE, it's good;
         * otherwise, it's not.
         */
        retrievedReport = strBuf.toString();
        if (!retrievedReport.startsWith("<!DOCTYPE"))
        {
            retrievedReport = "No reports available for " +
                cityName + ".";
        }
        input.close( );
    }
    catch (Exception e)
    {
        /*
         * We can get an exception when the connection
         * hits end of file; this test makes sure we
         * only report true errors.
```

```
        */
        if (e.getMessage() != null)
        {
            retrievedReport = null;
        }
    }
    return retrievedReport;
}
```

The following routine is a utility routine for sending header information back to the caller.

```
/*
 * Send back a header of the given contentType;
 * add lots of checks to avoid caching.
 */
public void headerInfo( HttpServletRequest request,
    HttpServletResponse response, String contentType)
{
    response.setContentType( contentType );
    response.setHeader("Cache-Control",
        "no-cache, no-store, must-revalidate");
    response.setHeader("Cache-Control",
        "post-check=0, pre-check=0");

    /*
     * Netscape has problems with Pragma: no-cache,
     * so only send it to Explorer.
     */
    String agent = request.getHeader("User-Agent").toLowerCase();
    if (agent.indexOf("explorer") > -1){
        response.setHeader("Pragma", "no-cache");
    }
    response.setHeader("Expires", "Thu, 01 Dec 1994 16:00:00 GMT");
}
```

Sending the SVG is trivial; it's already ready and waiting in a string.

```
public void emitSVG ( HttpServletRequest request,
    HttpServletResponse response, String svgString )
{
    headerInfo( request, response, "image/svg+xml");
    try {

        response.getWriter().write( svgString );
        response.getWriter().flush();
    }
    catch (Exception e)
    {
        e.printStackTrace();
    }
}
```

Sending back the JPG and PNG requires one extra step: invoking the appropriate Batik transcoder to convert the SVG into an array of bytes, which we send directly to the response's output stream. `response.getWriter()` is used for text; `response.getOutputStream()` is used for binary data.

```
public void emitJPG( HttpServletRequest request,
    HttpServletResponse response, String svgString )
{
    headerInfo( request, response, "image/jpeg");

    JPEGTranscoder t = new JPEGTranscoder();
    t.addTranscodingHint(JPEGTranscoder.KEY_QUALITY,
                    new Float(.8));

    TranscoderInput input =
        new TranscoderInput( new StringReader(svgString) );
    try {
        TranscoderOutput output =
            new TranscoderOutput(response.getOutputStream());
        t.transcode(input, output);
        response.getOutputStream().close();
    }
    catch (Exception e)
    {
        e.printStackTrace();
    }
}

public void emitPNG ( HttpServletRequest request,
    HttpServletResponse response, String svgString )
{
    headerInfo( request, response, "image/png");

    PNGTranscoder t = new PNGTranscoder();

    TranscoderInput input =
        new TranscoderInput( new StringReader(svgString) );
    try {
        TranscoderOutput output =
            new TranscoderOutput(response.getOutputStream());
        t.transcode(input, output);
        response.getOutputStream().close();
    }
    catch (Exception e)
    {
        e.printStackTrace();
    }
}
```

We are now left with one interesting problem—handling errors. In the Weather servlet, we were creating an HTML page, so the error trapping simply generated a different HTML page with the error message on it. In this case, though, the servlet is expecting image data, and sending back HTML text won't do. The client wants image data, so that's what we'll give it. If the user requested an SVG graphic, we'll send back the following "error image" from a text file:

```
<?xml version="1.0" encoding="UTF-8"?>
<!DOCTYPE svg PUBLIC "-//W3C//DTD SVG 1.0//EN"
    "http://www.w3.org/TR/2001/REC-SVG-20010904/DTD/svg10.dtd">
<svg viewBox="0 0 350 200" height="200" width="350">
    <rect x="1" y="1" width="348" height="198"
        style="fill: none; stroke: black;"/>
    <text x="175" y="112"
        style="font-size: 18pt; text-anchor: middle;">
    Unable to retrieve data.
    </text>
</svg>
```

If the user requested a JPG or PNG image, we'll send back a JPG version of the error image, shown at half size in Figure 13-4. We send back a JPG image because that format is supported by even the oldest browsers.

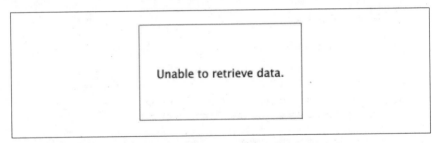

Figure 13-4. Screenshot of error image

Here's the code. Again, the SVG, being text, is sent to `response.getWriter()`, and the JPG, being binary, is sent to `response.getOutputStream()`. If there's any error during *this* process, we log the error and let the bits fall where they may.

```
public void errorExit( HttpServletRequest request,
    HttpServletResponse response, String msg )
{
    try {
        if (request.getParameter( "imgtype" ).equals( "SVG" ))
        {
            response.setContentType("image/svg+xml");
            String title = rb.getString( "svgErrFile" );
            BufferedReader input =
                new BufferedReader(new FileReader(title));
            String str;
```

```
                while (null != ((str = input.readLine()))))
                {
                     response.getWriter().write( str );
                }
                input.close();
                response.getWriter().close();
           }
           else
           {
                response.setContentType("image/jpeg");
                String title = rb.getString( "imgErrFile" );
                byte [] buffer = new byte[8192];

                FileInputStream input =
                     new FileInputStream( title );
                while (input.read( buffer ) >= 0)
                {
                     response.getOutputStream().write( buffer );
                }
                input.close();
                response.getOutputStream().close();
           }
      }
      catch (Exception e)
      {
           if (e.getMessage() != null)
           {
                log( "Cannot output error image" );
                log( e.getMessage() );
           }
      }
 }
```

The XSLT File

The XSLT file used to transform the OMF records to SVG has one major
enhancement; it must receive the parameter that was passed to it in the
doPost method. Note that we give a default value of UTC so that the result
will show up in Greenwich Mean Time if no parameter is passed to the
XSLT file.

```
<xsl:param name="timeZone" select="UTC"/>
```

The XSLT extensions we wrote in Chapter 12 in the section "Extending
XSLT in Java" must also be modified to use the time zone parameter when
returning the date and time. These extensions are in the *XSLTUtils.java*
file, which will be compiled and stored in a file named *XSLTUtils.jar*
(rather than *TimeUtils.class* as in the original example).

```java
import java.util.Calendar;
import java.util.Date;
import java.util.TimeZone;
import java.text.DateFormat;

public class XSLTUtils
{

    public static String getDate(String timeStampString,
        String timeZoneString)
    {
        DateFormat d = DateFormat.getDateInstance();
        d.setTimeZone( TimeZone.getTimeZone( timeZoneString ));
        long milliseconds = Long.parseLong( timeStampString ) * 1000;
        return
            d.format(new Date(milliseconds));
    }

    public static Double getHour(String timeStampString,
        String timeZoneString)
    {
        long milliseconds = Long.parseLong( timeStampString ) * 1000;
        Calendar c = Calendar.getInstance(
            TimeZone.getTimeZone( timeZoneString ));
        c.setTime( new Date( milliseconds ) );
        return new Double( c.get( Calendar.HOUR_OF_DAY ) );
    }

    public static Double getMinute(String timeStampString,
        String timeZoneString)
    {
        long milliseconds = Long.parseLong( timeStampString ) * 1000;
        Calendar c = Calendar.getInstance(
            TimeZone.getTimeZone( timeZoneString ));
        c.setTime( new Date( milliseconds ) );
        return new Double( c.get( Calendar.MINUTE ) );
    }

}
```

The XSLT can then call upon these functions when drawing the clock and date.

```xml
<text font-size="10pt" x="345" y="20" text-anchor="end">
    <xsl:value-of select="java:XSLTUtils.getDate( $tstamp, $timeZone )"/>
</text>

<xsl:call-template name="draw-time-and-clock">
    <xsl:with-param name="hour"
        select="java:XSLTUtils.getHour( $tstamp, $timeZone )"/>
    <xsl:with-param name="minute"
        select="java:XSLTUtils.getMinute( $tstamp, $timeZone )"/>
</xsl:call-template>
```

Setting up the Server

We chose the Tomcat servlet container implementation from the Apache Software Foundation, found at *http://jakarta.apache.org/index.html*, to run these servlets. As with all the other software mentioned in this appendix, it is cross-platform and open source. It can run as a standalone server, serving web pages, servlets, and JavaServer Pages. It can also be used in conjunction with the Apache web server, Microsoft's Internet Information Server (IIS), Microsoft's Personal Web Server, or Netscape's Netscape Enterprise Server.*

We did our testing with Tomcat running in standalone mode on a Linux system. We changed the *tomcat.sh* shell script as follows:

- We explicitly set the JAVA_HOME and TOMCAT_HOME variables:

    ```
    JAVA_HOME=/usr/local/j2sdk1.3.0
    TOMCAT_HOME=/usr/local/jakarta-tomcat
    ```

- To run our servlets, Tomcat's classpath needs access to Xalan and Xerces for the XSLT transformations, and it also needs access to the Batik .jar files. The normal Tomcat classpath setup is also in *conf/tomcat.sh*. It saves your current CLASSPATH, creates a new one with the paths that it wants, and then re-appends the classpath that you had specified. We modified that code to create a new classpath and entirely ignore the old one, which had some duplications and many unnecessary paths. Our changes are shown in boldface.

    ```
    oldCP=$CLASSPATH
    unset CLASSPATH

    #
    # The latest versions of Xalan and Xerces which we
    # want to use must come first!
    #
    CLASSPATH=/usr/local/xmljar/xalan.jar:/usr/local/xmljar/xerces.jar
    CLASSPATH=${CLASSPATH}:/usr/local/xmljar/bsf.jar
    CLASSPATH=${CLASSPATH}:/usr/local/xmljar/XSLTUtils.jar

    #
    # Add all the .jar files in the Batik library
    # to the classpath
    #
    for i in /usr/local/batik/lib/* ; do
    ```

---

* This isn't the only choice available. You can also use a Java-based delivery framework such as Cocoon, available from the Apache Software Foundation at *http://xml.apache.org/cocoon/*, or the Perl-based AxKit system, available at *http://217.158.50.178*.

```
CLASSPATH=${CLASSPATH}:$i
done


#
# Add all the .jar files in Tomcat's library directory
# to the classpath. The "else" branch will never be
# taken, but it's needed in Tomcat's code, so we decided
# to leave it intact here
#
for i in ${TOMCAT_HOME}/lib/* ; do
  if [ "$CLASSPATH" != "" ]; then
    CLASSPATH=${CLASSPATH}:$i
  else
    CLASSPATH=$i
  fi
done

if [ -f ${JAVA_HOME}/lib/tools.jar ] ; then
    # We are probably in a JDK1.2 environment
    CLASSPATH=${CLASSPATH}:${JAVA_HOME}/lib/tools.jar
fi

# Backdoor classpath setting for development purposes when all classes
# are compiled into a /classes dir and are not yet jarred.
if [ -d ${TOMCAT_HOME}/classes ]; then
    CLASSPATH=${TOMCAT_HOME}/classes:${CLASSPATH}
fi

# Ignore old classpath altogether
#
#if [ "$oldCP" != "" ]; then
#    CLASSPATH=${CLASSPATH}:${oldCP}
#fi
```

- We added a new context to the *conf/server.xml* so we could put our files in a directory other than the *webapps/examples* directory. We set `reloadable` to true because we were doing a lot of recompiling and testing. In a production environment you would probably want to set this to `false` to avoid the overhead of checking for updates every time a request comes to the server.

```
<Context path="/omf_j"
         docBase="/home/httpd/html/omf_j"
         crossContext="false"
         debug="0"
         reloadable="true" >
</Context>
```

The XML You Need for SVG

The purpose of this appendix is to introduce you to XML. A knowledge of XML is essential if you wish to write SVG documents directly rather than having them generated by some graphics utility.

If you're already acquainted with XML, you don't need to read this appendix. If not, read on. The general overview of XML given in this appendix should be more than sufficient to enable you to work with the SVG documents that you will create. For further information about XML, the O'Reilly books, *Learning XML* by Erik T. Ray and *XML in a Nutshell* by Elliotte Rusty Harold and W. Scott Means, are invaluable guides, as is the weekly online magazine *XML.com*.

Note that this appendix makes frequent reference to the formal XML 1.0 specification, which can be used for further investigation of topics that fall outside the scope of SVG. Readers are also directed to the "Annotated XML Specification," written by Tim Bray and published online at *http://XML.com/*, which provides illuminating explanation of the XML 1.0 specification; and to "What is XML?" by Norm Walsh, also published on *XML.com*.

What Is XML?

XML, the Extensible Markup Language, is an Internet-friendly format for data and documents, invented by the World Wide Web Consortium (W3C). The "Markup" denotes a way of expressing the structure of a document within the document itself. XML has its roots in a markup language called SGML (Standard Generalized Markup Language), which is used in publishing and shares this heritage with HTML. XML was created to do for machine-readable documents on the Web what HTML did for human-readable documents—that is, provide a commonly agreed-upon syntax so that processing the underlying format becomes a commodity and documents are made accessible to all users.

Unlike HTML, though, XML comes with very little predefined. HTML developers are accustomed both to the notion of using angle brackets < > for denoting elements (that is, *syntax)*, and also to the set of element names themselves (such as head, body, etc.). XML shares only the former feature (i.e., the notion of using angle brackets for denoting elements). Unlike HTML, XML has no predefined elements, but is merely a set of rules that lets you write other languages like HTML.* Because XML defines so little, it is easy for everyone to agree to use the XML syntax, and then to build applications on top of it. It's like agreeing to use a particular alphabet and set of punctuation symbols, but not saying which language to use. However, if you're coming to XML from an HTML background, then prepare yourself for the shock of having to choose what to call your tags!

Knowing that XML's roots lie with SGML should help you understand some of XML's features and design decisions. Note that, although SGML is essentially a document-centric technology, XML's functionality also extends to data-centric applications, including SVG. Commonly, data-centric applications do not need all the flexibility and expressiveness that XML provides and limit themselves to employing only a subset of XML's functionality.

Anatomy of an XML Document

The best way to explain how an XML document is composed is to present one. The following example shows an XML document you might use to describe two authors:

```
<?xml version="1.0" encoding="us-ascii"?>
<authors>
    <person id="lear">
        <name>Edward Lear</name>
        <nationality>British</nationality>
    </person>
    <person id="asimov">
        <name>Isaac Asimov</name>
        <nationality>American</nationality>
```

---

* To clarify XML's relationship with SGML: XML is an *SGML subset.* By contrast, HTML is an *SGML application.* SVG uses XML to express its operations and thus is an *XML application.*

```
      </person>
      <person id="mysteryperson"/>
    </authors>
```

The first line of the document is known as the *XML declaration*. This tells a processing application which version of XML you are using (the version indicator is mandatory) and which character encoding you have used for the document. In the previous example, the document is encoded in ASCII. (The significance of character encoding is covered later in this chapter.) If the XML declaration is omitted, a processor will make certain assumptions about your document. In particular, it will expect it to be encoded in UTF-8, an encoding of the Unicode character set. However, it is best to use the XML declaration wherever possible, both to avoid confusion over the character encoding and to indicate to processors which version of XML you're using.

Elements and Attributes

The second line of the example begins an *element*, which has been named "authors." The contents of that element include everything between the right angle bracket (>) in <authors> and the left angle bracket (<) in </authors>. The actual syntactic constructs <authors> and </authors> are often referred to as the element *start tag* and *end tag*, respectively. Do not confuse tags with elements! Note that elements may include other elements, as well as text. An XML document must contain exactly one *root element*, which contains all other content within the document. The name of the root element defines the type of the XML document.

Elements that contain both text and other elements simultaneously are classified as *mixed content*. The SVG <text> element is such an element; it can contain text and <tspan> elements.

The sample "authors" document uses elements named person to describe the authors themselves. Each person element has an *attribute* named id. Unlike elements, attributes can only contain textual content. Their values must be surrounded by quotes. Either single quotes (') or double quotes (") may be used, as long as you use the same kind of closing quote as the opening one.

Within XML documents, attributes are frequently used for *metadata* (i.e., "data about data")—describing properties of the element's contents. This is the case in our example, where id contains a unique identifier for the person being described.

As far as XML is concerned, it does not matter in what order attributes are presented in the element start tag. For example, these two elements contain exactly the same information as far as an XML 1.0 conformant processing application is concerned:

```
<animal name="dog" legs="4"/>
<animal legs="4" name="dog"/>
```

On the other hand, the information presented to an application by an XML processor on reading the following two lines will be different for each animal element because the ordering of elements is significant:

```
<animal><name>dog</name><legs>4</legs></animal>
<animal><legs>4</legs><name>dog</name></animal>
```

XML treats a set of attributes like a bunch of stuff in a bag—there is no implicit ordering—while elements are treated like items on a list, where ordering matters.

New XML developers frequently ask when it is best to use attributes to represent information and when it is best to use elements. As you can see from the "authors" example, if order is important to you, then elements are a good choice. In general, there is no hard-and-fast "best practice" for choosing whether to use attributes or elements.

The final author described in our document has no information available. All we know about this person is his or her ID, mysteryperson. The document uses the XML shortcut syntax for an empty element. The following is a reasonable alternative:

```
<person id="mysteryperson"></person>
```

Name Syntax

XML 1.0 has certain rules about element and attribute names. In particular:

- Names are case-sensitive: e.g., <person/> is not the same as <Person/>.

- Names beginning with "xml" (in any permutation of uppercase or lowercase) are reserved for use by XML 1.0 and its companion specifications.

- A name must start with a letter or an underscore, not a digit, and may continue with any letter, digit, underscore, or period.*

---

* Actually, a name may also contain a colon, but the colon is used to delimit a *namespace prefix* and is not available for arbitrary use. Knowledge of namespaces is not required for understanding SVG, but for more information, see Tim Bray's "XML Namespaces by Example," published at *http://www.xml.com/pub/a/1999/01/namespaces.html.*

A precise description of names can be found in Section 2.3 of the XML 1.0 specification, at *http://www.w3.org/TR/REC-xml#sec-common-syn.*

Well-Formed

An XML document that conforms to the rules of XML syntax is known as *well-formed.* At its most basic level, well-formedness means that elements should be properly matched, and all opened elements should be closed. A formal definition of well-formedness can be found in Section 2.1 of the XML 1.0 specification, at *http://www.w3.org/TR/REC-xml#sec-well-formed.* Table A-1 shows some XML documents that are not well-formed.

Table A-1. Examples of poorly formed XML documents

Document	Reason why it's not well-formed

`<foo>`
  `<bar>`
  `</foo>`
`</bar>`
	The elements are not properly nested because foo is closed while inside its child element bar.

`<foo>`
  `<bar>`
`</foo>`
	The bar element was not closed before its parent, foo, was closed.

`<foo baz>` `</foo>`	The baz attribute has no value. While this is permissible in HTML (e.g., `<table border>`), it is forbidden in XML.
`<foo baz=23>` `</foo>`	The baz attribute value, 23, has no surrounding quotes. Unlike HTML, all attribute values must be quoted in XML.

Comments

As in HTML, it is possible to include *comments* within XML documents. XML comments are intended to be read only by people. With HTML, developers have occasionally employed comments to add application-specific functionality. For example, the server-side include functionality of most web servers uses instructions embedded in HTML comments. XML provides other means of indicating application processing instructions,[*] so comments should not be used for any purpose other than those for which they were intended.

---

[*] A discussion of *processing instructions (PIs)* is outside the scope of this book. For more information on PIs, see Section 2.6 of the XML 1.0 specification, at *http://www.w3.org/TR/REC-xml#sec-pi.*

The start of a comment is indicated with `<!--`, and the end of the comment with `-->`. Any sequence of characters, aside from the string `--`, may appear within a comment.

Comments tend to be used more in XML documents intended for human consumption than those intended for machine consumption. The `<desc>` and `<title>` elements in SVG obviate much of the need for comments.

Entity References

Another feature of XML that is occasionally useful when writing SVG documents is the mechanism for *escaping* characters.

Because some characters have special significance in XML, there needs to be a way to represent them. For example, in some cases the `<` symbol might really be intended to mean "less than" rather than to signal the start of an element name. Clearly, just inserting the character without any escaping mechanism would result in a poorly formed document because a processing application would assume you were starting another element. Another instance of this problem is needing to include both double quotes and single quotes simultaneously in an attribute's value. Here's an example that illustrates both these difficulties:

```
<badDoc>
  <para>
    I'd really like to use the < character
  </para>
  <note title="On the proper 'use' of the " character"/>
</badDoc>
```

XML avoids this problem by the use of the *predefined entity reference*. The word *entity* in the context of XML simply means a unit of content. The term *entity reference* means just that, a symbolic way of referring to a certain unit of content. XML predefines entities for the following symbols: left angle bracket (`<`), right angle bracket (`>`), apostrophe (`'`), double quote (`"`), and ampersand (`&`).

An entity reference is introduced with an ampersand (`&`), which is followed by a name (using the word "name" in its formal sense, as defined by the XML 1.0 specification), and terminated with a semicolon (`;`). Table A-2 shows how the five predefined entities can be used within an XML document.

Table A-2. Predefined entity references in XML 1.0

Literal character	Entity reference
<	&lt;
>	&gt;
'	&apos;
"	&quot;
&	&amp;

Here's our problematic document revised to use entity references:

```
<badDoc>
  <para>
    I'd really like to use the &lt; character
  </para>
  <note title="On the proper &apos;use&apos; of the &quot;character"/>
</badDoc>
```

Being able to use the predefined entities is all you need for SVG; in general, entities are provided as a convenience for human-created XML. XML 1.0 allows you to define your own entities and use entity references as "shortcuts" in your document. Section 4 of the XML 1.0 specification, available at *http://www.w3.org/TR/REC-xml#sec-physical-struct*, describes the use of entities.

Character References

You are likely to find *character references* in the context of SVG documents. Character references allow you to denote a character by its numeric position in Unicode character set (this position is known as its *code point*). Table A-3 contains a few examples that illustrate the syntax.

Table A-3. Example character references in UTF-8

Actual character	Character reference
1	&#48;
A	&#65;
Ñ;	&#xD1;
®	&#xAE;

Note that the code point can be expressed in decimal or, with the use of x as a prefix, in hexadecimal.

Character Encodings

The subject of character encodings is frequently a mysterious one for developers. Most code tends to be written for one computing platform and, normally, to run within one organization. Although the Internet is changing things quickly, most of us have never had cause to think too deeply about internationalization.

XML, designed to be an Internet-friendly syntax for information exchange, has internationalization at its very core. One of the basic requirements for XML processors is that they support the Unicode standard character encoding. Unicode attempts to include the requirements of all the world's languages within one character set. Consequently, it is very large!

Unicode Encoding Schemes

Unicode 3.0 has more than 57,700 code points, each of which corresponds to a character.* If one were to express a Unicode string by using the position of each character in the character set as its encoding (in the same way as ASCII does), expressing the whole range of characters would require 4 octets† for each character. Clearly, if a document is written in 100 percent American English, it will be four times larger than required—all the characters in ASCII fitting into a 7-bit representation. This places a strain both on storage space and on memory requirements for processing applications.

Fortunately, two encoding schemes for Unicode alleviate this problem: *UTF-8* and *UTF-16*. As you might guess from their names, applications can process documents in these encodings in 8- or 16-bit segments at a time. When code points are required in a document that cannot be represented by one chunk, a bit-pattern is used that indicates that the following chunk is required to calculate the desired code point. In UTF-8 this is denoted by the most significant bit of the first octet being set to 1.

This scheme means that UTF-8 is a highly efficient encoding for representing languages using Latin alphabets, such as English. All of the ASCII character set is represented natively in UTF-8—an ASCII-only document and its equivalent in UTF-8 are byte-for-byte identical.

---

* You can obtain charts of all these characters online by visiting *http://www.unicode.org/charts/*.

† An *octet* is a string of 8 binary digits, or bits. A *byte* is commonly, but not always, considered the same thing as an octet.

This knowledge will also help you debug encoding errors. One frequent error arises because of the fact that ASCII is a proper subset of UTF-8—programmers get used to this fact and produce UTF-8 documents, but use them as if they were ASCII. Things start to go awry when the XML parser processes a document containing, for example, characters such as Á. Because this character cannot be represented using only one octet in UTF-8, this produces a two-octet sequence in the output document; in a non-Unicode viewer or text editor, it looks like a couple of characters of garbage.

Other Character Encodings

Unicode, in the context of computing history, is a relatively new invention. Native operating system support for Unicode is by no means widespread. For instance, although Windows NT offers Unicode support, Windows 95 and 98 do not have it.

XML 1.0 allows a document to be encoded in any character set registered with the Internet Assigned Numbers Authority (IANA). European documents are commonly encoded in one of the *ISO Latin* character sets, such as ISO-8859-1. Japanese documents commonly use *Shift-JIS*, and Chinese documents use *GB2312* and *Big 5*.

A full list of registered character sets may be found at *http://www.isi.edu/ in-notes/iana/assignments/character-sets*.

XML processors are not required by the XML 1.0 specification to support any more than UTF-8 and UTF-16, but most commonly support other encodings, such as US-ASCII and ISO-8859-1. Although most SVG transactions are currently conducted in ASCII (or the ASCII subset of UTF-8), there is nothing to stop SVG documents from containing, say, Korean text. You will, however, probably have to dig into the encoding support of your computing platform to find out if it is possible for you to use alternate encodings.

Validity

In addition to well-formedness, XML 1.0 offers another level of verification, called *validity*. To explain why validity is important, let's take a simple example. Imagine you invented a simple XML format for your friends' telephone numbers:

```
<phonebook>
  <person>
    <name>Albert Smith</name>
    <number>123-456-7890</number>
  </person>
  <person>
    <name>Bertrand Jones</name>
    <number>456-123-9876</number>
  </person>
</phonebook>
```

Based on your format, you also construct a program to display and search your phone numbers. This program turns out to be so useful, you share it with your friends. However, your friends aren't so hot on detail as you are, and try to feed your program this phone book file:

```
<phonebook>
  <person>
    <name>Melanie Green</name>
    <phone>123-456-7893</phone>
  </person>
</phonebook>
```

Note that, although this file is perfectly well-formed, it doesn't fit the format you prescribed for the phone book, and you find you need to change your program to cope with this situation. If your friends had used number as you did to denote the phone number, and not phone, there wouldn't have been a problem. However, as it is, this second file is not a valid phonebook document.

For validity to be a useful general concept, we need a machine-readable way of saying what a valid document is; that is, which elements and attributes must be present and in what order. XML 1.0 achieves this by introducing *document type definitions* (DTDs). For the purposes of SVG, you don't need to know much about DTDs. Rest assured that SVG does have a DTD, and it spells out in detail exactly which combinations of elements and attributes make up a valid document.

Document Type Definitions (DTDs)

The purpose of a DTD is to express the allowed elements and attributes in a certain document type and to constrain the order in which they must appear within that document type. A DTD is generally composed of one file, which contains declarations defining the element types and attribute lists. (In theory, a DTD may span more than one file; however, the mechanism for including one file inside another—parameter entities—is outside the scope of this book.) It is common to mistakenly conflate element and element types. The distinction is that an element is the actual instance of the structure as found in an XML document, whereas the element type is the kind of element that the instance is.

Putting It Together

What *is* important to you is knowing how to link a document to its defining DTD. This is done with a document type declaration `<!DOCTYPE ...>`, inserted at the beginning of the XML document, after the XML declaration in our fictitious example:

```
<?xml version="1.0" encoding="us-ascii"?>
<!DOCTYPE authors SYSTEM "http://example.com/authors.dtd">
<authors>
    <person id="lear">
        <name>Edward Lear</name>
        <nationality>British</nationality>
    </person>
    <person id="asimov">
        <name>Isaac Asimov</name>
        <nationality>American</nationality>
    </person>
    <person id="mysteryperson"/>
</authors>
```

This example assumes the DTD file has been placed on a web server at *example.com*. Note that the document type declaration specifies the root element of the document, not the DTD itself. You could use the same DTD to define "person," "name," or "nationality" as the root element of a valid document. Certain DTDs, such as the DocBook DTD for technical documentation,* use this feature to good effect, allowing you to provide the same DTD for multiple document types.

A validating XML processor is obliged to check the input document against its DTD. If it does not validate, the document is rejected. To return to the phone book example, if your application validated its input files against a phone book DTD, you would have been spared the problems of debugging your program and correcting your friend's XML because your application would have rejected the document as being invalid. Most of the programs that read SVG files have a validating XML processor built into them to assure they have valid input (and to keep you honest!). The kinds of XML processors that are available are discussed in the section "Tools for Processing XML."

---

* See *http://www.docbook.org*.

XML Namespaces

XML 1.0 lets developers create their own elements and attributes, but leaves open the potential for overlapping names. "Title" in one context may mean something entirely different than "Title" in a different context. The Namespaces in XML specification (which can be found at *http://www.w3.org/TR/REC-xml-names/*) provides a mechanism developers can use to identify particular vocabularies using Uniform Resource Identifiers (URIs).

SVG uses the URI *http://www.w3.org/2000/svg* for its namespace. The URI is just an identifier—opening that page in a Web browser reveals some links to the SVG, XML 1.0, and Namespaces in XML specifications. Programs processing documents with multiple vocabularies can use the namespaces to figure out which vocabulary they are handling at any given point in a document.

SVG applies the namespace in the root element of SVG documents:

```
<svg xmlns="http://www.w3.org/2000/svg" width="100" height="100">
....
</svg>
```

The xmlns attribute, which defines the namespace, is actually provided as a default value by the SVG DTD, so the declaration isn't required to appear in SVG documents. (If it does appear, it must have the exact value shown earlier.) The namespace declaration applies to all of the elements contained by the element in which the declaration appears, including the containing element. This means that the element named "svg" is in the namespace *http://www.w3.org/2000/svg*.

SVG uses the "default namespace" for its content, using the SVG element names without any prefix. Namespaces can also be applied using prefixes, as shown here:

```
<svgns:svg xmlns:svgns="http://www.w3.org/2000/svg"
    width="100" height="100">
....
</svgns:svg>
```

In this case, the namespace URI *http://www.w3.org/2000/svg* would apply to all elements using a prefix of "svgns". The SVG 1.0 DTD won't validate against such documents, but future versions of SVG may support this feature. Appendix F shows examples of how to use namespaces to integrate SVG with other XML vocabularies.

Namespaces are very simple on the surface but are a well-known field of combat in XML arcana. For more information on namespaces, see *XML In a Nutshell* or *Learning XML*.

Tools for Processing XML

Many parsers exist for using XML with many different programming languages. Most are freely available, the majority being Open Source.

Selecting a Parser

An XML parser typically takes the form of a library of code that you interface with your own program. The SVG program hands the XML over to the parser, and it hands back information about the contents of the XML document. Typically, parsers do this either via events or via a document object model.

With event-based parsing, the parser calls a function in your program whenever a parse event is encountered. Parse events include things like finding the start of an element, the end of an element, or a comment. Most Java event-based parsers follow a standard API called SAX, which is also implemented for other languages such as Python and Perl. You can find more about SAX at *http://www.megginson.com/SAX/*.

Document object model (DOM) based parsers work in a markedly different way. They consume the entire XML input document and hand back a tree-like data structure that the SVG software can interrogate and alter. The DOM is a W3C standard; documentation is available at *http://www.w3.org/DOM/*.

As XML matures, hybrid techniques that give the best of both worlds are emerging. If you're interested in finding out what's available and what's new for your favorite programming language, keep an eye on the following online sources:

XML.com Resource Guide
  http://xml.com/pub/resourceguide/

XMLhack XML Developer News
  http://xmlhack.com

Free XML Tools Guide
  http://www.garshol.priv.no/download/xmltools/

XSLT Processors

Many XML applications involve transforming one XML document into another or into HTML. The W3C has defined a special language called XSLT for doing transformations. XSLT processors are becoming available for all major programming platforms.

XSLT works by using a *stylesheet*, which contains templates that describe how to transform elements from an XML document. These templates typically specify what XML to output in response to a particular element or attribute. Using a W3C technology called XPath gives you the flexibility to say not only "do this for every 'person' element," but to give instructions as complex as "do this for the third 'person' element whose 'name' attribute is 'Fred.'"

Because of this flexibility, some applications have sprung up for XSLT that aren't really transformation applications at all, but take advantage of the ability to trigger actions on certain element patterns and sequencers. Combined with XSLT's ability to execute custom code via extension functions, the XPath language has enabled applications such as document indexing to be driven by an XSLT processor. You can see a brief introduction to XSLT in Chapter 12 in the section "Using XSLT to Convert XML Data to SVG."

The W3C specifications for XSLT and XPath can be found at *http://w3.org/TR/xslt* and *http://w3.org/xpath*, respectively.

B

Introduction to Stylesheets

As mentioned in Chapter 4, some attributes of SVG elements control the element's geometry. An example of one such attribute would be the `cx` (center x) attribute of a `<circle>`. Other attributes, such as `fill`, control the element's presentation. Stylesheets provide a way for you to separate the presentation from the geometric structure; this lets you control the visual display of many different SVG elements (and even documents) by changing one stylesheet referenced by all the documents.

Anatomy of a Style

A style is a specification of a visual property for an element and the value that you would like that property to have. The property name and the value are separated by a colon. For example, to say that you want the stroke color for some element to be blue, the appropriate style specifier would be `stroke: blue`.

To specify multiple properties in a style, you separate the specifiers with semicolons. The following style specifier sets the stroke color to red, the stroke width to three pixels, and the fill color to a light blue. The last property-value pair is followed by a semicolon. This is not necessary, but is done to give the style a more consistent look.

```
stroke: red; stroke-width: 3px; fill: #ccccff;
```

Style Selectors

Once you have determined the visual properties you'd like, you must select the element or elements to which they apply. The simplest way to apply a style specification to a single element is to make that specification the value of a style attribute. So, if you want the preceding specification to apply to a particular <circle> in your document, you write:

```
<circle cx="50" cy="40" r="12"
    style="stroke: red; stroke-width: 3px; fill: #ccccff;"/>
```

Internal Stylesheets

If you want the style specification to apply to all <circle> elements in a single document, add an internal stylesheet. A style sheet consists of *selectors* (the names of the elements you want to affect) and the style specifications for those selectors. The style specification is enclosed in curly braces. The following applies styles to <circle> and <rect> elements:

```
<style type="text/css"><![CDATA[
    circle {
        stroke: red; stroke-width: 3px;
        fill: #ccccff;
    }
    rect { fill: gray; stroke: black; }
]]></style>
```

When you put a <style> element into an SVG document, you should enclose its contents within <![CDATA[and]]>. This notation tells XML parsers that the contents are pure character *data* and should not, under any circumstances, be treated as information for XML to parse.

Because this stylesheet is within a document, it applies to that document alone. If you have many documents, all of whose circles and rectangles appear as specified in the preceding example, take the specifiers, without any of the tags, and put them into a separate *myStyle.css* file. In each SVG document, insert the following processing instruction:

```
<?xml-stylesheet href="myStyle.css" type="text/css"?>
```

Then, at a later point, if you decide that all rectangles should be filled with a light green and outlined in dark green, you can simply change the specification in *myStyle.css* to read:

```
rect {fill: #ccffcc; stroke: #006600; }
```

and all your documents, once redisplayed, will have green rectangles instead of gray rectangles.

Style Selector Classes

The preceding stylesheet affects all `<rect>` and `<circle>` elements. Let's say, though, that you want only some circles in your documents to be styled. Write your stylesheet with a class specifier as follows, where the dot after `circle` indicates that the following identifier is a class name:

```
circle.special {
  stroke: red; stroke-width: 3px;
  fill: #ccccff;
}
```

If, in your SVG document, you had the following elements, the first circle would show up as the default (black fill, no stroke), and the second would take on the style attributes as its class name matches the class identifier in the stylesheet.

```
<circle cx="40" cy="40" r="20"/>
<circle cx="60" cy="20" r="10" class="special"/>
```

It is possible to specify a generic class that can apply to any element. Presume that several different graphic objects serve as warning symbols. You would like them to have a yellow fill and a red border. You could write this selector, which consists only of a class name and its style specifier:

```
.warning { fill: yellow; stroke: red; }
```

This generic class may now be applied to any SVG element. In the following example, both the rectangle and triangle will have yellow interiors and red outlines.

```
<rect class="warning" x="5" y="10" width="20" height="30"/>
<polygon class="warning" points="40 40, 40 60, 60 50"/>
```

The `class` attribute may contain the names of several classes; their combined properties will be applied to the element in question. We will add a generic class named seeThrough for translucency to the previous example, and then apply both classes to the polygon.

```
<svg width="100" height="100" viewBox="0 0 100 100">
    <style type="text/css"><![CDATA[
        .warning { fill: yellow; stroke: red; }
        .seeThrough { fill-opacity: 0.25; stroke-opacity: 0.5; }
    ]]></style>
    <rect class="warning" x="5" y="10" width="20" height="30"/>
    <polygon class="warning seeThrough" points="40 40, 40 60, 60 50"/>
</svg>
```

Using CSS with SVG

The question then becomes: which attributes in SVG elements can also be specified in a stylesheet? Table B-1 is a list of the properties you may use in a stylesheet, the valid values (with default value shown in boldface where appropriate), and the elements to which they may be applied. It is a modified version of the property index from the SVG specification at *http://www.w3.org/TR/SVG/*.*

Table B-1. CSS property table for SVG

Name	Values	Applies to
alignment-baseline	auto | baseline | before-edge | text-before-edge | middle | after-edge | text-after-edge | ideographic | alphabetic | hanging | mathematical	\<tspan>, \<tref>, \<altGlyph>, \<textPath>
baseline-shift	**baseline** | sub | super | percentage | length	\<tspan>, \<tref>, \<altGlyph>, \<textPath> elements
clip	shape | **auto**	Elements which establish a new viewport, \<pattern> elements and \<marker> elements
clip-path	uri	Container elements and graphics elements
clip-rule	nonzero | evenodd | class=noxref	Graphics elements within a \<clipPath> element
color	color	Elements to which properties fill, stroke, stop-color, flood-color, lighting-color apply
color-interpolation	auto | **sRGB** | linearRGB	Container elements, graphics elements and \<animateColor>

Table B-1. CSS property table for SVG (continued)

Name	Values	Applies to
color-interpolation-filters	auto | sRGB | **linearRGB**	Filter primitives
color-profile	**auto** | sRGB | *name* | *uri*	<image> elements that refer to raster images
color-rendering	auto | optimizeSpeed | optimizeQuality	Container elements, graphics elements and <animateColor>
cursor	*uri* | **auto** | crosshair | default | pointer | move | e-resize | ne-resize | nw-resize | n-resize | se-resize | sw-resize | s-resize | w-resize | text | wait | help	Container elements and graphics elements
direction	**ltr** | rtl	<text>, <tspan>, <tref> and <textPath> elements
display	**inline** | block | list-item | run-in | compact | marker | table | inline-table | table-row-group | table-header-group | table-footer-group | table-row | table-column-group | table-column | table-cell | table-caption | none	<svg>, <g>, <switch>, <a>, <foreignObject>, graphics elements (including the <text> element) and text sub-elements (i.e., <tspan>, <tref>, <altGlyph>, <textPath>)
dominant-baseline	**auto** | use-script | no-change | reset-size | alphabetic | hanging | ideographic | mathematical | central | middle | text-after-edge | text-before-edge | text-top | text-bottom	Text content elements
enable-background	**accumulate** | new [*x y width height*]	Container elements
fill	*paint* (default black)	Shapes and text content elements
fill-opacity	*opacity-value* (default 1)	Shapes and text content elements

Table B-1. CSS property table for SVG (continued)

Name	Values	Applies to
fill-rule	**nonzero** | evenodd	Shapes and text content elements
filter	*uri* | **none**	Container elements and graphics elements
flood-color	currentColor | *color specifier* (default black)	<feFlood> elements
flood-opacity	*alphavalue* (default 1)	<feFlood> elements
font	font-style, font-variant, font-weight, font-size line-height, font-family | caption | icon | menu | message-box | small-caption | status-bar	Text content elements
font-family	series of *family-name* or *generic-family*	Text content elements
font-size	*absolute-size* | *relative-size* | *length* | *percentage*	Text content elements
font-size-adjust	*number* | **none**	Text content elements
font-stretch	**normal** | wider | narrower | ultra-condensed | extra-condensed | condensed | semi-condensed | semi-expanded | expanded | extra-expanded | ultra-expanded	Text content elements
font-style	**normal** | italic | oblique	Text content elements
font-variant	**normal** | small-caps	Text content elements
font-weight	**normal** | bold | bolder | lighter | 100 | 200 | 300 | 400 | 500 | 600 | 700 | 800 | 900	Text content elements
glyph-orientation-horizontal	*angle* (default 0deg)	Text content elements
glyph-orientation-vertical	**auto** | *angle*	Text content elements
image-rendering	**auto** | optimizeSpeed | optimizeQuality	images
kerning	**auto** | *length*	Text content elements
letter-spacing	**normal** | *length*	Text content elements

Table B-1. CSS property table for SVG (continued)

Name	Values	Applies to
lighting-color	currentColor | *color specification* (default white)	<feDiffuseLighting> and <feSpecularLighting> elements
marker, marker-end, marker-mid, marker-start	**none** | *uri*	<path>, <line>, <polyline> and <polygon> elements
mask	*uri* | **none**	Container elements and graphics elements
opacity	*alphavalue* (default 1)	Container elements and graphics elements
overflow	visible | hidden | scroll | auto	Elements which establish a new viewport, <pattern> elements and <marker> elements
pointer-events	**visiblePainted** | visibleFill | visibleStroke | visible | painted | fill | stroke | all | none	Graphics elements
shape-rendering	**auto** | optimizeSpeed | crispEdges | geometricPrecision	Shapes
stop-color	currentColor | *color specification* (default black)	<stop> elements
stop-opacity	*alphavalue* (default 1)	<stop> elements
stroke	*paint*	Shapes and text content elements
stroke-dasharray	**none** | *dasharray*	Shapes and text content elements
stroke-dashoffset	*dashoffset* (default 0)	Shapes and text content elements
stroke-linecap	**butt** | round | square	Shapes and text content elements
stroke-linejoin	**miter** | round | bevel	Shapes and text content elements
stroke-miterlimit	*miterlimit* (default 4)	Shapes and text content elements

Table B-1. CSS property table for SVG (continued)

Name	Values	Applies to
stroke-opacity	*opacity-value* (default 1)	Shapes and text content elements
stroke-width	*width* (default 1)	Shapes and text content elements
text-anchor	**start** | middle | end	Text content elements
text-decoration	**none** | underline | overline | line-through | blink	Text content elements
text-rendering	**auto** | optimizeSpeed | optimizeLegibility | geometricPrecision	<text> elements
unicode-bidi	**normal** | embed | bidi-override	Text content elements
visibility	**visible** | hidden | collapse	Graphics elements (including the <text> element) and text sub-elements (i.e., <tspan>, <tref>, <altGlyph>, <textPath> and <a>)
word-spacing	**normal** | *length*	Text content elements
writing-mode	**lr-tb** | rl-tb | tb-rl | lr | rl | tb	<text> elements

C

Programming Concepts

Many graphic designers want to use the scripting capability of SVG as described in Chapter 11. If they're not familiar with programming, they tend to practice what might be called "voodoo scripting." In the popular-culture stereotype,* voodoo works by reciting a mysterious spell and hoping that your enemies die horribly. Voodoo scripting works by copying someone else's mysterious script into your SVG document and hoping that your document continues to live. We're under no illusion (nor even a spell) that reading this brief, purposely oversimplified summary will turn you into a master programmer. Our goal is simply to introduce enough of the elementary programming concepts to remove some of the mystery from the scripts that you copy and modify. The particular programming language that we will discuss in this appendix is called ECMA Script;† the concepts used in ECMA Script are common to many other programming languages.

Constants

A constant is a fancy word for a number or string of characters that never changes. Examples are 2, 2.71828, "message", and 'communication'. The last two are called string constants. In ECMA Script, you can use either single or double quotes to mark the boundaries of a string. This is good if you ever need to write things like "O'Reilly & Associates" or 'There is no "there" there.'.

---

* Unlike the actual practice of Santería and voudon, which are much more complex and not inherently evil.

† It is the standardized version of the JavaScript language.

You will sometimes see the two Boolean constants true and false, which are used for "yes-or-no" situations.

Variables

A variable is a block of memory reserved to hold some value that may change from time to time. You can think of it as a mailbox with a name on it; the mailbox holds a slip of paper with information written on it. Let's say you need to keep track of the current width of a rectangle and need to store a changeable message; in ECMA Script you define these variables like this:

```
var currentWidth;
var message;
```

You may visualize them as shown in Figure C-1.

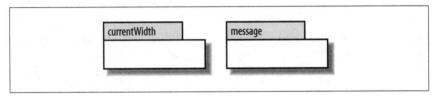

Figure C-1. Two empty variables

Variables defined this way have nothing in their "mailbox;" the technical term is that these variables contain the null value. Variable names must start with a letter or an underscore and can contain only letters, digits, and underscores. They are case sensitive, so width, Width, and WIDTH are names of three different variables.

Assignment and Operators

You can put a value into a variable by using an assignment statement, which starts with a variable name, an equal sign, and the value. Examples:

```
currentWidth = 32;
message = "I love SVG.";
```

You can read these as "set the value of currentWidth equal to 32" and "set the value of message equal to "I love SVG." In reality, this statement works from right to left; whatever is on the righthand side of the equal sign is placed into the variable on the lefthand side. Note that all our ECMA Script statements end with a semicolon. There are cases where you don't need one, but we'd rather have the semicolon and not need it than need it and not have it. Figure C-2 shows the "after" picture for these assignments.

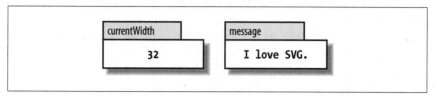

Figure C-2. Two assigned variables

Actually, we told you a small lie a few sentences ago. Whatever the right-hand side of the equal sign *works out to* goes into the variable on the left-hand side. This lets us do mathematical operations, as in the following code.

```
var info; ❶
info = 7 + 2; ❷
info = 7 * 2; ❸
info = info + 1; ❹
info = "door"; ❺
info = info + "bell" ❻
```

❶ Create an empty variable named `info`.

❷ `info` will now contain the value 9 (seven plus two). You use the minus sign – for subtraction.

❸ The asterisk is used for multiplication, since the multiplication symbol is too easily confused with the letter x. `info` will contain 14 (seven times two). The previous value of nine will be discarded. You use the forward slash / for division.

❹ This is illegal in high school algebra, but not in ECMA Script. We start with the righthand side of the equal sign: take the current value of `info`, which is 14, and add one to it. The righthand side works out to 15. This result goes into the variable on the left side of the equal, which just happens to be `info`. At the end of this statement, `info` will contain the value 15.

❺ This takes the string `"door"` and puts it into `info`. In ECMA Script, a variable can hold any sort of information at any time.

❻ This takes the current value of `info`, which is `"door"`, and "adds" (appends) the string constant `"bell"` to the end of it. The resulting value is the word `"doorbell"`, which goes back into `info` on the left side of the equal sign. The plus sign is the only operator that works with strings; you can't subtract, multiply, or divide them.

You can define a variable and set its initial value all in one fell swoop. This is called initializing a variable. You can have more than one operation on the righthand side of the equal sign. In the following code, an empty variable named `celsius` is created, then a variable named `fahrenheit` with value 212, then the Fahrenheit temperature is converted to Celsius.

```
var celsius;
var fahrenheit = 212;
celsius = ((fahrenheit - 32) / 9 ) * 5;
```

Arrays

An array is an ordered collection of data, indexed by number. We compared a simple variable to a mailbox (send mail to the "Smith Residence"). An array is like a set of numbered apartment mailboxes (send mail to the "A-List Apartments, #12"). The only difference is that array index numbers start at zero rather than one.* Here's a declaration of an array of radius sizes for circles. This form initializes the array. The second statement sets the value of the last element of the array to 9. You access one of the "slots" of an array by putting its index number in square brackets. Figure C-3 shows the results after the code has finished.

```
var radiusSizes = new Array( 8.5, 6.4, 12.2, 7 );
radiusSizes[3] = 9;
```

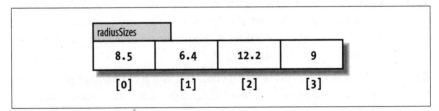

Figure C-3. Depiction of an array

---

* This is not done to be contrary; it's because programs often use a mathematical formula to select the relevant item. These formulas are invariably easier when you start counting at zero.

Comments

Comments provide a way to document your programs so that other people can figure out what you did. There are two kinds of comments in ECMA Script. If you place two forward slashes in a row (//) they and everything to the end of that line are considered to be a comment. If you want a multi-line comment, start with /* and end with */ as shown here:

```
var interest;   // this is accumulated on a daily basis
var rate;       // expressed as a decimal; 75% is a rate of 0.75

/* Figure out the payment amount given a principal
   of $10,000 and 180 monthly payments. */
```

Conditional Statements

Ordinarily, your program statements are carried out in the order in which they appear. Sometimes you may want to do different calculations depending upon some condition. You use the if statement to do this. Here's a calculation for wages that depends upon the number of hours worked. We presume that all the var statements have been set up appropriately.

```
if (hours <= 40) ❶
{
    pay = hours * rate; ❷
}
else ❸
{
    pay = 40 * rate + (hours - 40) * rate * 1.5; ❹
}
```

❶ The expression in the parentheses is called the condition. It always asks a yes-or-no question. In this case, the question is "is the value of the hours variable less than or equal to 40?" Other comparison operations are less than (<), greater than (>) greater than or equal (>=), exactly equal (==), and not equal (!=). Note that asking if two things are equal to each other requires two equal signs, not one!

❷ If the answer to the question is "yes," then the program will do everything between the opening and closing braces { and }...

❸ ...otherwise (else)...

❹ ...do everything between the other set of curly braces. The curly braces are used to signify that one or more statements should be grouped together, much in the way that XML opening and closing tags tell where content begins and end.

Repeated Actions

Sometimes you want to repeat an action a specific number of times ("fill ten two-liter containers from a large water tank"). You use a for loop to do the first sort of task. It's called a loop because, if you were to draw arrows representing the path the computer takes through your program, they would form a loop as the program repeated the actions. Here's the container-filling scenario translated into ECMA Script, with variables for the water tank and the containers presumed to be defined. The loop body, that is, the actions we want repeated, are enclosed in curly braces.

```
var i;               // a counter variable
for (i = 0;          // start counting at zero
    i < 10;          // up to (but not including) 10
    i++)             // add one to the count at every repetition
{
    tank[i] = 2;                  // fill container number "i"
    waterTank = waterTank - 2;    // take 2 liters out of the tank
}
```

Other times you want to repeat an action as long as some condition is true ("keep filling two-liter containers from a large water tank as long as there is any water left"). For this, you use a while loop.

```
i = 0;                     // start with container number zero
while ( waterTank > 0 )    // while there is water left
{
    tank[i] = 2;                  // fill container number "i"
    waterTank = waterTank - 2;    // take 2 liters out of the tank
    i = i + 1;                    // move on to the next container
}
```

Functions

You can accomplish some surprisingly sophisticated tasks with this small number of programming concepts. You collect sets of ECMA Script statements designed to perform a specific task into functions. Think of a function as a recipe card that gives a list of ingredients and instructions which, when followed, create a specific dish. A function starts with the keyword function followed by the function name. The name should be indicative of the task that it does, and it follows the same rules that variable names do. Following the function name, in parentheses, are the parameters of the function. A parameter is extra information that the function needs when it does its task. Consider this imaginary recipe:

Korean Kimch'i Surprise

Take 100 grams of kimch'i per serving, 25 grams of ko-ju-jang red pepper paste per serving, and 50 grams of mushrooms per serving. Mix well. Serve.

Before you can make the recipe, you have to supply some extra information—the number of servings you intend to make. Our script might look like this:

```
function makeKimchiSurprise( numberOfServings )
{
    var kimchi = 100 * numberOfServings;
    var kojujang = 25 * numberOfServings;
    var mushrooms = 50 * numberOfServings;
    var surprise = kimchi + kojujang + mushrooms;
}
```

This is only the definition of the function. It does absolutely **nothing** until it is invoked, or called on. (You may have hundreds of recipe cards in a file box at home. They just sit there, inactive, until someone asks you to pull one card out and perform the cooking tasks.) You will often call a function as the result of an event. In the following example a click on the blue rectangle will call the function. The number 5 in the parentheses will fill in the "extra information" required by the numberOfServings parameter.

```
<rect x="10" y="10" width="100" height="30" style="fill: blue;"
    onclick="makeKimchiSurprise( 5 )" />
```

Even if the function doesn't need any parameters, you still have to put the parentheses after its name. This is how ECMA Script can tell the difference between a variable named **area** and a function called **area()**.

Some functions can also call other functions. For example, a function that calculates compound interest might need to call upon another function that determines whether a year is a leap year or not. A parameter lets the interest function tell the leap year function what year it's interested in. The return statement will let the leap year function communicate its result back to the caller. This allows you to modularize a program into generally useful building blocks. In cooking terms, the makeHollandaiseSauce function can be called from the makeEggsBenedict function as well as from makeChickenFlorentine.

Objects, Properties, and Methods

Take a power supply with its on-off switch, a plastic dial, a lever with a spring, and a metal chassis with rectangular slots and coils of wire in it. Put all these parts together, and you get a toaster.

Each of these parts is an object. Some of them have characteristics that are of interest to us: The power supply has a voltage of 110 or 220 volts; the chassis has a color and a number of slots, and the dial has a minimum and maximum setting. (The lever has no interesting characteristics.)

You do actions with each of these objects: you push the lever down or pop it up, you insert bread into the slots, you turn the power supply on or off, and you turn the dial to the desired setting.

Let's take this toaster into the world of ECMA Script. Now our mailboxes don't just hold slips of paper; they can hold entire other mailboxes (just as objects have little objects inside them). We'll also let a mailbox hold recipe cards (functions) so that they can perform actions. When a variable is inside another variable, we call the inner variable a *property*. When a function is inside a mailbox, we call it a *method*. The diagram for the toaster looks like Figure C-4.

We now have a very flexible way of modeling a toaster, but it's introduced a problem. We can't just say things like:

```
color = "gold";
voltage = 220;
popUp();
```

to set the toaster's color or voltage or to pop out the bread because the color property is nested inside the toaster variable, the voltage really belongs to the powerSupply inside the toaster, and it's the toaster's lever that does the popUp function. Instead, we must say:

```
toaster.color = "gold";
toaster.powerSupply.voltage = 220;
toaster.lever.popUp();
```

These are easy to figure out if we read them from right to left and say "of" whenever we see a period: "Put gold into the color of the toaster." "Put 220 into the voltage of the power supply of the toaster." "Call the pop up

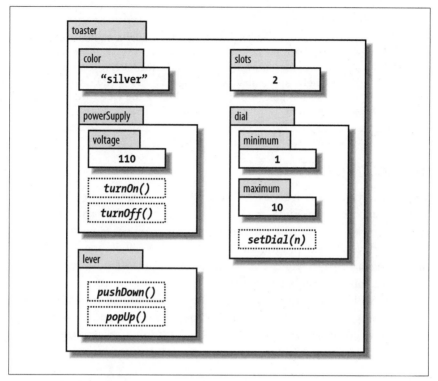

Figure C-4. The object diagram for a toaster

method of the lever of the toaster."* Think of this as the grown-up version of nested objects and methods that you learned as a child: "this is the dog that chased the cat that killed the rat that ate the malt that lay in the house that Jack built."

We have just used objects to model the behavior of a toaster; we've built a Toaster Object Model. Similarly, there is a Document Object Model (DOM) that lets ECMA Script access a document's properties and invoke its methods. Almost all of your access to an SVG document will be through methods that begin with the word set or get. For example, if you receive a mouse click event and want to find its *x*-coordinate, you would write evt.getClientX(). To set the radius of a <circle> element with an id of wheel, you might write svgDocument.getElementById("wheel").setAttribute("r", 3).

---

* If you insist upon reading left to right, adapt the suggestion for reading path names made by Elizabeth Castro in her book, *Visual Quickstart Guide to HTML for the World Wide Web*: read the period as "contains." Then toaster.powerSupply.voltage = 220; is read as "the toaster contains a power supply, which contains a voltage. Set that voltage to 220."

The SVG Document Object Model is actually a superset of the XML Document Object Model; once you learn to manipulate the structure of an SVG document, you can immediately apply that knowledge to other XML documents, so the time you spend in learning the DOM will be amply repaid.

What, Not How

We've given you an overview of the *what* of programming, which can serve as a base for reading programs that other people have written and making sense of them (the programs, not the people). *How* you define a task and lay out the programming steps to solve it is another problem altogether, and far beyond the scope of this book. If you enjoy solving crossword puzzles or brain teasers, or just solving problems in general, you may well enjoy writing programs. If you would like to learn to write original programs in ECMA Script, I strongly recommend Danny Goodman's excellent *JavaScript Bible*, which is chock full of examples.

D

Matrix Algebra

Matrix algebra is a branch of mathematics that defines operations on matrices, which are series of numbers arranged in rows and columns. In addition to its many uses in science and engineering, matrix algebra makes the computations for graphic operations very efficient. The purpose of this appendix is to introduce you to the fundamental concepts of matrix algebra that SVG uses "behind the scenes."

Matrix Terminology

We describe a matrix by its number of rows and columns. Figure D-1 displays a matrix that arranges a series of daily temperatures over a two-week period into two rows of seven columns each. This matrix is called a "two-by-seven" matrix. Matrices are enclosed in square brackets when written.

$$\begin{bmatrix} 22.3 & 26 & 27.2 & 24.8 & 28 & 25 & 28.2 \\ 30.3 & 30.4 & 28 & 26.4 & 29.9 & 27.2 & 26 \end{bmatrix}$$

Figure D-1. 2 by 7 matrix of daily temperatures

Here are some other terms that you may encounter when dealing with matrix operations: A square matrix is a matrix with the same number of rows as columns. A vector is a matrix with only one row, and a column vector is a matrix with only one column. The individual entries in a matrix are called entries, and the technical term for a plain number is a scalar. Now you can bring these sure-fire conversation stoppers to the next party you attend.

Applying the concept of a matrix to SVG, you might express a set of x and y coordinates as a two-by-one matrix. This isn't the way we'll ultimately end up representing coordinates, but it's a good place to start, as it's easy to understand. In this representation, the point (3, 5) is expressed as shown in Figure D-2.

$$\begin{bmatrix} 3 \\ 5 \end{bmatrix}$$

Figure D-2. Coordinates expressed as a matrix

Matrix Addition

The easiest matrix operation is addition. To add two matrices, you add their corresponding elements. This, of course, requires that your matrices have exactly the same number of rows and columns. Figure D-3 shows the addition of 2 matrices, each 3-by-2.

$$\begin{bmatrix} 1 & 2 \\ 3 & 4 \\ 5 & 6 \end{bmatrix} + \begin{bmatrix} 7 & 8 \\ 9 & 10 \\ 11 & 12 \end{bmatrix} = \begin{bmatrix} 1+7 & 2+8 \\ 3+9 & 4+10 \\ 5+11 & 6+12 \end{bmatrix} = \begin{bmatrix} 8 & 10 \\ 12 & 14 \\ 16 & 18 \end{bmatrix}$$

Figure D-3. Addition of two 3 by 2 matrices

We see that the `translate` transformation in SVG could be accomplished easily by matrix addition. For example, the matrix addition in Figure D-4 would implement `transform="translate(7, 2)"` for any point (x, y).

$$\begin{bmatrix} x \\ y \end{bmatrix} + \begin{bmatrix} 7 \\ 2 \end{bmatrix} = \begin{bmatrix} x+7 \\ y+2 \end{bmatrix}$$

Figure D-4. Simple method to translate coordinates

The order in which you add matrices doesn't matter. Technically, we say that matrix addition is commutative (A + B = B + A). It is also associative; given three matrices A, B, and C, (A + B) + C is the same as A + (B + C). There is such a thing as matrix subtraction; just subtract the corresponding elements of the two matrices. Just as with regular subtraction, matrix subtraction is not commutative.

Matrix Multiplication

You may be thinking that matrix multiplication works in a similar manner, and that's how you can do a `scale()` transformation. Unfortunately, the easy way doesn't work this time. Matrix multiplication is significantly more complicated than matrix addition. In the first examples that follow, this complexity appears to be needless. As we proceed, you'll see that the usefulness of matrix multiplication far outweighs its difficulty.

In order to multiply two matrices, the number of *columns* of the first matrix must equal the number of *rows* of the second matrix. Such matrices are called compatible. This means you can multiply a 3-by-5 matrix times a 5-by-4 matrix, but not a 3-by-5 matrix times a 3-by-2 matrix. The matrices we will multiply in Figure D-5 are compatible.

$$\begin{bmatrix} 1 & 2 & 3 \\ 4 & 5 & 6 \end{bmatrix} \bullet \begin{bmatrix} 7 & 10 \\ 8 & 11 \\ 9 & 12 \end{bmatrix}$$

Figure D-5. Two matrices to be multiplied

The resulting matrix will have the same number of rows as the first matrix, and the same number of columns as the second matrix. Thus, the example's 2-by-3 matrix times the 3-by-2 matrix will result in a 2-by-2 matrix.

The entry that will go in row one, column one of our result matrix is the cross product of the first row of the first matrix and the first column of the second matrix. "Cross product" is a fancy way of saying "add up the products of the corresponding entries in a row and column" as shown in Figure D-6.

To find the quantity to place in row two, column one (the lower left) of the result matrix, take the cross product of row two in the first matrix and column one in the second matrix, as shown in Figure D-7.

$$
\begin{bmatrix} 1 & 2 & 3 \\ 4 & 5 & 6 \end{bmatrix} \bullet \begin{bmatrix} 7 & 10 \\ 8 & 11 \\ 9 & 12 \end{bmatrix} = \begin{bmatrix} 1 \cdot 7 + 2 \cdot 8 + 3 \cdot 9 & - \\ - & - \end{bmatrix} = \begin{bmatrix} 50 & - \\ - & - \end{bmatrix}
$$

Figure D-6. First entry in multiplied matrices

$$
\begin{bmatrix} 1 & 2 & 3 \\ 4 & 5 & 6 \end{bmatrix} \bullet \begin{bmatrix} 7 & 10 \\ 8 & 11 \\ 9 & 12 \end{bmatrix} = \begin{bmatrix} 1 \cdot 7 + 2 \cdot 8 + 3 \cdot 9 & - \\ 4 \cdot 7 + 5 \cdot 8 + 6 \cdot 9 & - \end{bmatrix} = \begin{bmatrix} 50 & - \\ 122 & - \end{bmatrix}
$$

Figure D-7. Second entry in multiplied matrices

Calculating the remaining items produces the result shown in Figure D-8.

$$
\begin{bmatrix} 1 & 2 & 3 \\ 4 & 5 & 6 \end{bmatrix} \bullet \begin{bmatrix} 7 & 10 \\ 8 & 11 \\ 9 & 12 \end{bmatrix} = \begin{bmatrix} 1 \cdot 7 + 2 \cdot 8 + 3 \cdot 9 & 1 \cdot 10 + 2 \cdot 11 + 3 \cdot 12 \\ 4 \cdot 7 + 5 \cdot 8 + 6 \cdot 9 & 4 \cdot 10 + 5 \cdot 11 + 6 \cdot 12 \end{bmatrix} = \begin{bmatrix} 50 & 68 \\ 122 & 167 \end{bmatrix}
$$

Figure D-8. Completed multiplication of matrices

Given this information, we can now use matrix multiplication to express the calculations needed to scale a point (x, y) by a factor of 3 horizontally and a factor of 1.5 vertically. Our transformation matrix will have to have two rows and two columns so it is compatible with our two row by one column coordinates, as shown in Figure D-9.

$$
\begin{bmatrix} 3 & 0 \\ 0 & 1.5 \end{bmatrix} \bullet \begin{bmatrix} x \\ y \end{bmatrix} = \begin{bmatrix} 3 \cdot x + 0 \cdot y \\ 0 \cdot x + 1.5 \cdot y \end{bmatrix} = \begin{bmatrix} 3x \\ 1.5y \end{bmatrix}
$$

Figure D-9. Simple scaling by multiplying matrices

Unlike multiplication of single numbers, matrix multiplication is not commutative. If two matrices, A and B, aren't square matrices, then A·B won't have the same number of rows and columns as B·A (if they're even compatible in both directions). Even if A and B are both 3-by-3 square matrices, there's no guarantee that A times B will result in the same answer as B times A. In fact, they'll come out equal in only a very few special cases.

There is another limited form of multiplication; multiplying a matrix by a scalar (a plain number) will multiply every item in the matrix by the scalar, as shown in Figure D-10. We didn't mention this in conjunction with scaling, since this construct scales uniformly, and SVG scaling isn't always the same horizontally and vertically.

$$5 \bullet \begin{bmatrix} 3 & 2 \\ 5 & 6 \end{bmatrix} = \begin{bmatrix} 15 & 10 \\ 25 & 30 \end{bmatrix}$$

Figure D-10. Multiplying a scalar by a matrix

There is no such thing as matrix division as such. There is a construct called a matrix inverse, which is analogous to the reciprocal of a number, but it's very complicated to calculate, and SVG doesn't make any great use of it.

How SVG Uses Matrix Algebra for Transformations

The approach we've taken to translation and scaling works, but it's not ideal. For instance, if we want to translate a point and then scale it, we need to do one matrix addition and then a matrix multiplication. SVG uses a clever trick to represent coordinates and transformation matrices so you can do scaling and translation all with one operation. First, it adds a third value, which is always equal to one, to the coordinate matrix. This means that the point (3, 5) will be represented as shown in Figure D-11.

SVG uses a 3-by-3 matrix, again set up with extra zeroes and ones, to specify the transformation. Figure D-12 shows a matrix that translates a point by a horizontal distance of tx and a vertical distance of ty.

$$\begin{bmatrix} 3 \\ 5 \\ 1 \end{bmatrix}$$

Figure D-11. SVG representation of a coordinate

$$\begin{bmatrix} 1 & 0 & tx \\ 0 & 1 & ty \\ 0 & 0 & 1 \end{bmatrix} \bullet \begin{bmatrix} 3 \\ 5 \\ 1 \end{bmatrix} = \begin{bmatrix} 1 \cdot 3 + 0 \cdot 5 + tx \cdot 1 \\ 0 \cdot 3 + 1 \cdot 5 + ty \cdot 1 \\ 0 \cdot 3 + 0 \cdot 5 + 1 \cdot 1 \end{bmatrix} = \begin{bmatrix} 3 + tx \\ 5 + ty \\ 1 \end{bmatrix}$$

Figure D-12. SVG representation of translation

Figure D-13 shows a transformation matrix that will scale a point by a factor of sx in the horizontal direction and sy in the vertical direction.

$$\begin{bmatrix} sx & 0 & 0 \\ 0 & sy & 0 \\ 0 & 0 & 1 \end{bmatrix} \bullet \begin{bmatrix} 3 \\ 5 \\ 1 \end{bmatrix} = \begin{bmatrix} sx \cdot 3 + 0 \cdot 5 + 0 \cdot 1 \\ 0 \cdot 3 + sy \cdot 5 + 0 \cdot 1 \\ 0 \cdot 3 + 0 \cdot 5 + 1 \cdot 1 \end{bmatrix} = \begin{bmatrix} sx \cdot 3 \\ sy \cdot 5 \\ 1 \end{bmatrix}$$

Figure D-13. SVG representation of scaling

What we've bought with this is a consistent notation; all our transformations, including rotation and skewing, can be represented with 3-by-3 matrices. Furthermore, since everything is 3-by-3, we can construct a chain of transformations by multiplying those matrices together; they're guaranteed to be compatible. For example, to do a translation followed by a scaling, we multiply the matrices in that order (see Figure D-14).

$$\begin{bmatrix} 1 & 0 & tx \\ 0 & 1 & ty \\ 0 & 0 & 1 \end{bmatrix} \bullet \begin{bmatrix} sx & 0 & 0 \\ 0 & sy & 0 \\ 0 & 0 & 1 \end{bmatrix} \bullet \begin{bmatrix} 3 \\ 5 \\ 1 \end{bmatrix}$$

Figure D-14. Translation followed by scaling

Again, it seems as if we're needlessly complicating matters. In order to transform the point (3, 5), we now need two matrix multiplications. To transform another point would require two more multiplications. Given a `<path>` element with several hundred points, this could run into some serious computing time.

Here's where SVG does something clever: it multiplies the first two matrices together, and stores that result, as shown in Figure D-15.

$$
\begin{bmatrix} 1 & 0 & tx \\ 0 & 1 & ty \\ 0 & 0 & 1 \end{bmatrix} \bullet \begin{bmatrix} sx & 0 & 0 \\ 0 & sy & 0 \\ 0 & 0 & 1 \end{bmatrix} = \begin{bmatrix} sx & 0 & tx \\ 0 & sy & ty \\ 0 & 0 & 1 \end{bmatrix}
$$

Figure D-15. Result of multiplying translation and scaling matrices

This "pre-multiplied" matrix now embodies both of the transformations. By multiplying this new matrix times a coordinate point's matrix, we can do the translation and scaling with a single matrix multiplication (see Figure D-16). Now conversion of a hundred points would require only one hundred multiplications, not two hundred.

$$
\begin{bmatrix} sx & 0 & tx \\ 0 & sy & ty \\ 0 & 0 & 1 \end{bmatrix} \bullet \begin{bmatrix} 3 \\ 5 \\ 1 \end{bmatrix} = \begin{bmatrix} sx \cdot 3 + 0 \cdot 5 + tx \cdot 1 \\ 0 \cdot 3 + sy \cdot 5 + ty \cdot 1 \\ 0 \cdot 3 + 0 \cdot 5 + 1 \cdot 1 \end{bmatrix} = \begin{bmatrix} sx \cdot 3 + tx \\ sy \cdot 5 + ty \\ 1 \end{bmatrix}
$$

Figure D-16. Result of premultiplying translation and scaling matrices

If we had to do a translation followed by a rotation followed by a scale, we'd create three 3-by-3 matrices; one to do the translation, one to do the rotation, and one to do the scaling. We'd multiply them all together (in that order), and the resulting matrix would embody all the calculations needed to do all three transformations.

As we mentioned in the section "Matrix Multiplication," matrix multiplication is not commutative. If we change the order of the transformation matrices, we get a different result. This is the mathematics behind the fact that the sequence of transformations makes a difference in the resulting graphic, as described in Chapter 5 in the section "Sequences of Transformations."

This, then, is the power of matrix algebra; it lets us combine the information about as many transformations as we want into one single 3-by-3 matrix, thus dramatically reducing the amount of calculation necessary to transform points. The matrices in Figure D-17 are the ones used to specify a rotation by an angle a, a skew along the *x*-axis of ax, and a skew along the *y*-axis of ay.

$$\begin{bmatrix} \cos(a) & -\sin(a) & 0 \\ \sin(a) & \cos(a) & 0 \\ 0 & 0 & 1 \end{bmatrix} \begin{bmatrix} 1 & \tan(ax) & 0 \\ 0 & 1 & 0 \\ 0 & 0 & 1 \end{bmatrix} \begin{bmatrix} 1 & 0 & 0 \\ \tan(ay) & 1 & 0 \\ 0 & 0 & 1 \end{bmatrix}$$

Figure D-17. Rotate, skew x, and skew y transformation matrices

SVG also uses matrix algebra quite heavily in the calculations associated with filters, which are described in Chapter 10. There, a pixel's red, green, blue, and alpha (opaqueness) values are described as a matrix with five rows and one column. It also adds a fifth row so that a 5-by-5 transformation matrix can add a constant amount to any of the values as well as multiply them by any desired factor. The economies of scale we get by pre-multiplying coordinate transformation matrices work equally well when pre-multiplying pixel manipulation matrices.

The <feColorMatrix> filter, described in Chapter 10 in the section "The feColorMatrix Element," lets you specify all twenty values and places them in the pixel transformation matrix as shown in Figure D-18.

$$\begin{bmatrix} a_0 & a_1 & a_2 & a_3 & a_4 \\ a_5 & a_6 & a_7 & a_8 & a_9 \\ a_{10} & a_{11} & a_{12} & a_{13} & a_{14} \\ a_{15} & a_{16} & a_{17} & a_{18} & a_{19} \\ 0 & 0 & 0 & 0 & 1 \end{bmatrix}$$

Figure D-18. Color transformation matrix

E

Creating Fonts

The fonts built into the system that renders your SVG documents will take care of the vast majority of your needs. Sometimes, though, you will want to use a custom font. It is possible to create a font for use with SVG from scratch. In brief, you use a `<font>` element tag to describe the origin and default width of the font's glyphs. Inside the `<font>` is the `<font-face>` element, which has an immense number of attributes that describe the font's dimensions in excessive detail. These attributes are summarized in the SVG specification at *http://www.w3.org/TR/SVG/fonts.html*. Following the `<font-face>` are `<glyph>` elements, which contain path descriptions for each of the glyphs you wish to have in your font.

While it is possible to create fonts from scratch, it's a lot of work, and often a duplication of effort, since the glyphs you need may be in an already-existing font. If you already have a True Type font with the desired glyphs, you are in luck.

The ttf2svg Utility

The Apache Batik project has created a utility that will convert your True Type fonts to SVG. The following summary is adapted from the Batik project's documentation and is Copyright (C) 2000 The Apache Software Foundation. All rights reserved.

If you are using the Batik binary distribution, type the following at the command line:

```
java -jar batik-ttf2svg.jar [options]
```

If you are using the Batik developer distribution, type the following at the command line:

```
build ttf2svg [options]
```

In both cases, the options are the same:

```
ttf-path
[-l range-begin]
[-h range-end]
[-ascii] [id id]
[-o output-path]
[-testcard]
```

The options have the following meaning:

ttf-path
>   Specifies the True Type font file that contains the characters to be converted.

-l *range-begin*
-h *range-end*
>   The low and high value of the range of characters to be converted to SVG. (ASCII or Unicode values.)

-ascii
>   Forces usage of the ASCII character map.

-id *id*
>   Specifies the value for the id attribute of the generated <font> element.

-o *output-path*
>   Specifies the path for the generated SVG Font file. If not specified, output goes to the Java console.

-testcard
>   Specifies that a set of SVG <text> elements should be appended to the SVG Font file to visualize and test the characters in the SVG Font. This provides an easy way to validate the generated SVG Font file visually.

For example, to convert characters 48 to 57, that is, '0' to '9', in the *myFont.ttf* into their SVG equivalent in the *mySVGFont.svg* file, appending a test card so that the font can be visualized easily, you would use this command:

```
java -jar batik-ttf2svg.jar /usr/home/myFont.ttf -l 48 -h 57
    -id MySVGFont -o mySVGFont.svg -testcard
```

Make sure you have the right to embed a font before you embed it in an SVG file. True Type Font files contain a flag that defines the "embeddability" of a font, and there are tools for checking that flag.

F

Using SVG with Other
XML Applications

John Donne said that no man is an island, and likewise SVG is not the only XML application in the universe. In fact, as an XML application, SVG is *intended* to be used with other XML applications. We'll explore several such uses in this appendix.

Referring to an SVG Document in HTML

OK, so we lied. HTML isn't an XML application, but you'll still want to put SVG graphics in a web page. For most browsers, this is done by using a plug-in. As of this writing, Adobe's SVG viewer plugin is available for Windows and Macintosh systems. To have a plug-in display in an SVG file within an HTML document, you use the <embed> element. The src attribute specifies the file in which the SVG resides, and the width and height attributes tell how much screen space to reserve for the graphic. The graphic will be centered in the space that you specify. You must also specify a type attribute with a value of image/svg+xml.

```
<embed src="some_file.svg" width="100" height="200"
    type="image/svg+xml" />
```

Additionally, you may specify a pluginspage attribute whose value is a URL where users may download the plug-in.

Referring to an SVG Document in XHTML

This is where things get interesting. First, the `<embed>` element is deprecated in HTML 4.0, and nonexistent in HTML 4.01 and XHTML. Obviously, this calls for other measures. In place of `<embed>`, you must use the `<object>` element. It also needs a `height`, `width`, and `type`, but it uses the `data` attribute to specify where the SVG document lives. Any content between the opening and closing `<object>` tags will be displayed if the browser doesn't support the type of object you've specified.

```
<object data="some_file.svg" width="100" height="200"
    type="image/svg+xml">
    <p>
    Sorry, but your browser doesn't support
    SVG objects. What a pity.
    </p>
</object>
```

If you use `<object>`, be aware that it doesn't work at all in many browsers with version numbers less than 4.0, and is subject to annoying oddities in all but the latest browsers.

Placing SVG Directly Within XHTML Documents

Of course, the ultimate goal is to place SVG elements directly within an XHTML document. Whenever you mix elements from two different markup languages, you must differentiate them so that a browser or parser can tell which elements belong to which language. This is done by putting a namespace prefix on the markup for at least one of the two languages.*

The other joker in the deck is that only the very latest browsers allow you to mix SVG and XHTML. Microsoft's Internet Explorer version 5.5 and above, and an SVG-enabled version of Mozilla, available at *http://www.croczilla.com/svg/index.html*, permit you to do this intermixing. Example F-1 shows the setup for Internet Explorer.

---

* The technical term for this is namespaces. Appendix A describes namespaces in more detail.

Example F-1. XHTML and SVG in one cocument

```
<html xmlns:svg="http://www.w3.org/2000/svg"> ❶

<object id="AdobeSVG" ❷
   CLASSID="clsid:78156a80-c6a1-4bbf-8e6a-3cd390eeb4e2">
</object>
<?import namespace="svg" implementation="#AdobeSVG"?>
<head><title>SVG Example</title></head> ❸
<body>
<p>
   Behold SVG mixed with XHTML.
</p>
<svg:svg width="100px" height="100px" viewBox="0 0 100 100"> ❹
    <svg:rect x="10" y="20" width="30" height="40"
        fill="blue" stroke="none"/>
</svg:svg>
<p> ❺
   More XHTML
</p>
</body>
</html>
```

❶ The attribute in this element establishes that any element beginning with svg is associated with the SVG specification.

❷ These four lines are a Microsoft magic spell that loads the appropriate code to handle SVG. This magic spell is part of something that Microsoft calls "binary behaviors" and they are a proprietary method of emulating XML namespaces. This goes totally counter to the philosophy and practice of XML, but, because it does exist and people will insist upon using it, we have to mention it. If you're using the SVG-enabled version of Mozilla, you don't need these lines.

❸ Standard XHTML. Nothing to look at here; keep moving along.

❹ All the tags associated with SVG are preceded with the prefix svg:, just as we stated in the first line of the document. *This includes the closing tags as well as the opening tags.*

❺ More XHTML at the end of the document.

If you have an existing SVG document that you want to insert in an XHTML document, and you need to prefix all the tags, follow these steps in your favorite text editor:

1. Replace all `</` with `%%/`, presuming that `%%/` does not occur elsewhere in your text.

2. Replace all `<` with `<svg:`. If you have any `<![CDATA[..]]<` sections, make sure you don't replace the less than signs inside them.

3. Replace all `%%/` with `</svg:`.

Embedding SVG in XSL Formatting Objects

The other XML application that supports inline SVG is Extensible Stylesheet Language Formatting Objects (XSL-FO). This is a markup language used to specify page formatting of text. You may use the Apache Software Foundation's FOP software tool to take a document written in XSL-FO and transform it to Adobe's PDF (Portable Document Format). You may see the XSL-FO specification at *http://www.w3.org/TR/xsl/* or read a brief introduction in Chapter 13 of *XML in a Nutshell* by Elliotte Rusty Harold and W. Scott Means. FOP is available at *http://xml.apache.org*.

Example F-2 lays out a document with text and SVG graphics for the cover of what must surely be one of the more eccentric Compact Discs ever recorded. The graphic has nothing whatsoever to do with the subject of the disc; it's merely an existence proof.

Once we run this file through FOP, we can display it in our favorite PDF viewer. Figure F-1 shows a screenshot.

Example F-2. Combined XSL-FO and SVG markup

```
<?xml version="1.0" encoding="UTF-8"?>
<fo:root xmlns:fo="http://www.w3.org/1999/XSL/Format"> ❶
<fo:layout-master-set> ❷
<fo:simple-page-master ❸
    margin-right="0.5cm"
    margin-left="0.5cm"
    margin-bottom="0.5cm"
    margin-top="0.5cm"
    page-height="12cm" page-width="12cm"
    master-name="cdcover">
```

Figure F-1. PDF output

Example F-2. Combined XSL-FO and SVG markup (continued)

```
<fo:region-body/> ❹
</fo:simple-page-master>
</fo:layout-master-set>

<fo:page-sequence master-name="cdcover"> ❺
<fo:flow flow-name="xsl-region-body" font-family="Times"> ❻

    <fo:block font-size="12pt" font-style="italic" space-after="12pt"> ❼
    The Peoria Bagpipe and Timpani Ensemble Performs
    </fo:block>

    <fo:block font-size="24pt" font-weight="bold" space-after="24pt"
        text-align="center">
    Beethoven on Broadway!
    </fo:block>

    <fo:block text-align="center"> ❽
    <fo:instream-foreign-object width="140px" height="140px"> ❾
    <!-- Simple geometric design -->
    <svg xmlns="http://www.w3.org/2000/svg" width="140px" height="140px"> ❿
        <polygon points="0 0 140 0 0 140" style="fill: #cccccc;"/>
        <polygon points="0 140 140 140 140 0" style="fill: #666666;"/>
```

Example F-2. Combined XSL-FO and SVG markup (continued)

```
            <circle cx="70" cy="70" r="35"
                style="fill: white; stroke: black;"/>
        </svg>
        </fo:instream-foreign-object>
        </fo:block>

        <fo:block text-align="center" font-size="9pt" space-before="2.5cm"> ⓫
        Copyright 2001 O'Reilly &amp; Associates
        </fo:block>
    </fo:flow>
    </fo:page-sequence>
    </fo:root>
```

❶ It is customary to prefix all of the tags in an XSL-FO document with fo, and that is what the xmlns:fo attribute does. The root element of the document, therefore, is <fo:root>.

❷ The document begins by specifying templates for pages. This layout will contain only one page template.

❸ The <fo:simple-page-master> lets you specify the page dimensions and margins, and an identifying name.

❹ Every page template is divided into regions for a header, footer, left edge content, right edge content, and the page body. The <fo:region-body> must always be specified. This region, too, can have margins, but we aren't going to bother with those here. We won't have headers or footers, so we won't specify any other regions than the body.

❺ After the page templates are specified, we can begin entering content that will go into a sequence of pages that are laid out according to the given master-name template.

❻ Content flows into each region that has been specified for a page sequence. Since we've specified only one region (the body), that's where text will flow into.

❼ <fo:block> is one of the most important elements you can have in the flow. Each new block begins on a new line. Any attributes you specify in this element will be applied to the text in the block. This block and the next one contain simple text.

❽ Unlike the preceding two blocks, this one will be horizontally centered on the screen.

❾ And, it will contain an <fo:instream-foreign-object>—namely, our SVG graphic. The incarnation of FOP that we used, version 0.20.1, is very finicky about its measurements. We recommend that you specify the width and height of the graphic in pixels, and that it exactly match...

❿ ... the dimensions that you use in your <svg> element. Our attempts to use millimeters as width and height units in conjunction with a view-Box were entirely unsuccessful. The xmlns attribute has been set up so that tags from SVG do *not* need any prefix.

⓫ Once the <fo:instream-foreign-object> and its containing <fo:block> have finished, we return to a normal <fo:block> for a copyright notice.

If you wish to keep your SVG graphic in a separate file but still include it within an XSL-FO document, you may do so using the <fo:external-graphic> element. If, in the preceding example, we had put the graphics in a separate file named design.svg, we could replace the entire <fo:instream-foreign-object> element with:

```
<fo:external-graphic src="design.svg"
    content-width="140px" content-height="140px"/>
```

Index

A

a element, 194
actions, repeating, 188, 304
  (see also animation)
adding matrices, 310
Adobe Illustrator, 6
  Bézier curves and, 88
Adobe SVG viewer, xiii
  plugin for, 184
aligning
  scaled images vis-a-vis viewport, 20
  text, 122
alpha channel, 149
alpha value, 141
animate element, 184
animateColor element, 190
animateMotion element, 192
animateTransform element, 190
animation, 183–195
  beginning/ending, 183
  duration of, 183
    how time is measured, 186
  repeating, 188
  scripting and, 209–211
Apache Software Foundation, xiii, 323
appendChild, 232

arc, elliptical (see elliptical arcs)
arrays, 302
ascent, 119
aspect ratio, preserving, 20–24
assignment statement, 300
assignments, 300–302
associative matrix addition, 311
attributeName, 184
attributes
  changing for objects, 196–200
  presentation, 48
  specifying styles as, 8
  text, 119–122
  XML and, 279
attributeType, 184

B

background, accessing, 172
BackgroundAlpha, 172
BackgroundImage, 172
baseline, 119
baseline-shift style property, 125
basic shapes (see shapes)
Batik SVG viewer, xii
Batik transcoders, 271

We'd like to hear your suggestions for improving our indexes. Send email to *index@oreilly.com.*

327

About the Author

J. **David Eisenberg** is a programmer and instructor living in San Jose, California with his cat, Tabitha. David has a talent for teaching and explaining. He has developed courses on CSS, JavaScript, CGI, and beginning XML. He also teaches at De Anza Community College in Cupertino. David has written articles for xml.com and alistapart.com on topics such as JavaScript and the Document Object Model, XML validation, XSL Transformations and Formatting Objects, and (surprise) SVG. His online courses at *http://langintro.com* provide introductory tutorials for Korean, Modern Greek, and Russian.

When not programming, David enjoys digital photography, reading science fiction, and riding his bicycle.

Colophon

Our look is the result of reader comments, our own experimentation, and feedback from distribution channels. Distinctive covers complement our distinctive approach to technical topics, breathing personality and life into potentially dry subjects.

The animal on the cover of *SVG Essentials* is a great argus pheasant (*Argusianus argus*). This pheasant can be found in Malaysia, Thailand, Sumatra, and Borneo, where it lives in tropical rainforests. The males have blue faces, black crowns, and short crests; their under parts are mottled brown. The iridescent spots on their wings and tail feathers aid in attracting females. Female argus pheasants are smaller than males and lack their ornate plumage.

The great argus pheasant's wings can continue to grow into the bird's sixth year. Its tail feathers are the longest of all birds, measuring up to 5.7 feet. Some cultures use these feathers in their headdresses.

Jeffrey Holcomb was the production editor, and Ellie Cutler was the copyeditor for *SVG Essentials*. Sue Willing was the proofreader. Jane Ellin, Darren Kelly, and Claire Cloutier provided quality control. Derek Di Matteo provided production assistance. J. David Eisenberg and Brenda Miller wrote the index.

Ellie Volckhausen designed the cover of this book, based on a series design by Edie Freedman. The cover image is a 19th-century engraving from the Dover Pictorial Archive. Emma Colby produced the cover layout with QuarkXPress 4.1 using Adobe's ITC Garamond font.

David Futato designed the interior layout based on a series design by Nancy Priest. The print version of this book was created by translating the DocBook XML markup of its source files into a set of groff macros using a filter developed at O'Reilly & Associates by Norman Walsh. Steve Talbott designed and wrote the underlying macro set on the basis of the GNU troff –mgs macros; Lenny Muellner adapted them to XML and implemented the book design. The GNU groff text formatter Version 1.11.1 was used to generate PostScript output. The text and heading fonts are ITC Garamond Light and Garamond Book; the code font is Constant Willison. The illustrations that appear in the book were produced by Robert Romano and Jessamyn Read using Macromedia FreeHand 9 and Adobe Photoshop 6. This colophon was written by Linley Dolby.

More Titles from O'Reilly

XML

XML in a Nutshell

By Elliotte Rusty Harold & W. Scott Means
1st Edition December 2000
400 pages, ISBN 0-596-00058-8

XML in a Nutshell is just what serious XML developers need in order to take full advantage of XML's incredible potential: a comprehensive, easy-to-access desktop reference to the fundamental rules that all XML documents and authors must adhere to. This book details the grammar that specifies where tags may be placed, what they must look like, which element names are legal, how attributes attach to elements, and much more.

Java and XSLT

By Eric M. Burke
1st Edition September 2001
528 pages, ISBN 0-596-00143-6

Learn how to use XSL transformations in Java programs ranging from stand-alone applications to servlets. *Java and XSLT* introduces XSLT and then shows you how to apply transformations in real-world situations, such as developing a discussion forum, transforming documents from one form to another, and generating content for wireless devices.

Java & XML, 2nd Edition

By Brett McLaughlin
2nd Edition September 2001
528 pages, ISBN 0-596-00197-5

New chapters on Advanced SAX, Advanced DOM, SOAP, and data binding, as well as new examples throughout, bring the second edition of *Java & XML* thoroughly up to date. Except for a concise introduction to XML basics, the book focuses entirely on using XML from Java applications. It's a worthy companion for Java developers working with XML or involved in messaging, web services, or the new peer-to-peer movement.

XSLT

By Doug Tidwell
1st Edition August 2001
473 pages, ISBN 0-596-00053-7

XSLT (Extensible Stylesheet Language Transformations) is a critical bridge between XML processing and more familiar HTML, and dominates the market for conversions between XML vocabularies. Useful as XSLT is, its complexities can be daunting. Doug Tidwell, a developer with years of XSLT experience, eases the pain by building from the basics to the more complex and powerful possibilities of XSLT, so you can jump in at your own level of expertise.

XML Pocket Reference, 2nd Edition

By Robert Eckstein
with Michel Casabianca
2nd Edition April 2001
102 pages, ISBN 0-596-00133-9

The *XML Pocket Reference* is both a handy introduction to XML terminology and syntax, and a quick reference to XML instructions, attributes, entities, and datatypes. Although XML itself is complex, its basic concepts are simple. This small book combines a perfect tutorial for learning the basics of XML with a reference to the XML and XSL specifications. The new edition introduces information on XSLT (Extensible Stylesheet Language Transformations) and Xpath.

Learning XML

By Erik T. Ray with Christopher R.Maden
1st Edition January 2001
368 pages, ISBN 0-596-00046-4

XML (Extensible Markup Language) is a flexible way to create "self-describing data"—and to share both the format and the data on the World Wide Web, intranets, and elsewhere.

In *Learning XML*, the authors explain XML and its capabilities succinctly and professionally, with references to real-life projects and other cogent examples. *Learning XML* shows the purpose of XML markup itself, the CSS and XSL styling languages, and the XLink and XPointer specifications for creating rich link structures.

O'REILLY®

XML

HTML & XHTML: The Definitive Guide, 4th Edition

By Chuck Musciano & Bill Kennedy
4th Edition August 2000
677 pages, ISBN 0-596-00026-X

This complete guide is full of examples, sample code, and practical hands-on advice for creating truly effective web pages and mastering advanced features. Web authors learn how to insert images, create useful links and searchable documents, use Netscape extensions, design great forms, and much more. The fourth edition covers XHTML 1.0, HTML 4.01, Netscape 6.0, and Internet Explorer 5.0, plus all the common extensions.

DocBook: The Definitive Guide

By Norman Walsh & Leonard Muellner
1st Edition October 1999
648 pages, Includes CD-ROM
ISBN 1-56592-580-7

DocBook is a Document Type Definition (DTD) for use with XML (the Extensible Markup Language) and SGML (the Standard Generalized Markup Language). DocBook lets authors in technical groups exchange and reuse technical information. This book contains an introduction to SGML, XML, and the DocBook DTD, plus the complete reference information for DocBook.

Programming Jabber

By DJ Adams
1st Edition December 2001 (est.)
300 pages (est.), ISBN 0-596-00202-5

This book will offer programmers a chance to learn and understand the Jabber technology and protocol from an implementer's point of view. Every detail of every part of the Jabber client protocol is introduced, explained, discussed, and covered in the form of recipes, mini-projects or simple and extended examples in Perl, Python, and Java. *Programming Jabber* provides a walk-through of the foundation elements that are common to any messaging solution, including a detailed overview of the Jabber server architecture.

Programming Web Services with XML-RPC

By Simon St.Laurent, Joe Johnston
& Edd Dumbill
Foreword by Dave Winer
1st Edition June 2001
230 pages, ISBN 0-596-00119-3

XML-RPC, a simple yet powerful system built on XML and HTTP, lets developers connect programs running on different computers with a minimum of fuss. Java programs can talk to Perl scripts, which can talk to ASP applications, and so on. With XML-RPC, developers can provide access to functionality without having to worry about the system on the other end, so it's easy to create web services.

Programming Web Services with SOAP

By James Snell, Doug Tidwell
& Pavel Kulchenko
1st Edition December 2001 (est.)
352 pages (est.), ISBN 0-596-00095-2

In typical O'Reilly fashion this book moves beyond the theoretical and explains how to build and implement SOAP web services. The book begins with a solid introduction to SOAP, detailing its history and structure, followed by an introduction to the three major types of SOAP applications: SOAP-RPC, SOAP-Messaging, and SOAP-Intermediaries. Each SOAP application is illustrated with an in-depth implementation.

Building Oracle XML Applications

By Steve Muench
1st Edition September 2000
810 pages, Includes CD-ROM
ISBN 1-56592-691-9

Building Oracle XML Applications gives Java and PL/SQL developers a rich and detailed look at the many tools Oracle provides to support XML development. It shows how to combine the power of XML and XSLT with the speed, functionality, and reliability of the Oracle database. The author delivers nearly 800 pages of entertaining text, helpful and timesaving hints, and extensive examples that developers can put to use immediately to build custom XML applications.

How to stay in touch with O'Reilly

1. Visit Our Award-Winning Web Site

http://www.oreilly.com/

★ "Top 100 Sites on the Web" —PC Magazine
★ "Top 5% Web sites" —Point Communications
★ "3-Star site" —The McKinley Group

Our web site contains a library of comprehensive product information (including book excerpts and tables of contents), downloadable software, background articles, interviews with technology leaders, links to relevant sites, book cover art, and more. File us in your Bookmarks or Hotlist!

2. Join Our Email Mailing Lists

New Product Releases
To receive automatic email with brief descriptions of all new O'Reilly products as they are released, send email to:
ora-news-subscribe@lists.oreilly.com
Put the following information in the first line of your message (not in the Subject field):
subscribe ora-news

O'Reilly Events
If you'd also like us to send information about trade show events, special promotions, and other O'Reilly events, send email to:
ora-news-subscribe@lists.oreilly.com
Put the following information in the first line of your message (not in the Subject field):
subscribe ora-events

3. Get Examples from Our Books via FTP

There are two ways to access an archive of example files from our books:

Regular FTP
• ftp to:
ftp.oreilly.com
(login: anonymous
password: your email address)
• Point your web browser to:
ftp://ftp.oreilly.com/

FTPMAIL
• Send an email message to:
ftpmail@online.oreilly.com
(Write "help" in the message body)

4. Contact Us via Email

order@oreilly.com
For answers to problems regarding your order or our products. To place an order online visit:
http://www.oreilly.com/order_new/

subscriptions@oreilly.com
To place an order for any of our newsletters or periodicals.

books@oreilly.com
General questions about any of our books.

booktech@oreilly.com
For book content technical questions or corrections.

proposals@oreilly.com
To submit new book or software proposals to our editors and product managers.

international@oreilly.com
For information about our international distributors or translation queries. For a list of our distributors
outside of North America check out:
http://www.oreilly.com/distributors.html

5. Work with Us

Check out our website for current employment opportunites:
http://jobs.oreilly.com/

O'Reilly & Associates, Inc.
1005 Gravenstein Hwy North
Sebastopol, CA 95472 USA
TEL 707-829-0515 or 800-998-9938
     (6am to 5pm PST)
FAX 707-829-0104

O'REILLY®

International Distributors

http://international.oreilly.com/distributors.html • international@oreilly.com

UK, EUROPE, MIDDLE EAST, AND AFRICA (EXCEPT FRANCE, GERMANY, AUSTRIA, SWITZERLAND, LUXEMBOURG, AND LIECHTENSTEIN)

INQUIRIES
O'Reilly UK Limited
4 Castle Street
Farnham
Surrey, GU9 7HS
United Kingdom
Telephone: 44-1252-711776
Fax: 44-1252-734211
Email: information@oreilly.co.uk

ORDERS
Wiley Distribution Services Ltd.
1 Oldlands Way
Bognor Regis
West Sussex PO22 9SA
United Kingdom
Telephone: 44-1243-843294
UK Freephone: 0800-243207
Fax: 44-1243-843302 (Europe/EU orders)
or 44-1243-843274 (Middle East/Africa)
Email: cs-books@wiley.co.uk

FRANCE

INQUIRIES & ORDERS
Éditions O'Reilly
18 rue Séguier
75006 Paris, France
Tel: 33-1-40-51-71-89
Fax: 33-1-40-51-72-26
Email: france@oreilly.fr

GERMANY, SWITZERLAND, AUSTRIA, LUXEMBOURG, AND LIECHTENSTEIN

INQUIRIES & ORDERS
O'Reilly Verlag
Balthasarstr. 81
D-50670 Köln, Germany
Telephone: 49-221-973160-91
Fax: 49-221-973160-8
Email: anfragen@oreilly.de (inquiries)
Email: order@oreilly.de (orders)

CANADA
(FRENCH LANGUAGE BOOKS)
Les Éditions Flammarion ltée
375, Avenue Laurier Ouest
Montréal (Québec) H2V 2K3
Tel: 1-514-277-8807
Fax: 1-514-278-2085
Email: info@flammarion.qc.ca

HONG KONG
City Discount Subscription Service, Ltd.
Unit A, 6th Floor, Yan's Tower
27 Wong Chuk Hang Road
Aberdeen, Hong Kong
Tel: 852-2580-3539
Fax: 852-2580-6463
Email: citydis@ppn.com.hk

KOREA
Hanbit Media, Inc.
Chungmu Bldg. 210
Yonnam-dong 568-33
Mapo-gu
Seoul, Korea
Tel: 822-325-0397
Fax: 822-325-9697
Email: hant93@chollian.dacom.co.kr

PHILIPPINES
Global Publishing
G/F Benavides Garden
1186 Benavides Street
Manila, Philippines
Tel: 632-254-8949/632-252-2582
Fax: 632-734-5060/632-252-2733
Email: globalp@pacific.net.ph

TAIWAN
O'Reilly Taiwan
1st Floor, No. 21, Lane 295
Section 1, Fu-Shing South Road
Taipei, 106 Taiwan
Tel: 886-2-27099669
Fax: 886-2-27038802
Email: mori@oreilly.com

INDIA
Shroff Publishers & Distributors Pvt. Ltd.
12, "Roseland", 2nd Floor
180, Waterfield Road, Bandra (West)
Mumbai 400 050
Tel: 91-22-641-1800/643-9910
Fax: 91-22-643-2422
Email: spd@vsnl.com

CHINA
O'Reilly Beijing
SIGMA Building, Suite B809
No. 49 Zhichun Road
Haidian District
Beijing, China PR 100080
Tel: 86-10-8809-7475
Fax: 86-10-8809-7463
Email: beijing@oreilly.com

JAPAN
O'Reilly Japan, Inc.
Yotsuya Y's Building
7 Banch 6, Honshio-cho
Shinjuku-ku
Tokyo 160-0003 Japan
Tel: 81-3-3356-5227
Fax: 81-3-3356-5261
Email: japan@oreilly.com

SINGAPORE, INDONESIA, MALAYSIA, AND THAILAND
TransQuest Publishers Pte Ltd
30 Old Toh Tuck Road #05-02
Sembawang Kimtrans Logistics Centre
Singapore 597654
Tel: 65-4623112
Fax: 65-4625761
Email: wendiw@transquest.com.sg

AUSTRALIA
Woodslane Pty., Ltd.
7/5 Vuko Place
Warriewood NSW 2102
Australia
Tel: 61-2-9970-5111
Fax: 61-2-9970-5002
Email: info@woodslane.com.au

NEW ZEALAND
Woodslane New Zealand, Ltd.
21 Cooks Street (P.O. Box 575)
Waganui, New Zealand
Tel: 64-6-347-6543
Fax: 64-6-345-4840
Email: info@woodslane.com.au

ARGENTINA
Distribuidora Cuspide
Suipacha 764
1008 Buenos Aires
Argentina
Phone: 54-11-4322-8868
Fax: 54-11-4322-3456
Email: libros@cuspide.com

ALL OTHER COUNTRIES
O'Reilly & Associates, Inc.
1005 Gravenstein Hwy North,
Sebastopol, CA 95472 USA
Tel: 707-829-0515
Fax: 707-829-0104
Email: order@oreilly.com

O'REILLY®

TO ORDER: **800-998-9938** • **order@oreilly.com** • **www.oreilly.com**
ONLINE EDITIONS OF MOST O'REILLY TITLES ARE AVAILABLE BY SUBSCRIPTION AT **safari.oreilly.com**
ALSO AVAILABLE AT MOST RETAIL AND ONLINE BOOKSTORES